PUBLIC PHILOSOPHY

PUBLIC PHILOSOPHY

ESSAYS ON MORALITY IN POLITICS

Michael J. Sandel

Harvard University Press • Cambridge, Massachusetts • London, England • 2005

Library of Congress Cataloging-in-Publication Data

Sandel, Michael J.
  Public philosophy : essays on morality in politics / Michael J. Sandel.
    p.   cm.
  Includes bibliographical references and index.
  ISBN 0-674-01928-8 (alk. paper)
    1. Political ethics–United States.   2. Political science–Philosophy.
  3. United States–Moral conditions.   4. United States–Politics and
  government–2001-   I. Title.

JK468.E7S36 2005
172–dc22   2005046260

For Kiku

CONTENTS

PUBLIC PHILOSOPHY

The re-election of President George W. Bush prompted a new wave of soul-searching among Democrats. Exit polls found that more voters based their presidential vote on "moral values" than on any other issue—more than terrorism, the war in Iraq, or the state of the economy. And those who cited moral values voted overwhelmingly (80 to 18 percent) for Bush over his opponent, John Kerry. Commentators were perplexed. "Somewhere along the line," a CNN reporter confessed, "all of us missed this moral values thing."

Skeptics warned against over-interpreting the "moral values" issue. They pointed out that the majority of voters did not share Bush's opposition to abortion and same-sex marriage, the most morally charged issues in the campaign. Other factors helped explain the Bush victory: Kerry's campaign had lacked a compelling theme; it is not easy to defeat an incumbent president during wartime; and Americans were still reeling from the terrorist attacks of September 11. Still, in the wake of the 2004 election, Democrats found themselves casting about for ways to speak more convincingly to Americans' moral and spiritual yearnings.

It was not the first time that Democrats had missed the "moral values thing." In the four decades following Lyndon Johnson's landslide victory in 1964, only two Democrats won the presidency. One was Jimmy Carter, a born-again Christian from Georgia who, in the wake of Watergate, promised to restore honesty and morality to government; the other was Bill Clinton who, despite his personal foibles, displayed a keen instinctive grasp of the religious and spiritual dimensions of politics. Other Democratic standard-bearers—Walter Mondale, Michael Dukakis, Al Gore, and John Kerry—eschewed soul talk, cleaving instead to the language of policies and programs. When Democrats in recent times have reached for moral and religious resonance, their efforts have taken two forms, neither wholly convincing. Some, following the example of George W. Bush, have sprinkled their speeches with religious rhetoric and biblical references. (Bush has employed this strategy more brazenly than any modern president; his inaugural addresses and State of the Union speeches mention God more frequently than even Ronald Reagan did.) So intense was the competition for divine favor in the 2000 and 2004 campaigns that a Web site, *beliefnet.com,* established a "God-o-meter" to track the candidates' references to God.

The second approach Democrats have taken is to argue that moral values in politics are not only about cultural issues, such as abortion, school prayer, same-sex marriage, and the display of the Ten Commandments in courthouses, but also about economic issues, such as health care, child care, education funding, and Social Security. John Kerry offered a version of this approach in his acceptance speech at the 2004 Democratic convention, using the V-words ("value" and "values") no less than 32 times.

Though the impulse is right, the hortatory fix for the values deficit comes across as stilted and unconvincing, for two reasons: First, Democrats have had trouble articulating, with clarity and conviction, the vision of economic justice that underlies their social and economic policies. Second, even a strong argument for economic justice does not by itself constitute a governing vision. Providing everyone a fair opportunity to reap the rewards of an affluent society is one aspect of the good society. But fairness isn't everything. It does not answer the hunger for a public life of larger meaning, because it does not connect the project of self-government with people's desire to participate in a common good greater than themselves.

Notwithstanding the outpouring of patriotism in the immediate aftermath of September 11, and the sacrifices being made by the soldiers in Iraq, American politics lacks an animating vision of the good society, and of the shared obligations of citizenship. A few weeks after the terrorist attacks of 2001, President Bush, who insisted on his tax cuts even as he led the nation into war, was asked why he had not called for any sacrifices from the American people as a whole. He replied that the American people were sacrificing by enduring longer lines at airports. In a 2004 interview in Normandy, France, on the anniversary of D-Day, NBC's Tom Brokaw asked the President why he was not asking the American people to sacrifice more so that they would feel connected with their fellow citizens fighting and dying in Iraq. Bush seemed mystified, replying, "What does that mean, 'sacrifice more'?" Brokaw offered the example of World War II rationing and restated his question: "There's a great sense, I think, that there's a disconnect between what American military people are doing overseas and what Americans are doing at home." Bush replied: "America has been sacrificing. Our economy hasn't [been] as strong as it should be, and there's—people haven't been working. Fortunately, our economy's now strong, and it's getting stronger."

That Democrats did not seize the theme of sacrifice, and that Bush scarcely understood the question, testifies to the dulled civic sensibilities of American politics in the early years of the twenty-first century. Without a compelling account of the public purpose, the electorate settled, in a time of terror, for the security and moral certitude they associated with the incumbent President.

The essays in this volume explore the moral and civic dilemmas that animate American public life. Part I, "American Civic Life," offers an overview of the American political tradition. It shows that the "moral values" predicament in which liberals find themselves today represents something of a reversal; conservatives have not always held a monopoly on the faith-based aspects of political argument. Some of the great movements of moral and political reform in American history—from the abolitionist movement to the Progressive era to the civil rights movement of the 1960s—drew powerfully on moral, religious, and spiritual sources. By recalling American political debates from Thomas Jefferson to the present, these essays show how liberalism lost its moral and civic voice, and ask whether the project of self-government can be rejuvenated in our time.

Part II, "Moral and Political Arguments," takes up some of the hotly contested moral and political issues of the last two decades, including affirmative action, assisted suicide, abortion, gay rights, stem cell research, pollution permits, presidential lying, criminal punishment, the moral limits of markets, the meaning of toleration and civility, individual rights and the claims of community, and the role of religion in public life. Running through the discussion of these controversies are several recurring questions: Individual rights and freedom of choice are the most prominent ideals in our moral and political life. But are they an adequate basis for a democratic society? Can we reason our way through the hard moral questions that arise in public life without recourse to controversial ideas about the good life? If (as I maintain) our political arguments cannot avoid questions of the good life, how can we contend with the fact that modern societies are teeming with disagreement about such questions?

Part III, "Liberalism, Pluralism, and Community," steps back from the particular moral and political controversies discussed in Part II to examine the varieties of liberal political theory prominent today, and to assess their strengths and weaknesses. It offers some examples of political theories that draw openly and explicitly on moral and religious ideals, and yet retain a commitment to pluralism. Connecting the themes running through the volume as a whole, the essays in this section argue for a politics that gives greater emphasis to citizenship, community, and civic virtue, and that grapples more directly with questions of the good life. Liberals often worry that inviting moral and religious argument into the public square runs the risk of intolerance and coercion. The essays in this volume respond to that worry by showing that substantive moral discourse is not at odds with progressive public purposes, and that a pluralist society need not shrink from engaging the moral and religious convictions its citizens bring to public life.

Many of these essays blur the line between political commentary and political philosophy. They constitute a venture in public philosophy, in two senses: they find in the political and legal controversies of our day an occasion for philosophy, and they represent an attempt to do philosophy in public—to bring moral and political philosophy to bear on contemporary public discourse. Most of the essays in this volume originally appeared in publications aimed at an audience beyond the academy, such as the *Atlantic Monthly,* the *New Republic,* the *New York Times,* and the *New York Review of Books.* Others appeared in law reviews or scholarly publications. But all are addressed to citizens as well as scholars, and seek to shed light on contemporary public life.

Part I

AMERICAN CIVIC LIFE

The essays in this section seek in the American political tradition sources of civic renewal for our time. Chapter 1, "America's Search for a Public Philosophy," is an essay in retrieval though not, I hope, in nostalgia. It shows that our political debates have not always focused on the size and distribution of the national product; nor is the consumerist, individualist understanding of freedom so familiar in our time the only way of conceiving liberty. From Thomas Jefferson to the New Deal, a more demanding, civic conception of freedom has also informed American political argument. The scale of political life in a global age complicates the civic project; we cannot invigorate self-government simply by reviving civic virtue as traditionally conceived. But recalling the civic strand of our tradition can help us reimagine present possibilities. At the very least, it can remind us of questions we have forgotten how to ask: How can powerful economic forces be brought to democratic account? Is self-government possible under conditions of a global economy? In a pluralist age marked by multiple identities and complex selves, what forms of commonality can democratic societies hope to inspire?

Chapters 2–7 are shorter essays that explore the changing terms of American political discourse in recent decades. "Beyond Individualism: Democrats and Community" was first published as Michael Dukakis and Gary Hart competed for the 1988 Democratic nomination. I argued that the Democratic Party had ceded to Ronald Reagan the language of community, and had lost its moral and civic voice. Not long after the article appeared, I received an appreciative letter from a reader in Little Rock. Bill Clinton, then the Governor of Arkansas, wrote that he had been making speeches around the country sounding similar themes, and was struck by two points in particular: "one, that we have something to learn from Reagan's conservative vision and his success in 'speaking the language of self-government and community,'" and second, "that we must focus less on macroeconomic issues and more on 'questions of economic structure' and 'building communities capable of self-government on a manageable scale.'"

Chapters 3–5 are essays written eight years later, in the midst of Clinton's presidency. They reflect on his partially successful attempt to wrest from Republicans the language of community and moral values and on his somewhat less successful attempt to articulate large governing themes for progressive politics at the end of the twentieth century. Both efforts were disrupted by the impeachment proceedings of 1998–99, touched off by a Clinton sex scandal involving a White House intern. Chapter 6 contrasts the largely partisan attempt by House Republicans to impeach Clinton with the more sober impeachment hearings that led to the resignation of Richard Nixon, hearings I had witnessed as a young journalist.

The section concludes with an essay recalling the civic voice of Robert F. Kennedy, drawn from a talk I gave at a gathering at the John F. Kennedy Library in 2000, celebrating the seventy-fifth anniversary of Robert Kennedy's birth.

one

AMERICA'S SEARCH FOR A PUBLIC PHILOSOPHY

LIBERAL VERSUS REPUBLICAN FREEDOM

The central idea of the public philosophy by which we live is that freedom consists in our capacity to choose our ends for ourselves. Politics should not try to form the character or cultivate the virtue of its citizens, for to do so would be to "legislate morality." Government should not affirm, through its policies or laws, any particular conception of the good life; instead it should provide a neutral framework of rights within which people can choose their own values and ends.

The aspiration to neutrality finds prominent expression in our politics and law. Although it derives from the liberal tradition of political thought, its province is not limited to those known as liberals, rather than conservatives, in American politics; it can be found across the political spectrum. Liberals invoke the ideal of neutrality when opposing school prayer or restrictions on abortion or attempts by Christian fundamentalists to bring their morality into the public square. Conservatives appeal to neutrality when opposing attempts by government to impose certain moral restraints—for the sake of workers' safety or environmental protection or distributive justice—on the operation of the market economy.

The ideal of free choice also figures on both sides of the debate over the welfare state. Republicans have long complained that taxing the rich to pay for welfare programs for the poor is a form of coerced charity that violates people's freedom to choose what to do with their own money. Democrats have long replied that government must assure all citizens a decent level of income, housing, education, and health care, on the grounds that those who are crushed by economic necessity are not truly free to exercise choice in other domains. Despite their disagreement about how government should act to respect individual choice, both sides assume that freedom consists in the capacity of people to choose their own ends.

So familiar is this vision of freedom that it might seem a permanent feature of the American political tradition. But as a reigning public philosophy, it is a recent arrival, a development of the past half century. Its distinctive character can best be seen by comparison with a rival public philosophy that it gradually displaced: a version of republican political theory.

Central to republican theory is the idea that liberty depends on sharing in self-government. This idea is not by itself inconsistent with liberal freedom. Participating in politics can be one among the ways in which people choose to pursue their individual ends. According to republican political theory, however, sharing in self-rule involves something more. It involves deliberating with fellow citizens about the common good and helping to shape the destiny of the political community. But to deliberate well about the common good requires more than the capacity to choose one's ends and to respect others' rights to do the same. It requires a knowledge of public affairs and also a sense of belonging, a concern for the whole, a moral bond with the community whose fate is at stake. To share in self-rule therefore requires that citizens possess, or come to acquire, certain civic virtues. But this means that republican politics cannot be neutral toward the values and ends its citizens espouse. The republican conception of freedom, unlike the liberal conception, requires a formative politics, a politics that cultivates in citizens the qualities of character that self-government requires.

Both the liberal and the republican understandings of freedom have been present throughout our political experience, but in shifting measure and relative importance. In recent decades the civic, or formative, aspect of our politics has given way to a procedural republic, concerned less with cultivating virtue than with enabling persons to choose their own values. This shift sheds light on our present discontent. For despite its appeal, the liberal vision of freedom lacks the civic resources to sustain self-government. The public philosophy by which we live cannot secure the liberty it promises, because it cannot inspire the sense of community and civic engagement that liberty requires.

THE POLITICAL ECONOMY OF CITIZENSHIP

If American politics is to recover its civic voice, it must find a way to debate questions we have forgotten how to ask. Consider the way we think and argue about economics today, in contrast to the way Americans debated economic policy through much of our history. These days most of our economic arguments revolve around two considerations: prosperity and fairness. Whatever tax policies or budget proposals or regulatory schemes people may favor, they usually defend them on the grounds that they will increase the size of the economic pie or distribute the pieces of the pie more fairly or both.

So familiar are these ways of justifying economic policy that they might seem to exhaust the possibilities. But our debates about economic policy have not always focused solely on the size and the distribution of the national product. Throughout much of American history they have also addressed a different question: What economic arrangements are most hospitable to self-government?

Thomas Jefferson gave classic expression to the civic strand of economic argument. In his *Notes on the State of Virginia* (1787) he argued against developing large-scale domestic manufactures on the grounds that the agrarian way of life made for virtuous citizens, well suited to self-government. "Those who labour in the earth are the chosen people of God," he wrote—the embodiments of "genuine virtue." The political economists of Europe claimed that every nation should manufacture for itself, but Jefferson worried that large-scale manufacturing would create a propertyless class, lacking the independence that republican citizenship requires: "Dependance begets subservience and venality, suffocates the germ of virtue, and prepares fit tools for the designs of ambition." Jefferson thought it better to "let our work-shops remain in Europe" and avoid the moral corruption they brought; better to import manufactured goods than the manners and habits that attended their production. "The mobs of great cities add just so much to the support of pure government, as sores do to the strength of the human body," he wrote. "It is the manners and spirit of a people which preserve a republic in vigour. A degeneracy in these is a canker which soon eats to the heart of its laws and constitution."

Whether to encourage domestic manufacturing or to retain the nation's agrarian character was the subject of intense debate in the early decades of the republic. In the end, Jefferson's agrarian vision did not prevail. But the republican assumption underlying his economics—that public policy should cultivate the qualities of character that self-government requires—found broader support and a longer career. From the Revolution to the Civil War the political economy of citizenship played a prominent role in American national debate. In fact, the civic strand of economic argument extended even into the twentieth century, when Progressives grappled with big business and its consequences for self-government.

THE CURSE OF BIGNESS

The political predicament of the Progressive Era bears a striking similarity to our own. Then as now, Americans sensed the unraveling of community and feared for the prospects of self-government. Then as now, there was a gap, or a lack of fit, between the scale of economic life and the terms in which people conceived their identities—a gap that many experienced as disorienting and disempowering. The threat to self-government at the turn of the century took two forms: the concentration of power amassed by giant corporations, and the erosion of those traditional forms of authority and community that had governed the lives of most Americans through the first century of the republic. A national economy dominated by vast corporations diminished the autonomy of local communities, traditionally the site of self-government. Meanwhile, the growth of large, impersonal cities, teeming with immigrants, poverty, and disorder, led many to fear that Americans lacked sufficient moral and civic cohesiveness to govern according to a shared vision of the good life.

Despite the dislocation they wrought, the new forms of industry, transportation, and communication seemed to offer a new, broader basis for political community. In many ways Americans of the early twentieth century were more closely connected than ever before. Railroads spanned the continent. The telephone, the telegraph, and the daily newspaper brought people into contact with events in distant places. And a complex industrial system connected people in a vast scheme of interdependence that coordinated their labors. Some saw in the new industrial and technological interdependence a more expansive form of community. "Steam has given us electricity and has made the nation a neighborhood," wrote William Allen White. "The electric wire, the iron pipe, the street railroad, the daily newspaper, the telephone, the lines of transcontinental traffic by rail and water . . . have made us all of one body—socially, industrially, politically. . . . It is possible for all men to understand one another."

More sober observers were not so sure. That Americans found themselves implicated in a complex scheme of interdependence did not guarantee that they would identify with that scheme or come to share a life with the unknown others who were similarly implicated. As the social reformer Jane Addams observed, "Theoretically, 'the division of labor' makes men more interdependent and human by drawing them together into a unity of purpose." But whether this unity of purpose is achieved depends on whether the participants take pride in their common project and regard it as their own; "the mere mechanical fact of interdependence amounts to nothing."

Political debate in the Progressive Era focused on two different responses to the power of big business. Some sought to preserve self-government by decentralizing economic power and thus bringing it under democratic control. Others considered economic concentration irreversible and sought to control it by enlarging the capacity of national democratic institutions. The decentralizing strand of progressivism found its ablest advocate in Louis D. Brandeis, who before his appointment to the Supreme Court was an activist attorney and an outspoken critic of industrial concentration. Brandeis's primary concern was with the civic consequences of economic arrangements. He opposed monopolies and trusts not because their market power led to higher consumer prices but because their political power undermined democratic government.

In Brandeis's view, big business threatened self-government in two ways—directly, by overwhelming democratic institutions and defying their control, and indirectly, by eroding the moral and civic capacities that equip workers to think and act as citizens. Brandeis brought long-standing republican themes into the twentieth-century debate: like Jefferson, he viewed concentrated power, whether economic or political, as inimical to liberty. His solution was not to confront big business with big government—that would only compound "the curse of bigness"—but to break up the trusts and restore competition. Only in this way would it be possible to preserve a decentralized economy of locally based enterprises amenable to democratic control.

Brandeis favored industrial democracy not for the sake of improving workers' incomes, desirable though that was, but for the sake of improving their civic capacities. For him, the formation of citizens capable of self-government was an end even higher than distributive justice. "We Americans are committed not only to social justice in the sense of avoiding . . . [an] unjust distribution of wealth; but we are committed primarily to democracy." The "striving for democracy" was inseparable from a "striving for the development of men," he said. "It is absolutely essential in order that men may develop that they be properly fed and properly housed, and that they have proper opportunities of education and recreation. We cannot reach our goal without those things. But we may have all those things and have a nation of slaves."

THE NEW NATIONALISM

The other branch of the Progressive movement offered a different response to the threat posed by corporate power. Rather than decentralize the economy, Theodore Roosevelt proposed a "New Nationalism" to regulate big business by increasing the capacity of the national government.

Like Brandeis, Roosevelt feared the political consequences of concentrated economic power. Where Roosevelt disagreed with the decentralizers was over how to reassert democratic authority. He considered big business an inevitable product of industrial development and saw little point in trying to recover the decentralized political economy of the nineteenth century. Since most big corporations operated in interstate or foreign commerce, beyond the reach of individual states, only the federal government was suited to the task of controlling them. The power of the national government had to grow to match the scale of corporate power.

Like republicans since Jefferson's time, Roosevelt worried about the civic consequences of economic arrangements. His aim was not only to reduce the domination of government by big business but also to enlarge the self-understanding of American citizens, to instill what he called "a genuine and permanent moral awakening," "a spirit of broad and far-reaching nationalism." More than a program of institutional reform, the New Nationalism was a formative project that sought to cultivate a new sense of national citizenship.

Roosevelt was the leading spokesman for the New Nationalism; Herbert Croly was its leading philosopher. In *The Promise of American Life* (1909), Croly laid out the political theory underlying the nationalist strand of progressivism: given "the increasing concentration of American industrial, political, and social life," American government "demands more rather than less centralization." But, according to Croly, the success of democracy also required the nationalization of politics. The primary form of political community had to be recast on a national scale. This was the way to ease the gap, felt so acutely in the Progressive Era, between the scale of American life and the terms of American identity. Given the national scale of the modern economy, democracy required "an increasing nationalization of the American people in ideas, in institutions, and in spirit."

Although Croly renounced Jefferson's notion that democracy depends on dispersed power, he shared Jefferson's conviction that economic and political arrangements should be judged by the qualities of character they promote. For him, the project of nationalizing the American character was "an essentially formative and enlightening political transformation." American democracy could advance only as the nation became more of a nation, which required in turn a civic education that inspired in Americans a deeper sense of national identity.

The decentralizing and nationalizing versions of Progressive reform found memorable expression in the 1912 contest between Woodrow Wilson and Theodore Roosevelt. In retrospect, however, the greater significance of that campaign lies in the assumptions the protagonists shared. Brandeis and Wilson on one side, and Croly and Roosevelt on the other, agreed despite their differences that economic and political institutions should be assessed for their tendency to promote or erode the moral qualities that self-government requires. Like Jefferson before them, they worried about the sort of citizens that the economic arrangements of their day were likely to produce. They argued, in different ways, for a political economy of citizenship. The economic arguments of our day bear little resemblance to the issues that divided the Progressive reformers. They were concerned with the structure of the economy and debated how to preserve democratic government in the face of concentrated economic power. We are concerned with the overall level of economic output and debate how to promote economic growth while assuring broad access to the fruits of prosperity. In retrospect it is possible to identify the moment when our economic questions displaced theirs. Beginning in the late New Deal and culminating in the early 1960s, the political economy of growth and distributive justice displaced the political economy of citizenship.

THE NEW DEAL AND THE KEYNESIAN REVOLUTION

As the New Deal began, political debate continued to reflect the alternatives defined in the Progressive Era. When Franklin D. Roosevelt took office, in the midst of the Depression, two traditions of reform offered competing approaches to economic recovery. One group of reformers, heirs to the philosophy of Louis Brandeis, sought to decentralize the economy through antitrust laws and other measures aimed at restoring competition. Another group, indebted to the New Nationalism of Teddy Roosevelt, sought to rationalize the economy through national economic planning. Despite their differences, both the antitrusters and the planners assumed that overcoming the Depression required a change in the structure of industrial capitalism. They also agreed that the concentration of power in the economy, left to its own devices, posed a threat to democratic government.

The competition between these approaches persisted, unresolved, through much of the New Deal. In different policies and different moods, Roosevelt experimented with both, never fully embracing or rejecting either. In the end neither the antitrusters nor the planners prevailed. Recovery, when it came, was due not to structural reform but to heavy government spending. The Second World War supplied the occasion for the spending, and Keynesian economics supplied the rationale. But Keynesian fiscal policy had political appeal even before the war demonstrated its economic success. For unlike the various proposals for structural reform, such as vigorous antitrust action or national economic planning, Keynesian economics offered a way for the government to control the economy without having to choose among controversial views of the good society. Where earlier reformers had sought economic arrangements that would cultivate citizens of a certain kind, Keynesians undertook no formative mission; they proposed simply to accept existing consumer preferences and to regulate the economy by manipulating aggregate demand.

By the end of the Second World War, the central issues of economic policy had little to do with the debates that had preoccupied Americans earlier in the century. The old debates about how to reform industrial capitalism faded from the scene, and the macroeconomic issues familiar in our day came to the fore. By 1960 most economists and policymakers agreed, as Herbert Stein has written, that "the chief economic problem of the country was to achieve and maintain high and rapidly rising total output." Steps to distribute income more equally were deemed desirable but secondary to the aim of full employment and economic growth.

Debate would continue, of course, about the relative claims of economic growth and distributive justice, about tradeoffs between inflation and unemployment, about tax policies and spending priorities. But these debates reflected the assumption that economic policy is concerned above all with the amount and the distribution of national wealth. With the triumph of fiscal policy, the political economy of citizenship gave way to the political economy of growth and distributive justice.

KEYNESIANISM AND LIBERALISM

The advent of the new political economy marked a decisive moment in the demise of the republican strand of American politics and the rise of contemporary liberalism. According to this liberalism, government should be neutral as to conceptions of the good life, in order to respect persons as free and independent selves, capable of choosing their own ends. Keynesian fiscal policy both reflected this liberalism and deepened its hold on American public life. Although those who practiced Keynesian economics did not defend it in precisely these terms, the new political economy displayed two features of the liberalism that defines the procedural republic. First, it offered policymakers and elected officials a way to "bracket," or set aside, controversial views of the good society, and so promised a consensus that programs for structural reform could not offer. Second, by abandoning the formative project, it denied government a stake in the moral character of its citizens and affirmed the notion of persons as free and independent selves.

The clearest expression of faith in the new economics as a neutral instrument of national governance was offered by President John F. Kennedy. In a commencement address at Yale University in 1962, he argued that modern economic problems could best be resolved if people set aside their ideological convictions. "The central domestic issues of our time," he observed, "are more subtle and less simple" than the large moral and political issues that commanded the nation's attention in earlier days. "They relate not to basic clashes of philosophy or ideology but to ways and means of reaching common goals. . . . What is at stake in our economic decisions today is not some grand warfare of rival ideologies which will sweep the country with passion but the practical management of a modern economy." Kennedy urged the country "to face technical problems without ideological preconceptions" and to focus on "the sophisticated and technical questions involved in keeping a great economic machinery moving ahead."

As Keynesian fiscal policy took hold in the 1960s, the civic strand of economic argument faded from American political discourse. Confronted with an economy too vast to admit republican hopes of mastery, and tempted by the prospect of prosperity, Americans of the postwar decades found their way to a new understanding of freedom. According to this understanding, our liberty depends not on our capacity as citizens to share in shaping the forces that govern our collective destiny but rather on our capacity as persons to choose our values and ends for ourselves.

From the standpoint of republican political theory, this shift represents a fateful concession; to abandon the formative ambition is to abandon the project of liberty as the republican tradition conceives it. But Americans did not experience the new public philosophy as disempowering—at least not at first. To the contrary, the procedural republic appeared to be a triumph of mastery and self-command. This was owing partly to the historical moment and partly to the promise of the liberal conception of freedom.

THE MOMENT OF MASTERY

The procedural republic was born at a rare moment of American mastery. At the end of the Second World War, the United States stood astride the world, an unrivaled global power. This power, combined with the buoyant economy of the postwar decades, accustomed a generation of Americans to seeing themselves as masters of their circumstances. John Kennedy's inaugural address gave stirring expression to a generation's conviction that it possessed powers of Promethean proportions. "The world is very different now," Kennedy proclaimed. "For man holds in his mortal hands the power to abolish all forms of human poverty and all forms of human life." We would "pay any price, bear any burden," to assure the success of liberty.

Beyond the bounty of American power, the promise of mastery in the postwar decades had another source in the public philosophy of contemporary liberalism itself. The image of persons as free and independent selves, unbound by moral or communal ties they have not chosen, is a liberating, even exhilarating, ideal. Freed from the dictates of custom or tradition, the liberal self is installed as sovereign, cast as the author of the only obligations that constrain. This image of freedom found expression across the political spectrum. Lyndon Johnson argued the case for the welfare state not in terms of communal obligation but instead in terms of enabling people to choose their own ends: "For more than thirty years, from Social Security to the war against poverty, we have diligently worked to enlarge the freedom of man," he said upon accepting the 1964 Democratic presidential nomination. "And as a result Americans tonight are freer to live as they want to live, to pursue their ambitions, to meet their desires . . . than at any time in all of our glorious history." Welfare-rights advocates opposed work requirements, mandatory job training, and family-planning programs for welfare recipients on the grounds that all people, including the poor, "should have the freedom to choose how they may express the meaning of their lives." For their part, conservative critics of Johnson's Great Society also made their arguments in the name of the liberal conception of freedom. The only legitimate functions of government, Barry Goldwater insisted, were those that made it "possible for men to follow their chosen pursuits with maximum freedom." The libertarian economist Milton Friedman opposed Social Security and other mandatory government programs on the grounds that they violated people's rights "to live their lives by their own values."

And so for a time the special circumstances of American life obscured the passing of the civic conception of freedom. But when the moment of mastery expired—when, in 1968, Vietnam, riots in the ghettos, campus unrest, and the assassinations of Martin Luther King Jr. and Robert Kennedy brought a shattering of faith—Americans were left ill equipped to contend with the dislocation that swirled about them. The liberating promise of the freely choosing self could not compensate for the loss of self-government more broadly conceived. Events spun out of control at home and abroad, and government seemed helpless to respond.

REAGAN'S CIVIC CONSERVATISM

There followed a season of protest that is with us still. As disillusionment with government grew, politicians groped to articulate the frustrations that the reigning political agenda did not address. The most successful, at least in electoral terms, was Ronald Reagan. Although he ultimately failed to allay the discontent he tapped, it is instructive nonetheless to consider the source of his appeal and the way it departed from the prevailing terms of political discourse.

Reagan drew, in different moods and moments, on both the libertarian and the civic strands of American conservatism. The most resonant part of his political appeal derived from the second of these, from his skillful evocation of communal values such as family and neighborhood, religion and patriotism. What set Reagan apart from laissez-faire conservatives also set him apart from the public philosophy of his day: his ability to identify with Americans' yearnings for a common life of larger meanings on a smaller, less impersonal scale than that the procedural republic provides.

Reagan blamed big government for disempowering citizens and proposed a "New Federalism" that would shift power to states and localities, recalling the long-standing republican worry about concentrated power. But Reagan revived this tradition with a difference. Previous advocates of republican political economy had worried about big government and big business alike. For Reagan, the curse of bigness attached to government alone. Even as he evoked the ideal of community, he had little to say about the corrosive effects of capital flight or the disempowering consequences of economic power organized on a vast scale.

Reagan-era Democrats did not challenge Reagan on this score, nor did they otherwise join the debate about community and self-government. Tied to the terms of rights-oriented liberalism, they missed the mood of discontent. The anxieties of the age concerned the erosion of those communities intermediate between the individual and the nation—families and neighborhoods, cities and towns, schools and congregations. But Democrats, once the party of dispersed power, had learned in recent decades to view intermediate communities with suspicion. Too often such communities had been pockets of prejudice, outposts of intolerance, places where the tyranny of the majority held sway. And so, from the New Deal to the civil-rights movement to the Great Society, the liberal project was to use federal power to vindicate individual rights that local communities had failed to protect. This unease with the middle terms of civic life, however honorably acquired, left Democrats ill equipped to attend to the erosion of self-government.

The civic strand of Reagan's rhetoric enabled him to succeed, where Democrats failed, in tapping the mood of discontent. In the end, however, Reagan's presidency did little to alter the conditions underlying the discontent. He governed more as a market conservative than as a civic conservative. The unfettered capitalism he favored did nothing to repair the moral fabric of families, neighborhoods, and communities and much to undermine them.

THE RISKS OF REPUBLICAN POLITICS

Any attempt to revitalize the civic strand of freedom must confront two sobering objections. The first doubts that it is possible to revive republican ideals; the second doubts that it is desirable. The first objection holds that given the scale and complexity of the modern world, it is unrealistic to aspire to self-government as the republican tradition conceives it. From Aristotle's polis to Jefferson's agrarian ideal, the civic conception of freedom found its home in small and bounded places, largely self-sufficient, inhabited by people whose conditions of life afforded the leisure, learning, and commonality to deliberate well about public concerns. But we do not live that way today. To the contrary, we live in a highly mobile continental society, teeming with diversity. Moreover, even this vast society is not self-sufficient but is situated in a global economy whose frenzied flow of money and goods, information and images, pays little heed to nations, much less neighborhoods. How, under conditions such as these, could the civic strand of freedom possibly take hold?

In fact, this objection continues, the republican strand of American politics, for all its persistence, has often spoken in a voice tinged with nostalgia. Even as Jefferson exalted the yeoman farmer, America was becoming a manufacturing nation. And so it was with the artisan republicans of Andrew Jackson's day, the apostles of free labor in Abraham Lincoln's time, and the shopkeepers and pharmacists Brandeis defended against the curse of bigness. In each of these cases—or so it is argued—republican ideals found their expression at the last moment, too late to offer feasible alternatives, just in time to offer an elegy for a lost cause. If the republican tradition is irredeemably nostalgic, then whatever its capacity to illuminate the defects of liberal politics, it offers little that could lead us to a richer civic life.

The second objection holds that even were it possible to recover republican ideals, to do so would not be desirable; given the difficulty of instilling civic virtue, republican politics always runs the risk of coercion. This peril can be glimpsed in Jean-Jacques Rousseau's account of the formative undertaking necessary to a democratic republic. The task of the republic's founder or great legislator, he writes, is no less than "to change human nature, to transform each individual . . . into a part of a larger whole from which this individual receives, in a sense, his life and his being." The legislator "must deny man his own forces" in order to make him reliant on the community as a whole. The more nearly each person's individual will is "dead and obliterated," the more likely that person is to embrace the general will. "Thus if each citizen is nothing and can do nothing except in concert with all the others . . . one can say that the legislation has achieved the highest possible point of perfection."

The coercive face of soulcraft is by no means unknown among American republicans. For example, Benjamin Rush, a signer of the Declaration of Independence, wanted "to convert men into republican machines" and to teach each citizen "that he does not belong to himself, but that he is public property." But civic education need not take so harsh a form. In practice, successful republican soulcraft involves a gentler kind of tutelage. For example, the political economy of citizenship that informed nineteenth-century American life sought to cultivate not only commonality but also the independence and judgment to deliberate well about the common good. It worked not by coercion but by a complex mixture of persuasion and habituation—what Alexis de Tocqueville called "the slow and quiet action of society upon itself."

The dispersed, differentiated character of American public life in Tocqueville's day and the indirect modes of character formation this differentiation allowed are what separate Rousseau's republican exertions from the civic practices Tocqueville described. Unable to abide disharmony, Rousseau's republican ideal seeks to collapse the distance between persons so that citizens stand in a kind of speechless transparence, or immediate presence to one another. Where the general will prevails, the citizens "consider themselves to be a single body" and there is no need for political argument. "The first to propose [a new law] merely says what everybody has already felt; and there is no question of intrigues or eloquence" to secure its passage.

It is this assumption, that the common good is unitary and uncontestable, not the formative ambition as such, that inclines Rous-

seau's politics to coercion. It is, moreover, an assumption that republican politics can do without. As America's experience with the
political economy of citizenship suggests, the civic conception of
freedom does not render disagreement unnecessary. It offers a way of
conducting political argument, not transcending it.

Unlike Rousseau's unitary vision, the republican politics Tocqueville described is more clamorous than consensual. It does not despise differentiation. Instead of collapsing the space between persons,
it fills this space with public institutions that gather people together
in various capacities, that both separate and relate them. These institutions include the townships, schools, religions, and virtue-sustaining occupations that form the "character of mind" and "habits of the
heart" a democratic republic requires. Whatever their more particular purposes, these agencies of civic education inculcate the habit of
attending to public things. And yet given their multiplicity, they prevent public life from dissolving into an undifferentiated whole.

So the civic strand of freedom is not necessarily coercive. It can
sometimes find pluralistic expression. To this extent the liberal objection to republican political theory is misplaced. But the liberal
worry does contain an insight that cannot be dismissed: republican
politics is risky politics, a politics without guarantees, and the risks it
entails inhere in the formative project. To accord the political community a stake in the character of its citizens is to concede the possibility that bad communities may form bad characters. Dispersed
power and multiple sites of civic formation may reduce these dangers but cannot remove them.

WHERE LIBERALS FEAR TO TREAD

What to make of this complaint depends on the alternatives. If there
were a way to secure freedom without attending to the character of
citizens, or to define rights without affirming a conception of the
good life, then the liberal objection to the formative project might be

decisive. But is there such a way? Liberal political theory claims that there is. The voluntarist conception of freedom promises to lay to rest, once and for all, the risks of republican politics. If liberty can be detached from the exercise of self-government and conceived instead as the capacity of persons to choose their own ends, then the difficult task of forming civic virtue can finally be dispensed with. Or at least it can be narrowed to the seemingly simpler task of cultivating toleration and respect for others.

In the voluntarist conception of freedom, statecraft no longer needs soulcraft, except in a limited domain. Tying freedom to respect for the rights of freely choosing selves dampens old disputes about how to form the habits of self-rule. It spares politics the ancient quarrels about the nature of the good life. Once freedom is detached from the formative project, "the problem of setting up a state can be solved even by a nation of devils," in Kant's memorable words. "For such a task does not involve the moral improvement of man."

But the liberal attempt to detach freedom from the formative project confronts problems of its own, problems that can be seen in both the theory and the practice of the procedural republic. The philosophical difficulty lies in the liberal conception of citizens as freely choosing, independent selves, unencumbered by moral or civic ties antecedent to choice. This vision cannot account for a wide range of moral and political obligations that we commonly recognize, such as obligations of loyalty or solidarity. By insisting that we are bound only by ends and roles we choose for ourselves, it denies that we can ever be claimed by ends we have not chosen—ends given by nature or God, for example, or by our identities as members of families, peoples, cultures, or traditions.

Some liberals concede that we may be bound by obligations such as these but insist that they apply to private life alone and have no bearing on politics. But this raises a further difficulty. Why insist on separating our identity as citizens from our identity as persons more broadly conceived? Why should political deliberation not reflect our best understanding of the highest human ends? Don't arguments about justice and rights unavoidably draw on particular conceptions of the good life, whether we admit it or not?

The problems in the theory of procedural liberalism show up in the practice it inspires. A politics that brackets morality and religion too completely soon generates its own disenchantment. Where political discourse lacks moral resonance, the yearning for a public life of larger meaning finds undesirable expression. The Christian Coalition and similar groups seek to clothe the naked public square with narrow, intolerant moralisms. Fundamentalists rush in where liberals fear to tread. The disenchantment also assumes more secular forms. Absent a political agenda that addresses the moral dimension of public questions, attention becomes riveted on the private vices of public officials. Political discourse becomes increasingly preoccupied with the scandalous, the sensational, and the confessional as purveyed by tabloids, talk shows, and eventually the mainstream media as well. It cannot be said that the public philosophy of contemporary liberalism is wholly responsible for these tendencies. But liberalism's vision of political discourse is too spare to contain the moral energies of democratic life. It creates a moral void that opens the way for intolerance and other misguided moralisms.

A political agenda lacking substantive moral discourse is one symptom of the public philosophy of the procedural republic. Another is a loss of mastery. The triumph of the voluntarist conception of freedom has coincided with a growing sense of disempowerment. Despite the expansion of rights in recent decades, Americans find to their frustration that they are losing control of the forces that govern their lives. This has partly to do with the insecurity of jobs in the global economy, but it also reflects the self-image by which we live. The liberal self-image and the actual organization of modern social and economic life are sharply at odds. Even as we think and act as freely choosing, independent selves, we confront a world governed by impersonal structures of power that defy our understanding and control. The voluntarist conception of freedom leaves us ill equipped to contend with this condition. Liberated though we may be from the burden of identities we have not chosen, entitled though we may be to the range of rights assured by the welfare state, we find ourselves overwhelmed as we turn to face the world on our own resources.

GLOBAL POLITICS AND PARTICULAR IDENTITIES

If the public philosophy of contemporary liberalism fails to address democracy's discontent, the question remains how a renewed attention to republican themes might better equip us to contend with our condition. Is self-government in the republican sense even possible under modern conditions, and if so, what qualities of character would be necessary to sustain it?

A partial, inchoate answer can be glimpsed in the shifting terms of contemporary political argument. Some conservatives, and recently some liberals, have gestured toward a revival of civic virtue, character formation, and moral judgment as considerations in public policy and political discourse. From the 1930s to the 1980s conservatives criticized the welfare state on libertarian grounds. Since the mid-1980s, however, the conservative argument has focused on the moral and civic consequences of federal social policy. Welfare is at odds with freedom, many conservatives now argue, not because it coerces taxpayers but because it breeds dependence and irresponsibility among recipients and so deprives them of the independence that full citizenship requires.

Liberals came more reluctantly to the revolt against the procedural republic, but they too have begun to articulate civic themes. In November of 1993, speaking in the Memphis church where Martin Luther King Jr. preached the night before his assassination, Bill Clinton ventured onto moral and spiritual terrain that liberals of recent times had sought to avoid. Restoring work to the life of the inner city was essential, he explained, not only for the income it would bring but also for its character-forming effects, for the discipline, structure, and pride that work confers on family life.

But suppose that the civic intimations present in our politics did find fuller voice and succeeded in reorienting the terms of political discourse. What is the prospect that a revitalized politics could actually alleviate the loss of mastery and the erosion of community that lie at the heart of democracy's discontent? Even a politics that engaged rather than avoided substantive moral discourse and managed to revive the formative project would confront a daunting obstacle. This obstacle consists in the formidable scale on which modern economic life is organized and the difficulty of achieving the democratic political authority necessary to govern it.

The difficulty actually involves two related challenges. One is to devise political institutions capable of governing the global economy. The other is to cultivate the civic identities necessary to sustain those institutions, to supply them with the moral authority they require. It is not obvious that both these challenges can be met.

In a world where capital and goods, information and images, pollution and people, flow across national boundaries with unprecedented ease, politics must assume transnational, even global, forms, if only to keep up. Otherwise, economic power will go unchecked by democratically sanctioned political power. Nation-states, traditionally the vehicles of self-government, will find themselves increasingly unable to bring their citizens' judgments to bear on the economic forces that govern their destinies. If the global character of the economy suggests the need for transnational forms of governance, however, it remains to be seen whether such political units can inspire the identification and allegiance—the moral and civic culture—on which democratic authority ultimately depends.

In striking ways, the challenge to self-government in the global economy resembles the predicament American politics faced in the early decades of the twentieth century. Then as now, new forms of commerce and communication spilled across familiar political boundaries and created networks of interdependence among people in distant places. But the new interdependence did not carry with it a new sense of community. Jane Addams's insight, that "the mere mechanical fact of interdependence amounts to nothing," is no less apt today. What railroads, telegraph wires, and national markets were to her time, satellite hookups, CNN, cyberspace, and global markets are to ours—instruments that link people without necessarily making them neighbors or fellow citizens or participants in a common venture.

Given the similarity between their predicament and ours, it is tempting to think that the logic of the Progressives' solution can be extended to our time. If the way to respond to a national economy was to strengthen the national government and cultivate a sense of national citizenship, perhaps the way to respond to a global economy is to strengthen global governance and cultivate a corresponding sense of global or cosmopolitan citizenship. Internationally minded reformers have already begun to articulate this impulse. The Commission on Global Governance, a group of twenty-eight public officials from around the world, recently published a report calling for greater authority for international institutions. The commission also called for efforts to inspire "broad acceptance of a global civic ethic," to transform "a global neighborhood based on economic exchange and improved communications into a universal moral community."

The analogy between the globalizing impulse of our time and the nationalizing project of the Progressives' time does hold to this extent: We cannot hope to govern the global economy without transnational political institutions, and we cannot expect to sustain such institutions without cultivating more-expansive civic identities. Human-rights conventions, global environmental accords, and world bodies governing trade, finance, and economic development are among the undertakings that will depend for public support on inspiring a greater sense of engagement in a shared global destiny.

But the cosmopolitan vision is wrong to suggest that we can re-store self-government simply by pushing sovereignty and citizenship upward. The hope for self-government today lies not in relocating sovereignty but in dispersing it. The most promising alternative to the sovereign state is not a cosmopolitan community based on the solidarity of humankind but a multiplicity of communities and political bodies—some more extensive than nations and some less—among which sovereignty is diffused. Only a politics that disperses sovereignty both upward and downward can combine the power required to rival global market forces with the differentiation required of a public life that hopes to inspire the allegiance of its citizens.

In some places dispersing sovereignty may entail according greater cultural and political autonomy to subnational communities—such as Catalans and Kurds, Scots and Quebecois—even while strengthening and democratizing the European Union and other transnational structures. Arrangements like these may avoid the strife that arises when state sovereignty is an all-or-nothing affair. In the United States, which never was a nation-state in the European sense, proliferating sites of political engagement may take a different form. America was born of the conviction that sovereignty need not reside in a single place. From the start the Constitution divided power among branches and levels of government. Over time, however, we too have pushed sovereignty and citizenship upward, in the direction of the nation.

The nationalizing of American political life occurred largely in response to industrial capitalism. The consolidation of economic power called forth the consolidation of political power. Present-day conservatives who rail against big government often ignore this fact. They wrongly assume that rolling back the power of the national government would liberate individuals to pursue their own ends, instead of leaving them at the mercy of economic forces beyond their control.

Conservative complaints about big government find popular resonance, but not for the reasons conservatives articulate. The American welfare state is politically vulnerable because it does not rest on a sense of national community adequate to its purpose. The nationalizing project that unfolded from the Progressive Era to the New Deal to the Great Society succeeded only in part. It managed to create a strong national government but failed to cultivate a shared national identity. As the welfare state developed, it drew less on an ethic of social solidarity and mutual obligation and more on an ethic of fair procedures and individual rights. But the liberalism of the procedural republic proved an inadequate substitute for the strong sense of citizenship that the welfare state requires.

If the nation cannot summon more than a minimal commonality, it is unlikely that the global community can do better, at least on its own. A more promising basis for a democratic politics that reaches beyond nations is a revitalized civic life nourished in the more particular communities we inhabit. In the age of NAFTA the politics of neighborhood matters more, not less. People will not pledge allegiance to vast and distant entities, whatever their importance, unless those institutions are somehow connected to political arrangements that reflect the identity of the participants.

BEYOND SOVEREIGN STATES AND SOVEREIGN SELVES

The growing aspiration for the public expression of communal identities reflects a yearning for political arrangements that can situate people in a world increasingly governed by vast and distant forces. For a time the nation-state promised to answer this yearning, to provide the link between identity and self-rule. In theory at least, each state was a more or less self-sufficient political and economic unit that gave expression to the collective identity of a people defined by a common history, language, or tradition. The nation-state laid claim to the allegiance of its citizens on the ground that its exercise of sovereignty expressed their collective identity.

In the contemporary world, however, this claim is losing its force. National sovereignty is eroded from above by the mobility of capital, goods, and information across national boundaries, the integration of world financial markets, and the transnational character of industrial production. And national sovereignty is challenged from below by the resurgent aspirations of subnational groups for autonomy and self-rule. As their effective sovereignty fades, nations gradually lose their hold on the allegiance of their citizens. Beset by the integrating tendencies of the global economy and the fragmenting tendencies of group identities, nation-states are increasingly unable to link identity and self-rule. Even the most powerful states cannot escape the imperatives of the global economy; even the smallest are too heterogeneous to give full expression to the communal identity of any one ethnic or national or religious group without oppressing others who live in their midst.

Since the days of Aristotle's polis, the republican tradition has viewed self-government as an activity rooted in a particular place, carried out by citizens loyal to that place and the way of life it embodies. Self-government today, however, requires a politics that plays itself out in a multiplicity of settings, from neighborhoods to nations to the world as a whole. Such a politics requires citizens who can abide the ambiguity associated with divided sovereignty, who can think and act as multiply situated selves. The civic virtue distinctive to our time is the capacity to negotiate our way among the sometimes overlapping and sometimes conflicting obligations that claim us, and to live with the tension to which multiple loyalties give rise.

The global media and markets that shape our lives beckon us to a world beyond boundaries and belonging. But the civic resources we need to master these forces, or at least to contend with them, are still to be found in the places and stories, memories and meanings, incidents and identities, that situate us in the world and give our lives their moral particularity. The task for politics now is to cultivate these resources, to repair the civic life on which democracy depends.

two

BEYOND INDIVIDUALISM
DEMOCRATS AND COMMUNITY

This essay appeared as the 1988 presidential primary season began. Michael Dukakis won the Democratic nomination that
year, and was defeated by George H. W. Bush in the general
election.

For half a century, the Democratic Party was sustained by the public
philosophy of New Deal liberalism. Democrats and Republicans debated the role of government in the market economy, and the responsibility of the nation for the collective provision of basic needs.
The Democrats won that debate, and elected every president but Eisenhower from 1932 to 1964.

In time the Republicans stopped attacking the welfare state and
argued instead that they could manage it better. But the New Deal
agenda continued to define the terms of debate, and the meaning of
liberalism and conservatism. Liberals favored a greater federal role in
the social and economic life of the nation, conservative less.

Between these alternatives flowed the rhythms of American politics. Arthur Schlesinger Jr. has written that American politics moves
in cycles, from activism to quietude and back again. Since progress
demands passions that cannot last for long, liberalism advances by
seasons, punctuated by conservative interludes that set the stage for
further reforms.

Thus the complacent Republican '20s gave way to the activism of

FDR and Truman, which receded in turn to the languid years of Eisenhower. A time of consolidation prepared the way for renewed political exertions, for Kennedy's call to "get the country moving again," and Lyndon Johnson's Great Society. By the end of the '60s, exhausted and divided, the country collapsed into Richard Nixon's awkward embrace.

This account of the political pendulum explains the predominance of the Democratic Party in recent times. Although it assigns to each party a distinctive vocation—the Democrats reform, the Republicans repose—it casts the Democratic Party as the primary agent of moral and political improvement. And so, for half a century, the Democrats have been. The welfare state took shape under Democratic auspices, and the great issues of the 1960s—civil rights and the Vietnam War—were fought out not between the parties but within the Democratic Party.

If the cycles of American politics hold up, 1988 should be a Democratic year. If the world turns as the conventional wisdom suggests, eight years of Ronald Reagan will have left a country ripe for reform.

But there is reason to think that the cycle has stalled, the pattern dissolved. By the 1970s the New Deal agenda had become obsolete. The alternatives it posed lost their capacity to inspire the electorate or animate meaningful debate. Voter turnout steadily declined from the '60s to the '80s, party loyalties eroded, and disillusion with government grew. Meanwhile, politicians groped to articulate frustrations and discontents that the reigning political agenda did not capture. From the left and the right came a politics of protest. In the 1972 primaries, pollsters found to their surprise that many supporters of George Wallace favored George McGovern as their second choice. Despite their ideological differences, both appealed to a tradition of populist protest.

In 1976 Jimmy Carter brought the Southern and progressive strands of populist protest together in a single candidacy. Like Wallace and McGovern, he campaigned as a political outsider, a critic of the federal bureaucracy and the Washington establishment. But Carter's presidency only deepened the discontent he had tapped as a candidate. Four years later another self-described political outsider, Ronald Reagan, ran for president by running against government, and won.

In different ways, both Carter and Reagan spoke to anxieties that the New Deal agenda failed to address. Both sensed a growing fear that, individually and collectively, we are less and less in control of the forces that govern our lives. Despite the extension of rights and entitlements in recent decades, and despite the expansion of the franchise, Americans increasingly find themselves in the grip of impersonal structures of power that defy their understanding and control.

By the 1970s a generation weaned on ever-rising standards of living and unrivaled American power suddenly confronted a world it could not summon or command. A decade of inflation and declining real wages undercut Americans' confidence that we could shape our personal destinies. Meanwhile, events in the world at large symbolized the loss of collective mastery—in Vietnam, a war we could not win, in Iran, a hostage-taking we could not avenge, and in 1987, a stock market crash that even the experts could not explain.

To make matters worse, the flow of power to large-scale institutions coincided with the decline of traditional communities. Families and neighborhoods, cities and towns, religious and ethnic and regional communities were eroded or homogenized, leaving the individual to confront the impersonal forces of the economy and the state without the moral or political resources that intermediate communities provide.

It is clear by now that Ronald Reagan's presidency has not addressed the worries and longings his candidacy so effectively evoked. For all the talk of "America standing tall," it neither restored our sense of self-mastery nor reversed the erosion of community. The

Marines killed in Lebanon, the failed attempt to trade arms for hostages, the Wall Street plunge, and a gaping trade deficit are Reagan-era reminders of a world spinning out of control.

Still, Democrats will not reap the fruits of Reagan's failures until they learn from his success at speaking the language of self-government and community. Oddly enough, a new public philosophy for American liberalism has something to learn from Ronald Reagan's conservative vision.

Political genius is more instinctive than deliberate, especially so in the case of Reagan. His genius was to bring together in a single voice two contending strands in American conservatism. The first is individualistic, libertarian, and laissez-faire, the second communal, traditionalist, and Moral Majoritarian. The first seeks a greater role for markets in public life, the second a greater role for morals.

Individualist conservatives believe people should be free to do as they please so long as they do not harm others. They are the conservatives who talk about "getting government off people's backs." Communal conservatives, by contrast, believe government should affirm moral and religious values. They want to ban abortion, restrict pornography, and restore prayer to public schools. While the first favor a volunteer army in the name of individual liberty, the second favor conscription in hopes of cultivating civic virtue. The first oppose the welfare state as a form of coerced charity; the second favor a welfare state that promotes conservative values.

Reagan managed to affirm both ethics without ever choosing between them. In his capacious conservatism, Milton Friedman met Jerry Falwell, and the two coexisted for a time. But Reagan's political achievement was not simply to make bedfellows of libertarian economists and fundamentalist preachers. It was to draw from conservative ideals a set of themes that spoke to the troubles of the time.

And here lies the lesson that American liberalism has still to learn: the themes that resonated most deeply came from the second strand, the communal strand of conservative thought. For all Reagan's talk of individual liberty and market solutions, the most potent part of his appeal was his evocation of communal values—of family and neighborhood, religion and patriotism. What Reagan stirred was a yearning for a way of life that seems to be receding in recent times— a common life of larger meanings, on a smaller, less impersonal scale than the nation-state provides.

To their political misfortune, Democrats in recent years have not spoken convincingly about self-government and community. More than a matter of rhetoric, the reasons run deep in liberal political theory. For, unlike conservatism, contemporary liberalism lacks a second voice, or communal strand. Its predominant impulse is individualistic.

Like laissez-faire conservatives, liberals believe that government should be neutral on moral and religious questions. Rather than affirm in law a particular vision of the good life, liberals would leave individuals free to choose their values for themselves. They believe government should protect people's rights, not promote civic virtue. It should offer a framework of rights, neutral among ends, within which its citizens may pursue whatever values they happen to have.

Though they share the ideal of a neutral state that protects individual rights, individualist conservatives and liberals disagree about what rights are fundamental, and about *what* political arrangements the ideal of neutrality requires. Conservatives emphasize private property rights, and claim that freedom of choice is most fully realized in an unfettered market economy. Liberals reply that genuine freedom requires certain social and economic prerequisites, and so argue for rights to welfare, education, employment, housing, health care, and the like.

And so, for half a century, the argument has gone. Locked in battle with laissez-faire conservatives, liberals defended the welfare state in the individualistic language of rights and entitlements. For example, the Social Security system was set up from the start to resemble a private insurance scheme rather than a social welfare program, funded by payroll "contributions," not general tax revenues. FDR rightly thought this would assure its political survival.

Compared with the social democracies of Europe, the American welfare state draws less on notions of communal obligation and social solidarity and more on notions of individual rights. Given the individualism of American political culture, this may have been the only way to win broad support for the public provision of basic human goods.

But political considerations aside, liberals are troubled in principle by strong notions of self-government and community. If government is not neutral, they ask, then what is to prevent an intolerant majority from imposing its values on those who disagree? Didn't the struggle for civil rights show that "local control" can be a code word for racism, that "community" is the first refuge of prejudice and intolerance? And hasn't the rise of the religious right taught the danger of mixing morality and politics?

When Democrats do speak of community, they usually mean the national community. FDR argued for "extending to our national life, the old principle of the local community," and encouraged Americans to think of themselves as "neighbors" bound in national community. More recently, Democrats have used the family as a metaphor for the ties of national citizenship. Urging the Great Society, Lyndon Johnson saw "America as a family, its people bound together by common ties of confidence and affection." In 1984 Walter Mondale and Mario Cuomo also compared the nation to a family. As Mondale proclaimed, "Let us be a community, a family where we care for each other, knit together by a band of love."

But the yearning for community can no longer be satisfied by depicting the nation as a family or a neighborhood. The metaphor is by now too strained to carry conviction. The nation is too vast to sustain more than a minimal commonality, too distant to permit more than occasional moments of participation.

Local attachments can serve self-government by engaging citizens in a common life beyond their private pursuits, and by cultivating the habit of attending to public things. They can enable citizens, in Tocqueville's phrase, to "practice the art of government in the small sphere within their reach."

Ideally at least, the reach extends as the sphere expands. Civic capacities first awakened in neighborhoods and town halls, churches and synagogues, trade unions and social movements, find national expression. For example, the civic education and social solidarity cultivated in the black Baptist churches of the South were a crucial prerequisite for the civil rights movement that ultimately unfolded on a national scale. What began as a bus boycott in Montgomery later became a general challenge to segregation in the South, which led in turn to a national campaign for equal citizenship and the right to vote. But more than a means of winning the vote, the movement itself was a moment of self-government, an instance of empowerment. It offered an example of the kind of civic engagement that can flow from local attachments and communal ties.

From the New Deal to the Great Society, the individualistic ethic of rights and entitlements offered an energizing, progressive force. But by the 1970s it had lost its capacity to inspire. Lacking a communal sensibility, liberals missed the mood of the discontent. They did not understand how people could be more entitled but less empowered at the same time.

The anxieties of the age concern the erosion of those communities intermediate between the individual and the nation, from families and neighborhoods to cities and towns to communities defined by religious or ethnic or cultural traditions. American democracy has long relied on communities like these to cultivate a public spirit that the nation alone cannot command. Self-government requires community, for people aspire to control their destiny not only as individuals, but as participants in a common life with which they can identify.

But the public philosophy of rights and entitlements left Democrats suspicious of intermediate communities. From the New Deal to the civil rights movement to the Great Society, the liberal project was to use the federal government to vindicate individual rights that local communities had failed to protect. Unable to fulfill the longing for self-government and community, Democrats allowed Ronald Reagan and the religious right to capture these aspirations and bend them to conservative purposes.

This abdication was politically costly, for as Reagan has shown, the communal dimension of politics is too potent to ignore. But it was also philosophically unnecessary, for there is nothing intrinsically conservative about family or neighborhood or community or religion. To the contrary, under modern conditions, traditional values cannot be vindicated by conservative policies. This can be seen in Reagan's failure to govern by the vision he evoked.

Reagan's proposed solution to the erosion of self-government was to shift power from the federal government to states and localities—to cut federal domestic spending, to decentralize and deregulate. A revitalized federal system would restore people's control over their lives by locating power closer to home. Meanwhile, a less activist federal judiciary would strengthen traditional values by allowing communities to legislate morality in the areas of abortion, pornography, homosexuality, and school prayer.

But this approach was bound to fail, because it ignored the conditions that led to the growth of federal power in the first place, including the growth of corporate power on a national, and now international, scale.

In its origins, federalism was designed to promote self-government by dispersing political power. But this arrangement presupposed the decentralized economy prevailing at the time. As national markets and large-scale enterprise grew, the political forms of the early republic became inadequate to self-government. Since the turn of the century, the concentration of political power has been a response to the concentration of economic power, an attempt to preserve democratic control.

Decentralizing government without decentralizing the economy, as Reagan proposed, is only half a federalism. And from the standpoint of self-government, half a federalism is worse than none. Leaving local communities to the mercy of corporate decisions made in distant places does not empower them; if anything it diminishes their ability to shape their destiny.

For similar reasons, conservative policies cannot answer the aspiration for community. The greatest corrosive of traditional values are not liberal judges but features of the modern economy that conservatives ignore. These include the unrestrained mobility of capital, with its disruptive effects on neighborhoods, cities, and towns; the concentration of power in large corporations unaccountable to the communities they serve; and an inflexible workplace that forces working men and women to choose between advancing their careers and caring for their children.

In the end, Reagan's presidency was an evocative success and a practical failure. In both respects, it offers insights that can inform a public philosophy for American liberalism.

First, liberalism must learn the language of self-government and community. It needs a vision of self-government that goes beyond voting rights, important though they are. And it needs a vision of community that embraces the rich array of civic resources intermediate between the individual and the nation.

Second, no amount of exhortation can rejuvenate communities unless people identify with them and have reason to participate in them. So Democrats need a revitalized federalism of their own, and

should begin to debate the political responsibilities best suited to local control. A Democratic theory of federalism might begin by defining the basic rights of national citizenship, and seek ways, consistent
with those rights, of giving local communities a greater role in the
decisions that govern their lives. It might ask, for example, how to
enhance local control of schools consistent with nationally assured
rights to racial equality and a decent education for all citizens.

Third, Democrats must acknowledge, as Republicans do not, that
any meaningful devolution of political power requires reform in the
structure of the modern economy. They need policies to deal with
the unprecedented mobility of capital, the unaccountable power of
large corporations, and the adversarial relations of labor and management. A public philosophy that put self-government first would
focus less on macroeconomic issues such as budget deficits and tax
rates and more on questions of economic structure. And it would address these questions not only from the standpoint of maximizing
GNP, but also from that of building communities capable of self-
government on a manageable scale.

In this respect, it would recall an older debate in the progressive
tradition, a debate about the economic arrangements most amenable
to democratic government. Some New Dealers favored national economic planning as a way of preserving democracy in the face of
economic power, others anti-trust policy and economic decentraliza-
tion. Earlier in the century, the New Nationalism of Theodore Roosevelt opposed the New Freedom of Woodrow Wilson. Despite their
differences, the participants in those debates understood that economic policy was not only about consumption but also about self-
government. Democrats today would do well to recover that insight
of their progressive forebears.

Finally, Democrats should overcome the impulse to banish moral
and religious discourse from public life. They should reject the idea
that government can be neutral. A public life empty of moral mean-

ings and shared ideals does not secure freedom but offers an open invitation to intolerance. As the Moral Majority has shown, a politics whose moral resources are diminished with disuse lies vulnerable to those who would impose narrow moralisms. Fundamentalists rush in where liberals fear to tread. The answer for liberals is not to flee moral arguments but to engage them. In any case, liberals have long been making moral arguments, often explicitly so. The civil rights movement "legislated morality," and drew without apology on religious themes.

In recent years liberalism has faltered because of its failure to argue for a vision of the common good. This has conceded to conservatives the most potent resources of American politics. A public philosophy of self-government and community would reclaim those resources for liberal purposes, and enable Democrats to resume their career as the party of moral and political progress.

three

THE POLITICS
OF EASY VIRTUE

This essay and the next appeared during the presidential campaign of 1996, between Bill Clinton and his Republican challenger, Bob Dole. Clinton was re-elected by a comfortable margin.

Ever since Richard Nixon won the presidency by standing for law and order and against the counterculture, Democrats have been on the defensive about values. Until now. In one of the great reversals of contemporary American politics, Bill Clinton has seized the upper hand in the politics of virtue. Over the past year, Clinton has promoted the V-chip, curfews, and school uniforms, and condemned teenage pregnancy, smoking, and truancy. Some mock this agenda as a litany of small favors, and wonder when the president will come out against cussing. But, as Republicans have known for some time, easy virtue goes a long way in American politics, longer perhaps than more strenuous versions.

No one understood this better than Ronald Reagan. He skillfully evoked family and neighborhood, religion and patriotism, even while promoting an unfettered capitalism that undermined the traditions and communities he praised. Other Republicans followed. George H. W. Bush, who invoked values more out of strategy than conviction, posed in a flag factory and introduced us to Willie Horton. Dan Quayle criticized the television character Murphy Brown for bearing a child out of wedlock. William Bennett led a campaign against the violent lyrics of rap music. Patrick Buchanan demanded that we "take back our culture and take back our country." Democrats, meanwhile, resisted the politics of virtue, not by disputing conservatives' particular moral judgments but by rejecting the idea that moral judgments have a place in the public realm. When Republicans tried to ban abortion, oppose gay rights, or promote school prayer, liberals replied that government should not legislate morality or concern itself with the moral character of citizens. Turning statecraft into soulcraft, they argued, runs the risk of coercion. Politics should not be about telling people how to live but about giving people the freedom to choose for themselves.

The liberals' insistence that politics be neutral on moral and religious matters was misguided in principle and costly in practice. As a philosophical matter, it is by no means clear that government can or should be neutral on the pressing moral questions of the day. The civil rights laws legislated morality, and rightly so. Not only did they ban odious practices, like the segregation of lunch counters; they also aimed at changing moral sentiments.

Philosophy aside, the Democrats' rejection of the politics of virtue carried a high price, for it left conservatives with a monopoly on moral discourse in politics. This helped Republicans win five of the six presidential elections between 1968 and 1988. Bill Clinton finally broke the pattern, winning as a "New Democrat" who stressed responsibility as well as rights. But Clinton's success at wresting the values issue from Republicans became clear only in the summer of 1996.

Two things made it possible. The first was the Republican takeover of Congress in the mid-term elections. Once Clinton could no longer hope to legislate, he fell back on the presidency's rhetorical dimension. And with the bully pulpit comes an invitation to soulcraft.

The second was the nomination of Bob Dole, a man who lacks both the gift and the taste for talk of virtue. In his one valiant attempt to bring morals to bear on markets, he delivered a speech in Hollywood a year ago denouncing movie-makers for pandering to the public's taste for violence, sex, and depravity. But his heart was not in it. He recently returned to Hollywood to declare that there was no conflict between markets and morals after all. Movie-makers could make plenty of money by catering to our nobler instincts, as in the box office hit Independence Day, a high-tech shoot-up about alien space invaders. No longer the scolding prophet, Dole now spoke as an earnest public relations consultant. "In Hollywood today, the big story is that responsibility is good business. You can watch your ratings rise and your box-office receipts go up and still look yourself in the mirror." The ticket window, Dole argued, was a "cultural ballot box" that proved Americans' preference for "the good over the grotesque, excellence over exploitation, quiet virtue over gratuitous violence."

Faced with the need to energize his candidacy, Dole had to choose between the two great enthusiasms of modern Republican politics: the moral fervor of the religious right or the tax-cutting fervor of the supply-side true-believers. Weary of the abortion struggle that has divided his party, Dole opted for the second, leaving Clinton an opening on the values front. In an interview on values with USA Today, Dole could not conceal his impatience with the whole subject. His acceptance speech, he said, would be "pretty heavy on values." He would make the point that "it doesn't take a village, it takes a family. And whatever." But even this grudging concession to the politics of virtue seemed to offend his laconic sensibility. "What, do you run around saying, 'I'm the Values Candidate, c'mon in. I'll give you some values'?"

Clinton, hampered by no such reticence, had still to find some content for his soulcraft. How to do so was far from obvious. Previous presidents had mounted the bully pulpit to ask great sacrifices of their fellow citizens—to risk their lives in war, or to share their bounty with the less fortunate, or to forgo material consumption for the sake of civic virtue. And true to liberal worries, the most ambitious episodes of soulcraft often involved a measure of coercion, as in nineteenth-century efforts to Americanize immigrants and Progressive era attempts to combat poverty through settlement houses and other means of moral uplift.

But what kind of soulcraft is suited to a nation hungry for community but unwilling to abide restraint, yearning for moral purpose but in no mood for sacrifice? By design or intuition, Clinton has discovered a solution: don't impose moral restraints on adults; impose them on children. What V-chips, curfews, school uniforms, and campaigns against truancy, teenage pregnancy, and underage smoking have in common is that they all address people's anxieties about the erosion of moral authority by attending to the moral character of their children. Clinton's politics of virtue avoids the objection of paternalism by becoming, strictly speaking, paternal.

Some may complain that, compared to historic projects of moral and civic improvement, Clinton's sermonizing amounts to soulcraft lite, an exercise in easy virtue that does little to challenge the civic habits and dispositions of grown-ups. But perhaps that is all we can expect these days. Clinton's politics of virtue is at least an improvement over flag factories and Willie Horton. And it just might help make him become the first Democratic president since FDR to win re-election.

This presidential campaign offers a choice between one big, unworthy idea and many worthy little ones. The big but unworthy idea is at the heart of Bob Dole's proposed tax cut: people should keep more of what they earn. It is not clear why they should. First, given the budget deficit and unmet public needs, the government needs the money. Second, Americans already pay a smaller share of national income in taxes than do citizens of any other industrial democracy. Finally, by offering no higher purpose than lower taxes, Dole contradicts the admirable declaration in his acceptance speech that presidents should place moral considerations above material ones. Dole tries, on occasion, to elevate the moral status of tax cuts, arguing that too much taxation encroaches on liberty. But it is difficult to see how shifting a few hundred dollars per person to private consumption will make Americans more free.

Bill Clinton's campaign, bereft of big ideas, is littered with small ones—a volunteer literacy program, vouchers for job training, a ban on bullets that pierce bulletproof vests, new curbs on cigarettes, a law against forcing women out of maternity wards less than forty-eight hours after giving birth, a plan to reduce busy signals when people dial 911. These are good ideas, but they don't add up to a governing vision. Clinton has decided, probably rightly, that he does not need one to win.

This is the Dole campaign's most important failure: it has made life too easy for Clinton. It has absolved him of the challenge to re-think progressive politics or to grapple with the forces that, sooner or later, will transform American political debate. Had Pat Buchanan been the Republican nominee, Clinton would have been forced to confront the anxieties produced by the changing nature of work, the erosion of traditional communities, the rise of global markets, and the declining sovereignty of nations. Faced with a Republican whose political imagination runs in the well-worn grooves of tired party politics, however, Clinton can cleave to the conventional center with-out addressing the larger questions looming on the horizon. For all the president's talk of a bridge to the twenty-first century, this elec-tion will be remembered, if it is remembered at all, not as the begin-ning of a new era in American politics, but as the fading expression of an old one.

The defining election of the twenty-first century may not come for a decade or more. The questions that animate an age only be-come clear when, under pressure of events, people find ways of ex-plaining the new circumstances in which they live. The election that "built the bridge" to the twentieth century did not occur until 1912. It was then that Woodrow Wilson, the Democrat, and Theodore Roo-sevelt, running on the Bull Moose ticket, articulated the big ideas that gave shape to the politics of the twentieth century.

Their predicament was similar to ours. Then, as now, there was an uneasy fit between the scale of economic life and the terms of po-litical community. Railroads, telephones, telegraph wires, and daily newspapers spilled across local boundaries, bringing people into contact with events in distant places. National markets and a com-plex industrial system made workers and consumers interdependent. But Americans, accustomed to finding their bearings in small com-munities, felt powerless in the face of forces beyond their control. A decentralized political system, invented for a nation of farmers and shopkeepers, was dwarfed by the power of giant corporations.

How could a locally based democracy govern an economy national in scope? That question divided Wilson and Roosevelt. Wilson argued for breaking up the trusts and decentralizing economic power so it could be held accountable by local political units. Big business had become "vastly more centralized than the political organization of the country itself," Wilson declared. Corporations had bigger budgets than states "and loomed bigger than whole commonwealths in their influence over the lives and fortunes of entire communities of men." Simply to accept and regulate monopoly power was, according to Wilson, a kind of capitulation. "Have we come to a time," he asked, "when the President of the United States must doff his cap in the presence of this high finance, and say, 'You are our inevitable master, but we will see how we can make the best of it?'"

Teddy Roosevelt considered big business an inevitable product of industrial development and saw little point in trying to restore the decentralized economy of the nineteenth century. The only way to contend with national economic power, he argued, was to enlarge the capacity of national democratic institutions. The solution to big business was big government. Roosevelt sought to meet national economic power with national political power. But he insisted that a national democracy required more than the centralization of government; it also required the nationalization of politics. The political community had to be recast on a national scale. Roosevelt's "New Nationalism" sought to inspire in Americans "a genuine and permanent moral awakening," a new sense of national citizenship.

Wilson won the election, but Roosevelt's "New Nationalism" won the future. From the New Deal through the Great Society, and even to the age of Reagan and Gingrich, the nationalizing project gave energy and purpose to American political debate—to liberals who sought to expand the responsibilities of the federal government and to conservatives who sought to constrain them.

But today we face a new predicament similar to the one Americans confronted early in this century. Now, as then, new forms of commerce and communication spill across political boundaries, creating networks of interdependence while disrupting familiar forms of community. What railroads, telegraph wires, and national markets were to their time, cyberspace, CNN, and global markets are to ours—instruments that link people in distant places without making them neighbors, or fellow citizens, or participants in a common venture. Once again, the scale of economic life has outgrown the reach of existing democratic institutions. This explains the sense of disempowerment that hovers over our politics, the gnawing doubt that either party can do much to allay the anxieties of the age.

That we are not debating questions analogous to those that preoccupied Wilson and Roosevelt reveals the poverty of our politics. Is democracy possible within a global economy? How can emerging transnational arrangements from NAFTA to GATT to the International Court of Justice possibly inspire the loyalty of neighborhoods and nations? If civic virtues must be nourished closer to home—in schools, congregations, and workplaces—how can such communities equip us to exercise citizenship on a global scale? The bridge to the twenty-first century will not be built with a lot of small answers but by a few big questions.

five

THE PROBLEM
WITH CIVILITY

Worries about incivility and partisanship are a recurring motif of American politics. Such worries received renewed attention in the aftermath of the 1996 election, in which President
Clinton won re-election but Republicans retained control of
both houses of Congress.

Meanness is out of season in American life, and calls for civility echo
across the land. Fed up with attack ads, negative campaigns and partisan rancor, Americans are also distressed at the coarsening of everyday life—rudeness on the highways, violence and vulgarity in
Hollywood movies and popular music, the brazenly confessional fare
of daytime television, the baseball star who spits at an umpire.

Sensing the backlash against incivility, President Clinton and
Republican leaders promise to rise above partisanship and to seek
common ground. Members of Congress plan a bipartisan weekend
retreat to get to know one another better and to discuss ways of conducting their disagreements with greater civility. Meanwhile, a growing number of national commissions ponder ways of renewing citizenship and community.

Americans are right to worry about the erosion of civility in everyday life. But it is a mistake to think that better manners and decorum can solve the fundamental problems of American democracy. In
politics, civility is an overrated virtue.

The problem with civility is the very thing that tempts politicians to extol it: it is uncontroversial. But democratic politics, properly conducted, is filled with controversy. We elect politicians to debate hotly contested public questions—for example, how much to spend on education and defense and care for the poor, how to punish crime, whether to permit abortion. We should not recoil at the clamor and contention that result; it is the sound and the spectacle of democracy.

It is desirable, of course, that political debate be conducted in a spirit of mutual respect rather than enmity. But too often these days, the plea for more civility in politics is a high-minded way of pleading for less critical scrutiny of illicit campaign contributions or other misdeeds. Likewise, the call to rise above partisanship can blur legitimate policy differences or justify a politics that lacks principle or conviction.

From the New Deal to the civil rights movement, principled politics has always been partisan politics, at least in the sense of requiring the mobilization of like-minded citizens to fight for a cause that others oppose.

The incivility now rampant in American life will not be cured by exhortation or by a muting of political differences. It is a symptom of a problem with our public life more fundamental than can be solved by a softening of partisan voices. Americans' worries about incivility express a deeper fear that the moral fabric of community is unraveling around us. From families and neighborhoods to cities and towns to schools, congregations and trade unions, the institutions that traditionally provided people with moral anchors and a sense of belonging are under siege.

Taken together, these forms of community are sometimes described as the institutions of "civil society." A healthy civil society is important not only because it promotes civility (though this may be a welcome byproduct) but because it calls forth the habits, skills and qualities of character that make effective democratic citizens.

Of course, every institution of civil society has its own distinctive purposes. Schools are for educating the young, churches and synagogues for worship, and so on. But when we participate in schools or congregations, we also develop civic virtues, qualities that equip us to be good citizens. We learn, for example, how to think about the good of the whole, how to exercise responsibility for others, how to deal with conflicting interests, how to stand up for our views while respecting the views of others. Above all, the institutions of civil society draw us out of our private, self-interested concerns and get us in the habit of attending to the common good.

A century and a half ago, Alexis de Tocqueville praised America's vibrant civil society for producing the "habits of the heart" on which democracy depends. If Tocqueville was right, there is reason to worry about the health of civil society, even beyond its effect on the manners people display in stores and on the streets.

For if families, neighborhoods and schools are in ill repair, they may be failing to produce the active, public-spirited citizens a successful democracy requires. (The dismal turnout in the recent election may be one indication of this effect.)

This at least is the hunch underlying a profusion of national commissions sprouting up to explore ways to renew citizenship and community. They include the Penn National Commission on Society, Culture and Community, which convened this month in Philadelphia; the National Commission on Civic Renewal, led by William Bennett and retiring Senator Sam Nunn of Georgia; the National Commission on Philanthropy and Civic Renewal, whose chairman is former Education Secretary Lamar Alexander, and the Boston-based Institute for Civil Society, which recently announced a project on civic renewal to be led by retiring Representative Patricia Schroeder of Colorado.

Whether these efforts can help rejuvenate American civic life will depend on their willingness to grapple with hard, controversial questions about the factors that have undermined virtue-sustaining communities in the first place. They must resist the temptation, endemic to such commissions, to steer clear of politically charged questions.

On the surface, the project of renewing civil society has the same kind of nonpartisan appeal as the call for civility in public life. Who could oppose efforts to strengthen families, neighborhoods and schools? But the attempt to repair civil society will be uncontroversial only as long as it remains hortatory—the stuff of Fourth of July speeches and State of the Union addresses.

Any serious effort to shore up value-laden communities must face up to the forces that have undermined them. Conservatives like Mr. Bennett locate the threat to virtue-sustaining institutions in two sources: popular culture and big government.

Rap music and vulgar movies corrupt the youth, they argue, while big government and the welfare state sap individual initiative, enervate the impulse for local self-help, and pre-empt the role of mediating institutions. Prune the shade tree of big government, they insist, and families, neighborhoods and church-based charities will flourish in the sun and space now crowded out by the overgrown tree.

The cultural conservatives are right to worry about the coarsening effects of popular entertainment, which, taken together with the advertising that drives it, induces a passion for consumption and a passivity toward politics at odds with civic virtue. But they are wrong to ignore the most potent force of all—the corrosive power of an unfettered market economy.

When corporations use their power to extract tax reductions, zoning changes and environmental concessions from cities and states desperate for jobs, they disempower communities more profoundly than any federal mandate ever did. When the growing gap between rich and poor leads the affluent to flee public schools, public parks and public transportation for privileged enclaves, civic virtue becomes difficult to sustain, and the common good fades from view.

Any attempt to revitalize community must contend with the economic as well as the cultural forces eating away at the social fabric. We need a political philosophy that asks what economic arrangements are hospitable to self-government and the civic virtues that sustain it. The project of civic renewal is important, not because it offers a way of muting political differences but because the health of American democracy requires it. So, too, does the prospect of civility.

six

IMPEACHMENT— THEN AND NOW

This commentary appeared as the House began impeachment proceedings against Bill Clinton in 1998. The House, voting mainly along party lines, eventually approved two counts of impeachment. But Clinton retained popular support, and the Senate voted to acquit him.

I, too, was once a 21-year-old Washington intern. Between my junior and senior years of college, I worked as a reporter in the Washington bureau of the *Houston Chronicle*. It was the summer of 1974, and the House Judiciary Committee was considering the impeachment of Richard Nixon.

"Let others wallow in Watergate," Nixon once said. I was a happy wallower. On July 8, I sat in the Supreme Court chamber, listening to Leon Jaworski, the special prosecutor, and James St. Clair, the president's lawyer, debate whether Nixon should be compelled to turn over his tapes. (I actually heard only half of the oral argument. So intense was the crush of press coverage that most newspaper reporters had to share a seat in the Court chamber, rotating in and out every half-hour.) A few days later, the House Judiciary Committee released volumes of evidence prepared by its staff. Unlike the "document dumps" of today, which appear instantly on the Web, the volumes were often given out at the Capitol in the evening, embargoed for release the following morning. I volunteered to pick up the copies designated for our paper, lugged them to my apartment behind Capitol

Hill, and read late into the night, culling the massive tomes for new revelations. When the summer ended, I was allowed to keep one of our bureau's sets as a bulky souvenir.

The recent impeachment stirrings prompted me to pull the beige-covered volumes down from the shelf. Read in the light of the Starr report, the 1974 committee's "Statement of Information" is striking for its restraint. It consists solely of facts and supporting documents, without argument or conclusions. It also includes a parallel set of volumes, prepared by Nixon's lawyers and published by the committee, emphasizing evidence more favorable to the president.

Despite some surface similarities, the impeachment hearings I witnessed that summer differed in several ways from those now unfolding in Washington. Then, as now, the majority party in Congress was investigating a president of the opposing party serving his second term. The party balance on the committees was roughly the same—a 21–17 Democratic majority in Committee Chair Peter Rodino's day, a 21–16 Republican majority in Henry Hyde's. Rodino's inquiry, like the one House Republicans now propose, was not limited by time or subject matter. Almost six months passed from the authorization of the inquiry to the final vote. In the end, Rodino was able to secure a bipartisan majority for impeachment—and, with it, a national consensus.

Hyde's committee will not likely achieve either, for three reasons. The first has to do with changes in the Congress. Many have observed that the House today, and especially the Judiciary Committee, are more bitterly partisan than they were a quarter-century ago. To some extent, the comparison is clouded by nostalgia. The Nixon impeachment hearings were not devoid of partisan passions. Twelve of the Democrats on the committee, including Robert Drinan of Massachusetts, Charles Rangel and Elizabeth Holtzman of New York, and John Conyers Jr. of Michigan (who is now the committee's senior minority member), voted to impeach Nixon for his secret bomb-ing of Cambodia. (The article failed.) On the GOP side, Charles Wiggins, who represented Nixon's former district in California, and Charles Sandman Jr., a combative New Jersey Republican, vigorously defended their president to the bitter end. Then, as now, the minority complained about leaks and unfair treatment.

Still, the climate was less contentious. Party and ideology were less clearly aligned than they are today. Of the 21 Democrats on Rodino's committee, three were conservative Southern Democrats. Walter Flowers (Alabama), James Mann (South Carolina), and Ray Thornton (Arkansas) all came from districts that had voted heavily for Nixon in 1972, and their votes were in doubt until late in the pro-ceedings. The Republican ranks included Northern moderates such as William Cohen of Maine (now secretary of defense), Hamilton Fish Jr. of New York, and Tom Railsback of Illinois. The Southern Democrats and moderate Republicans met frequently, softening the partisan edge of the proceedings. In the end, all Democrats and seven Republicans voted to recommend impeachment.

The second big difference is in the nature of the presidential mis-deeds. Nixon's offenses—the cover-up of the Watergate burglary (Ar-ticle of Impeachment I) and the use of the FBI, CIA, and IRS against political enemies (Article of Impeachment II)—were classic exam-ples of the "serious offenses against the system of government" that, as the committee rightly argued, impeachment is designed to rem-edy. When Nixon released the "smoking gun" tape shortly after the committee's votes, proving his involvement in the Watergate cover-up conspiracy, even his ten die-hard Republican supporters on the committee announced that they favored impeachment. A president should be removed, they wrote in a minority addendum, "only for serious misconduct dangerous to the system of government estab-lished by the Constitution." Among the Nixon loyalists who endorsed that statement was Trent Lott, then a freshman representative. Hyde,

Lott, and their fellow Republicans will have a hard time persuading Democrats—and the country—that Clinton's misdeeds, deplorable though they are, pose a serious threat to our constitutional system.

A third factor that makes it difficult to imagine a national consensus for impeaching Bill Clinton has to do with the changing role of the presidency in American life. Vietnam, Watergate, and now the Clinton sex scandal have deflated the majesty and aura of the presidency. So has a style of media coverage that encourages presidential candidates to bare their souls and confess their foibles on national television. Bill Clinton is more liked but less revered than Richard Nixon. Paradoxically, this lack of reverence protects Clinton from the sense of outrage and injured idealism that made the impeachment of Nixon possible.

On the evening of July 27, I sat in Room 2141 of the Rayburn House Office Building as Chairman Rodino asked the clerk to call the roll. The room fell silent as, one by one, the members of the committee answered "aye" or "no." The "ayes" were softly spoken, barely audible. It was a moment of almost religious solemnity. When the first article of impeachment was voted, Rodino's gavel came down, and the press surged forward, as it always did, to the front of the room where the members sat. My task was to get a quote from the formidable Barbara Jordan, the Democratic congresswoman from Houston who had distinguished herself throughout the hearings with her forceful eloquence. "I don't want to talk to anyone about anything right now," she exploded. With tears in her eyes, she escaped to a back room. I retreated, shaken by the encounter. Even Democrats hostile to Nixon felt the awesome burden of impeaching him. It is difficult to imagine a similar moment of civic trembling today.

seven

ROBERT F. KENNEDY'S
PROMISE

Robert F. Kennedy was assassinated in 1968, on the night of his victory in the California primary. To recall his death is to wonder what might have been. For as he campaigned for the presidency, he was finding his way to a political vision that challenged the complacencies of postwar American liberalism. Had he lived, he might have set progressive politics on a new, more successful course. In the decades since his death, the Democratic Party has failed to recover the moral energy and bold public purpose to which RFK gave voice.

Despite his commitment to the poor and his opposition to the war in Vietnam, Kennedy was not, by temperament or ideology, a liberal. His political outlook was in some ways more conservative and in other ways more radical than the mainstream of his party. Unlike most liberals, he worried about the remoteness of big government, favored decentralized power, criticized welfare as "our greatest domestic failure," challenged the faith in economic growth as a panacea for social ills, and took a hard line on crime.

Some viewed RFK's departure from liberal orthodoxy as a shrewd attempt to win support from white working-class ethnic voters while retaining the support of minorities and the poor. It certainly had that effect. In the 1968 Indiana primary, Kennedy managed, remarkably, to win 86 percent of the black vote while also sweeping the counties that had given George Wallace his greatest support in 1964. The journalist Jack Newfield aptly described RFK as the only candidate of protest who "was able to talk to the two polarities of powerlessness at the same time."

But Kennedy's unease with the conventional wisdom of 1960s liberalism was more than a matter of political calculation. What gave his message its resonance was that it drew on a vision of citizenship and community that the managerial politics of the modern age had crowded from view. As he groped to articulate a public philosophy adequate to the turmoil of his times, RFK revived an older, more demanding vision of civic life. According to this ideal, freedom does not simply consist in fair access to the bounty of a consumer society; it also requires that citizens share in self-rule, that they participate in shaping the forces that govern their collective destiny.

The civic strand of Kennedy's politics enabled him to address anxieties of the late sixties that have persisted to our time—mistrust of government, a sense of disempowerment, and the fear that the moral fabric of community was unraveling. Liberals often cast their arguments in individualistic terms, or appeal to the ideal of national community. By contrast, Kennedy emphasized the importance for self-government of communities intermediate between the individual and the nation, and lamented the loss of such communities in the modern world: "Nations or great cities are too huge to provide the values of community . . . The world beyond the neighborhood has become more impersonal and abstract," beyond the reach of individual control. "Cities, in their tumbling spread, are obliterating neighborhoods and precincts. Housing units go up, but there is no place for people to walk, for women and their children to meet, for common activities. The place of work is far away through blackened tunnels or over impersonal highways. The doctor and lawyer and government official is often somewhere else and hardly known. In far too many places—in pleasant suburbs as well as city streets—the home is a place to sleep and eat and watch television; but the community is not where we live. We live in many places and so we live nowhere."

In addressing the nation's urban ills, Democrats of the sixties emphasized unemployment, while Republicans spoke of crime. Kennedy spoke convincingly about joblessness and crime, and linked both to civic themes. The tragedy of crime, he argued, was not only the danger it posed to life and limb but also its destructive effect on public spaces, such as neighborhoods and communities: "No nation hiding behind locked doors is free, for it is imprisoned by its own fear. No nation whose citizens fear to walk their own streets is healthy, for in isolation lies the poisoning of public participation." Similarly, unemployment posed a civic challenge, not just an economic one. The problem was not simply that the jobless lacked an income but that they could not share in the common life of citizenship: "Unemployment means having nothing to do—which means having nothing to do with the rest of us. To be without work, to be without use to one's fellow citizens, is to be in truth the Invisible Man of whom Ralph Ellison wrote."

Kennedy's clearest difference with mainstream liberal opinion was on the issue of welfare. Unlike conservatives, who opposed federal spending for the poor, Kennedy criticized welfare on the grounds that it corrupted the civic capacity of recipients. It rendered "millions of our people slaves to dependency and poverty, waiting on the favor of their fellow citizens to write them checks. Fellowship, community, shared patriotism—these essential values of our civilization do not come from just buying and consuming goods together. They come from a shared sense of individual independence and personal effort." The solution to poverty was not a guaranteed income paid by the government, but "dignified employment at decent pay, the kind of employment that lets a man say to his community, to his family, to his country, and most important, to himself, 'I helped to build this country. I am a participant in its great public ventures.'" A guaranteed income, whatever good it might do, "simply cannot provide the sense of self-sufficiency, of participation in the life of the community, that is essential for citizens of a democracy."

Had Democrats taken up RFK's toughness on crime, they would have deprived a generation of Republicans of one of its most effective issues. Had Democrats heeded Kennedy's worries about welfare, they could have reformed it without abandoning the poor, and avoided decades of public resentment toward welfare that fed a broader hostility toward government. Had Democrats learned from RFK the importance of community, self-government, and civic virtue, they would not have ceded these powerful ideals to conservatives like Ronald Reagan. Three decades later, the progressive impulse has yet to recover a compelling voice. We still need a strenuous idealism that recalls us to a citizenship that consists of something more than basic training for a consumer society.

Part II

MORAL AND POLITICAL ARGUMENTS

The essays in this section take up moral arguments prompted by recent legal and political controversies, ranging from affirmative action to pollution permits to stem cell research. A number of the essays deal with the moral limits of markets, a subject I plan to examine more systematically in a future book. In Chapters 8–13 I argue that market practices and commercial pressures can corrupt civic institutions and degrade the public realm. The growing tendency to fund education and other public purposes through state lotteries and commercial advertising in schools are two conspicuous examples. Less obvious but also insidious is the extension of branding, commercialism, and market imperatives into spheres of life (including government, sports, and universities) traditionally governed, at least to some extent, by non-market norms.

Chapter 14, "Should We Buy the Right to Pollute?", takes issue with the U.S. insistence that global environmental agreements include a tradable emissions scheme that would allow countries to buy and sell the right to pollute. This article brought a torrent of criticism from economists, for whom tradable pollution permits represent a cherished example of the way market mechanisms promote the public good. Soon after the article appeared, I received a note from my college economics professor. He was surprisingly sympathetic to my argument, but asked that I not publicly divulge that I had learned my economics from him.

More often than we realize, the question of moral desert lurks just below the surface of disputes about the just distribution of opportunities, honors, and rewards. Chapters 15–17 try to make sense of the competing notions of desert at stake in contemporary debates about the rights of the disabled, affirmative action, and criminal punishment. Chapter 18, "Clinton and Kant on Lying," uses President Clinton's alleged perjury about his sexual misconduct as an occasion to examine Immanuel Kant's moral distinction between lying and misleading.

When politicians, activists, and political commentators speak of morality in politics, they usually have in mind the morally and religiously charged issues that have figured in the culture wars—abortion, gay rights, assisted suicide, and, more recently, stem cell research. Chapters 19–21 deal with these issues. Running through these essays is the argument that liberal toleration is flawed insofar as it tries to adjudicate rights without attending to the substantive moral and religious claims in contention.

Some people claim it is not possible to conduct reasoned argument about deeply held moral and religious convictions, especially those involving the origins and sanctity of human life. These essays challenge that claim. Chapter 20, on the ethics of stem cell research, grew out of debates I encountered as a member of the President's Council on Bioethics, a body appointed by President George W. Bush to examine the ethical implications of new biomedical technologies. The debates I found myself engaged in with colleagues on the Council confirmed my sense that even questions as fraught as those concerning the moral status of the human embryo are susceptible to reasoned argument. (This is not to suggest that reasoned argument necessarily leads to agreement; the views expressed in this essay are mine alone, and do not represent those of the Council.) Chapter 21 takes up the hotly contested issues of abortion and gay rights. I assess the U.S. Supreme Court's reasoning on these subjects, from the privacy rights cases of the 1960s to a 2003 case that struck down a law banning gay and lesbian sexual practices.

AGAINST STATE LOTTERIES

Political corruption comes in two forms. Most familiar is the hand-in-the-till variety: bribes, payoffs, influence-peddling, lobbyists lining the pockets of public officials in exchange for access and favors. This corruption thrives in secrecy, and is usually condemned when exposed.

But another kind of corruption arises, by degree, in full public view. It involves no theft or fraud, but rather a change in the habits of citizens, a turning away from public responsibilities. This second, civic corruption, is more insidious than the first. It violates no law, but enervates the spirit on which good laws depend. And by the time it becomes apparent, the new habits may be too pervasive to reverse.

Consider the most fateful change in public finance since the income tax: the rampant proliferation of state lotteries. Illegal in every state for most of the century, lotteries have suddenly become the fastest-growing source of state revenue. In 1970, two states ran lotteries; today, forty states and the District of Columbia run them. Nationwide, lottery sales exceeded $48 billion a year by 2004, up from $9 billion in 1985.

The traditional objection to lotteries is that gambling is a vice. This objection has lost force in recent decades, partly because notions of sin have changed but also because Americans are more reluctant than they once were to legislate morality. Even people who find gambling morally objectionable shy away from banning it on that ground alone, absent some harmful effect on society as a whole.

Freed from the traditional, paternalistic objections to gambling, proponents of state lotteries advance three seemingly attractive arguments: first, lotteries are a painless way of raising revenue for important public services without raising taxes; unlike taxes, lotteries are a matter of choice, not coercion. Second, they are a popular form of entertainment. Third, they generate business for the retail outlets that sell lottery tickets (such as convenience stores, gas stations and supermarkets) and for the advertising firms and media outlets that promote them.

What, then, is wrong with state-run lotteries? For one thing, they rely, hypocritically, on a residual moral disapproval of gambling that their defenders officially reject. State lotteries generate enormous profits because they are monopolies, and they are monopolies because privately operated numbers games are prohibited, on traditional moral grounds. (In Las Vegas, where casinos compete with one another, the slot machines and blackjack tables pay out around 90 percent of their take in winnings. State lotteries, being monopolies, only pay out about 50 percent.) Libertarian defenders of state lotteries can't have it both ways. If a lottery is, like dry cleaning, a morally legitimate business, then why should it not be open to private enterprise? If a lottery is, like prostitution, a morally objectionable business, then why should the state be engaged in it?

Lottery defenders usually reply that people should be free to decide the moral status of gambling for themselves. No one is forced to play, they point out, and those who object can simply abstain. To those troubled by the thought that the state derives revenue from sin, advocates reply that government often imposes "sin taxes" on products (like liquor and tobacco) that many regard as undesirable. Lotteries are better than taxes, the argument goes, because they are wholly voluntary, a matter of choice.

But the actual conduct of lotteries departs sharply from this laissez-faire ideal. States do not simply provide their citizens the opportunity to gamble; they actively promote and encourage them to do so. The nearly $400 million spent on lottery advertising each year puts lotteries among the largest advertisers in the country. If lotteries are a form of "sin tax," they are the only kind in which the state spends huge sums to encourage its citizens to commit the sin.

Not surprisingly, lotteries direct their most aggressive advertising at their best customers—the working class, minorities and the poor. A billboard touting the Illinois lottery in a Chicago ghetto declared, "This could be your ticket out." Ads often evoke the fantasy of winning the big jackpot and never having to work again. Lottery advertising floods the airwaves around the first of each month, when Social Security and welfare payments swell the checking accounts of recipients. In sharp contrast to most other government amenities (say, police protection), lottery ticket outlets saturate poor and blue-collar neighborhoods and offer less service to affluent ones.

Massachusetts, with the highest grossing per capita lottery sales in the country, offers stark evidence of the blue-collar bias. A 1997 series in the *Boston Globe* found that Chelsea, one of the poorest towns in the state, has one lottery agent for every 363 residents; upscale Wellesley, by contrast, has one agent for every 3,063 residents. In Massachusetts, as elsewhere, this "painless" alternative to taxation is a sharply regressive way of raising revenue. Residents of Chelsea spent a staggering $915 per capita on lottery tickets last year, almost 8 percent of their income. Residents of Lincoln, an affluent suburb, spent only $30 per person, one-tenth of 1 percent of their income.

For growing numbers of people, playing the lottery is not the free, voluntary choice its promoters claim. Instant games such as scratch tickets and Keno (a video numbers game with drawings every five minutes), now the biggest money-makers for the lottery, are a leading cause of compulsive gambling, rivaling casinos and racetracks. Swelling the ranks of Gamblers Anonymous are lottery addicts, like the man who scratched $1,500 worth of tickets per day, exhausted his retirement savings and ran up debt on eleven credit cards.

Meanwhile, the state has grown as addicted to the lottery as its problem gamblers. Lottery proceeds now account for 13 percent of state revenues in Massachusetts, making radical change all but unthinkable. No politician, however troubled by the lottery's harmful effects, would dare raise taxes or cut spending sufficiently to offset the revenue the lottery brings in.

With states hooked on the money, they have no choice but to continue to bombard their citizens, especially the most vulnerable ones, with a message at odds with the ethic of work, sacrifice and moral responsibility that sustains democratic life. This civic corruption is the gravest harm that lotteries bring. It degrades the public realm by casting the government as the purveyor of a perverse civic education. To keep the money flowing, state governments across America must now use their authority and influence not to cultivate civic virtue but to peddle false hope. They must persuade their citizens that with a little luck they can escape the world of work to which only misfortune consigns them.

nine

COMMERCIALS
IN THE CLASSROOM

When the Boston Red Sox first installed a display of giant Coke bottles above the left field wall, local sportswriters protested that such tacky commercialism tainted the sanctity of Fenway Park. But ballparks have long been littered with billboards and ads. Today, teams routinely sell corporations the right to name the stadium: the Colorado Rockies, for example, play in Coors Field. However distasteful, such commercialism does not seem to corrupt the game or diminish the play.

The same cannot be said of the newest commercial frontier—the public schools. The corporate invasion of the classroom threatens to turn schools into havens for hucksterism. Eager to cash in on a captive audience of consumers-in-training, companies have flooded teachers with free videos, posters and "learning kits" designed to sanitize corporate images and emblazon brand names in the minds of children. Students can now learn about nutrition from curricular materials supplied by Hershey's Chocolate or McDonald's, or study the effects of the Alaska oil spill in a video made by Exxon. According to *Giving Kids the Business,* by Alex Molnar, a Monsanto video teaches the merits of bovine growth hormone in milk production, while Procter & Gamble's environmental curriculum teaches that disposable diapers are good for the earth.

Not all corporate-sponsored educational freebies promote ideological agendas; some simply plug the brand name. A few years ago, the Campbell Soup Company offered a science kit that showed students how to prove that Campbell's Prego spaghetti sauce is thicker than Ragu. General Mills distributed science kits containing free samples of its Gusher fruit snacks, with soft centers that "gush" when bitten. The teacher's guide suggested that students bite into the Gushers and compare the effect to geothermal eruptions. A Tootsie Roll kit on counting and writing recommends that, for homework, children interview family members about their memories of Tootsie Rolls.

While some marketers seek to insinuate brand names into the curriculum, others take a more direct approach: buying advertisements in schools. When the Seattle School Board faced a budget crisis a few years ago, it voted to solicit corporate advertising. School officials hoped to raise $1 million a year with sponsorships like "the cheerleaders, brought to you by Reebok" and "the McDonald's gym." Protests from parents and teachers forced the Seattle schools to suspend the policy, but such marketing is a growing presence in schools across the country.

Corporate logos now clamor for student attention from school buses to book covers. In Colorado Springs, advertisements for Mountain Dew adorn school hallways, and ads for Burger King decorate the sides of school buses. A Massachusetts firm distributes free book covers hawking Nike, Gatorade and Calvin Klein to almost 25 million students nationwide. A Minnesota broadcasting company pipes music into school corridors and cafeterias in fifteen states, with twelve minutes of commercials every hour. Forty percent of the ad revenue goes to the schools.

The most egregious example of the commercialization in schools is Channel One, a twelve-minute television news program seen by 8 million students in 12,000 schools. Introduced in 1990 by Whittle Communications, Channel One offers schools a television set for each classroom, two VCRs and a satellite link in exchange for an agreement to show the program every day, including the two minutes of commercials it contains. Since Channel One reaches over 40 percent of the nation's teenagers, it is able to charge advertisers a hefty $200,000 per thirty-second spot. In its pitch to advertisers, the company promises access to the largest teen audience in history in a setting free of "the usual distractions of telephones, stereos, remote controls, etc." The Whittle program shattered the taboo against outright advertising in the classroom. Despite controversy in many states, only New York has banned Channel One from its schools.

The rampant commercialization of schools is corrupting in two ways. First, most corporate-sponsored learning supplements are ridden with bias, distortion and superficial fare. A recent study by Consumers Union found that nearly 80 percent of classroom freebies are slanted toward the sponsor's product. An independent study of Channel One released earlier this year found that its news programs contributed little to students' grasp of public affairs. Only 20 percent of its airtime covers current political, economic or cultural events. The rest is devoted to advertising, sports, weather and natural disasters.

But, even if corporate sponsors supplied objective teaching tools of impeccable quality, commercial advertising would still be a pernicious presence in the classroom because it undermines the purposes for which schools exist. Advertising encourages people to want things and to satisfy their desires: education encourages people to reflect on their desires, to restrain or to elevate them. The purpose of advertising is to recruit consumers; the purpose of public schools is to cultivate citizens.

It is not easy to teach students to be citizens, capable of thinking critically about the world around them, when so much of childhood consists of basic training for a commercial society. At a time when children come to school as walking billboards of logos and labels and licensed apparel, it is all the more difficult—and all the more important—for schools to create some distance from a popular culture drenched in the ethos of consumerism.

But advertising abhors distance. It blurs the boundaries between places, and makes every setting a site for selling. "Discover your own river of revenue at the schoolhouse gates!" proclaims the brochure for the 4th Annual Kid Power Marketing Conference, held last May in New Orleans. "Whether it's first-graders learning to read or teenagers shopping for their first car, we can guarantee an introduction of your product and your company to these students in the traditional setting of the classroom!" Marketers are storming the schoolhouse gates for the same reason that Willie Sutton robbed banks—because that's where the money is. Counting the amount they spend and the amount they influence their parents to spend, 6- to 19-year-old consumers now account for $485 billion in spending per year.

The growing financial clout of kids is itself a lamentable symptom of parents abdicating their role as mediators between children and the market. Meanwhile, faced with property tax caps, budget cuts and rising enrollments, cash-strapped schools are more vulnerable to the siren song of corporate sponsors. Rather than raise the public funds we need to pay the full cost of educating our schoolchildren, we choose instead to sell their time and rent their minds to Burger King and Mountain Dew.

ten

BRANDING
THE PUBLIC REALM

The branding of public spaces has proliferated since 1998, when this article was written. "Municipal marketing" companies have sprung up to help cities sell naming rights. In 2003, the mayor of New York hired the city's first chief marketing officer. One of his first deals was a $166 million contract with Snapple to be the official drink of New York City.

It is getting hard to tell the difference between companies and countries. Earthwatch Inc. of Longmont, Colorado, recently launched the world's first commercial spy satellite into space. Now, anyone with a few hundred dollars can buy surveillance photos of missile sites in the Middle East or the swimming pool in a celebrity's backyard. Once the prerogative of governments, spying from space has become a commercial enterprise.

Even where countries retain their functions, governance and marketing are increasingly entangled. For decades, candidates for office have sold themselves like breakfast cereal. Today, entire countries do. Consider the "rebranding" of Britain. A few months ago, Prime Minister Tony Blair's advisers recommended that he update the country's image. It was time to "rebrand" Britain as "one of the world's pioneers rather than one of its museums." Red telephone booths are being replaced by transparent glass ones. The box-like London taxicab is getting a sleeker, aerodynamic design. "Rule Britannia!" is giving way to "Cool Britannia," the new slogan of the British Transit Authority, whose logo is now a jaunty Union Jack tinged with yellow and green for vibrancy. "The image of Britain," Blair explained, "which used to be bowler hats and pinstripe trousers and very old-fashioned and very stuffy, has been replaced by something far more dynamic and open and forward-looking. . . . I'm proud of my country's past, but I don't want to live in it." The "rebranding" of Britain is not an isolated episode but a sign of the times. It reflects a new image-savvy, commercialized approach to government that threatens to turn national identities into brand names, anthems into advertising jingles, flags into corporate logos.

Last year, the U.S. Postal Service issued a stamp of Bugs Bunny. Critics complained that stamps should honor historic figures, not commercial products. But the post office, facing stiff competition from email, fax machines, and Federal Express, sees licensing rights as key to its future. Every Bugs Bunny stamp that is saved rather than mailed contributes 32 cents to post office profits. And stamp collecting is the least of it. The licensing deal with Warner Bros. enables the Postal Service to market Looney Tunes ties, hats, videos, and other products at more than 500 postal stores nationwide.

Also for sale is a new product line called Postmark America that seeks to capitalize on the brand name of the Postal Service itself. Products include a $2.95 Pony Express youth cap, infantwear emblazoned with the logo "Just Delivered," and an airmail pilot's leather jacket—which sells for $345. A Postal Service executive explained that the retailing effort is modeled after companies like Warner Bros. and Walt Disney: "They've turned their icons into product lines. That's what we're trying to do. We're trying to key off our stamps and our stamp image."

Sometimes, however, the attempt to turn national symbols into brand names meets with resistance. In 1995, the Royal Canadian Mounted Police sold Disney the right to market the Mountie image worldwide. Disney paid Canada's federal police $2.5 million per year in marketing rights plus a share of the licensing fees for Mountie t-shirts, coffee mugs, teddy bears, maple syrup, diaper bags, and other merchandise. Many Canadians protested that the Mounties were selling out a sacred national symbol to a U.S. corporate giant. "It's not the price that rankles. It's the sale," complained an editorial in the Toronto-based *Globe and Mail.* "The Mounted Police have miscalculated on a crucial point. Pride."

Canada has learned to live with the marketing of the Mounties, but the critics had a point: there is reason to worry about an excessive commingling of governance and commerce. At a time when politics and government are widely disliked, public officials will inevitably seek to tap the appeal of popular culture, advertising, and entertainment. The problem is not that this borrowed authority fails, but that it succeeds too completely. According to polls, the two most popular agencies of the U.S. government are the post office and the military. Not coincidentally, perhaps, both advertise heavily on television. In a media-saturated world, citizens' judgments about government increasingly depend on the image it projects.

Not only is this unfair to government programs that lack advertising budgets (who ever saw a commercial for welfare?); it distorts the priorities of agencies that lavish money on their public image. After a time, their mission becomes indistinguishable from their marketing. Once the post office sold stamps and delivered the mail; today it sells stamp-related images and licensed apparel. Postmaster General Marvin Runyon articulated well the theory behind the new commercialized style of governance: "We have to be market-driven and customer-friendly, and make products that people want."

But citizens are not customers, and democracy is not simply a matter of giving people what they want. Self-government, properly practiced, leads people to reflect on their wants and to revise them in the light of competing considerations. Unlike customers, citizens sometimes sacrifice their wants for the sake of the common good. This is the difference between politics and commerce, between patriotism and brand loyalty.

When government leans too heavily on the borrowed appeal of cartoon characters and cutting-edge ads, it may boost its approval ratings but squander the dignity and authority of the public realm. And without a public realm in good repair, democratic citizens have little hope of directing the market forces and commercial pressures that quicken by the day and shape our lives in untold ways.

Margaret Thatcher, no friend of the rebranding of Britain, inadvertently contributed to this phenomenon when, as prime minister, she privatized the national airline. At a recent Conservative Party conference, she came upon a British Airways booth and was dismayed to find that the tail fin of the model plane on display no longer bore the Union Jack, but a multicultural motif designed to represent British Airways' new global identity. Drawing a tissue from her handbag, she covered the tail fin in protest. As Lady Thatcher should have known, markets, for all their glories, exact a price in honor and pride.

eleven

SPORTS AND CIVIC IDENTITY

When capitalism and community collide, as they increasingly do these days, community needs all the help it can get. Consider the case of sports. Like few institutions in American life, professional baseball, football, basketball, and hockey provide a source of social glue and civic pride. From Yankee Stadium to Candlestick Park, sports stadiums are the cathedrals of our civil religion, public spaces that gather people from different walks of life in rituals of loss and hope, profanity and prayer. The common sentiments reach beyond the ballpark or arena. When the Boston Celtics and the Los Angeles Lakers faced off in the NBA playoffs some years ago, one could walk the streets of Boston and from every open window hear the echoes of the game.

But professional sports is not only a source of civic identity. It is also a business. And these days the money in sports is driving out the community. Of course, when fans go to the ballpark, they don't go for the sake of a civic experience. They go to see Ken Griffey Jr. hit the ball a long way or make a sparkling catch in center field. But what they experience at the game are two important features of democratic public life: One is a broad equality of condition; another is a sense of belonging to a particular place. While box seats have always cost more than the bleachers, the ballpark is one of the few public places where CEOs sit side by side with mailroom clerks, where all eat the same soggy hot dogs, where rich and poor alike get wet when it rains, where all hearts sink and soar with the fate of the home team.

Or so it was until recently. Today, the allure of greater profit is leading team owners to transform their games in ways that destroy the class-mixing habits and sense of place on which sports and democracy thrive. The proliferation of luxury skyboxes segregates the upper crust from the common folk in the stands below. At the same time, owners are constantly relocating teams, or threatening to do so, if the home town is unwilling or unable to shell out huge public subsidies for stadiums.

The skybox trend began when the Dallas Cowboys installed luxury suites at Texas Stadium, where corporations pay up to 1.5 million dollars for the right to entertain executives and clients in posh settings above the crowd. Through the 1980s, more than a dozen teams followed the Cowboys' lead, cosseting privileged fans behind Plexiglas perches in the sky. In the late 1980s, Congress cut back on the tax deduction corporations could claim for skybox expenses, but this did not stem the demand for the climate-controlled retreats. Although skybox revenues represent a windfall for the teams, they change the fans' relation to the game and to one another. The sweaty, egalitarian intensity of the Boston Garden in Larry Bird's day has given way to Boston's commodious but class-stratified FleetCenter, where executive-suite patrons dine on pistachio-encrusted salmon in a restaurant so elevated that they cannot see the court below.

If skyboxes separate fans by class, relocation deprives a community of its home team, as the notorious case of the Cleveland Browns illustrates. Arthur Modell, for 35 years the owner of the Browns, could not complain about the Cleveland fans, who filled the 70,000 seats in Municipal Stadium game after game. But, in 1995, he announced he was moving his team to Baltimore, where local officials were offering him $65 million, a new stadium free of rent, and revenues from luxury boxes.

Cleveland is not the only community whose home-team loyalty

went unrequited by a profit-maximizing owner. In fact, Baltimore's extravagant bid for the Browns was prompted by a desire to replace its own beloved Baltimore Colts, who bolted for Indianapolis in 1984. ("This is my team," the Colt's owner bluntly declared at the time. "I own it, and I'll do whatever I want with it.") In the last six years, eight major-league teams have abandoned their host cities for sweeter deals elsewhere, and another 20 cities paid the blackmail teams demanded in the form of new or renovated stadiums. Many other teams are currently demanding subsidies as a condition of staying put. The Super Bowl champion Denver Broncos, for example, are threatening to leave unless taxpayers fork over $266 million for a new stadium.

From the standpoint of market principles, there is nothing wrong with selling teams to the highest bidder. Cities and states often compete with one another to attract new businesses to their communities. If it is all right to offer tax breaks and subsidies to persuade an auto plant to relocate, why not bid for a sports franchise as well? The answer is that all bidding wars among states are objectionable because they allow corporations to extract revenue that should go to education and other pressing public needs. In the case of sports, the bidding is doubly damaging because it mocks the loyalty and civic pride that communities invest in their teams.

What, if anything, can be done to render communities less vulnerable to extortion by the teams they love? David Morris, cofounder of a Minneapolis-based group called the Institute for Local Self-Reliance, suggests a promising solution: Since teams are now demanding subsidies that exceed the value of the teams, why not allow communities to take ownership themselves? The sole example of community ownership in big-league sports is the Green Bay Packers, incorporated in 1923 as a nonprofit organization. Despite their small market, the Packers have won three Super Bowls and sold out their games for more than 30 consecutive seasons. The waiting list for season tickets is 36,000 names long. Their 108,000 shareholder-fans know that they will not make a profit. But they do not need to worry that their Packers will leave town.

As Morris points out, the NFL now prohibits community ownership (with an exception for the Packers), and Major League Baseball has an informal policy against it. He therefore endorses legislation proposed by Representative Earl Blumenauer of Oregon that would require leagues to permit public ownership of teams. Leagues that refused would lose the valuable antitrust exemption that allows teams to collaborate in selling broadcast rights. The bill, dubbed the Give Fans a Chance Act, would also require teams to give 180 days notice before moving and afford local groups the opportunity to make ownership bids or other proposals to retain the team.

Whether or not Congress acts, the movement for community ownership may hold growing appeal for voters reluctant to subsidize millionaire owners and players as the price of keeping the home team at home. Activists in Denver plan a statewide initiative that would tie any stadium subsidy to a public share in the Broncos. In Minnesota, the danger of losing the Twins baseball franchise to Charlotte, North Carolina, has led some Minnesota legislators to propose a bill that would enable the state to buy the team and sell it to the fans. The drive for community ownership has won support both from conservatives who oppose stadium subsidies and from progressives who prize community and want government to level the playing field between private wealth and the public good.

twelve

HISTORY FOR SALE

The recent auction of John F. Kennedy memorabilia displayed two distasteful features of American culture in the 1990s: one is the obsession with celebrity; the other is the willingness to turn everything into a commodity. Among the items sold: a JFK rocking chair ($300,000), a sheet of presidential doodles ($12,250), the black alligator briefcase Kennedy carried with him to Dallas ($700,000), his Harvard sweater ($27,500), long underwear ($3,000), and a plastic comb ($1,100). The auction consisted largely of items that Robert L. White, an avid collector of JFK memorabilia, had inherited from Kennedy's longtime secretary, Evelyn Lincoln.

Kennedy's children, Caroline Kennedy and John F. Kennedy Jr., opposed the auction, disputing the ownership of some items and seeking to claim them for the John F. Kennedy Library in Boston. "Mrs. Lincoln never owned the vast majority of items that Mr. White received from her," they stated. "They once belonged to our father. They now belong to our family, to history, and to the American people." Defenders of the auction charged the Kennedy children with hypocrisy, citing their own $34.4 million auction of Jacqueline Kennedy Onassis's belongings two years ago. White's lawyer accused them of trying to "pick things out of the collection like it's an L.L. Bean catalog." The wrangle ended when White agreed to hand over two Kennedy diaries and other personal items in exchange for an agreement by the Kennedy children not to challenge the auction in court. Legal rights and wrongs aside, the auction reflects a tawdry trend that is gaining momentum by the day: the commodification of memory, the peddling of national pride and pain, the consignment of our past to mail-order catalogs and home shopping channels. In the case of Kennedy-related artifacts, the memorabilia market is fueled not only by sentiment but also by a lurid desire to possess the trappings of tragedy. Items related to the assassination are especially prized by collectors. Last year, an auction house sold a teletype printout of the Associated Press's report of the Kennedy assassination. Several years ago, the gun Jack Ruby used to kill Lee Harvey Oswald fetched $200,000.

Many feel a sense of moral queasiness at the spectacle of history on the auction block, but what exactly is wrong with selling presidential diaries, documents, and underwear to the highest bidder? At least two things, depending on the artifact: the first is that it privatizes what should be public; the second is that it publicizes what should be private.

When significant historical documents are at stake, selling them off to private collectors deprives the public of access (through libraries, museums, and archives) to sources of collective identity and memory. To commodify the past is to diminish the public realm. This is why many in the art world oppose the "deaccessioning," or selling off, of masterpieces from museum collections to raise funds for expenses. It is also reason to regret the sale to a private collector several years ago of a newly discovered first printing of the Declaration of Independence (for $2.4 million). Some scholars and civil rights figures have raised similar objections to efforts by the family of Martin Luther King Jr. to cash in on his legacy. Last year, the King family entered into a multimedia deal with Time Warner to market the words and image of Dr. King; the deal is projected to bring the estate $30 million to $50 million. Since the deal with Time Warner is to sell books, recordings, and cd-roms, it might be argued that commercialism in this case promotes, rather than restricts, public access.

But the aggressive marketing of King's legacy has coincided with severe limits on scholarly access to the King Center's archive. The estate has also been unusually stringent about enforcing its licensing rights. It sued CBS for selling a videotape containing footage of King's "I Have a Dream" speech and *USA Today* for publishing the speech without paying a licensing fee.

Of course, many of the things that collectors crave have less to do with history than celebrity. The public domain is not diminished by the fact that someone paid a fortune for a presidential comb. Still, there is something distasteful about buying and selling the personal effects of public figures. Perhaps it is the prying, prurient interest that lies behind the desire to possess such things. A few months ago, in another hotly disputed auction, Mickey Mantle's former agent and companion, Greer Johnson, sought to sell a bounty of Mantle memorabilia, including a lock of the Yankee slugger's hair, his American Express card, bathrobe, jockstrap, worn socks, golf shoes, and four vials of prescription decongestant. Under threat of a lawsuit from Mantle's family, Johnson agreed to withdraw some personal items from the sale, including the prescription bottles. In another celebrity auction last year, collectors from around the world bid via satellite and telephone in a Tokyo-based auction of Beatles memorabilia. Paul McCartney won a court order blocking the sale of a handwritten draft of his song "Penny Lane," but his birth certificate (once sold by his stepmother for $14,613) went for $73,064.

The worship of celebrities—sports heroes, rock stars, and movie idols—is nothing new. But the frenzied drive to commodify celebrity, to buy it and possess it, has reached unprecedented intensity. For generations, children came early to the ballpark in hopes of meeting a player and getting his autograph. Today, the autograph market is a $500 million industry, with dealers paying players to sign thousands of items, which are sold through catalog companies, cable television channels, mail-order houses, and sports-memorabilia stores in shopping malls across the country. In 1992, Mantle earned a reported $2.75 million for autographs and appearances, more than he made during his entire playing career with the Yankees.

Ironically, the cultural icons whose images and belongings are in greatest demand today—JFK, Mickey Mantle, the Beatles, Martin Luther King Jr.—are figures from the 1960s, a more innocent, idealistic time. It was a time before the personal foibles of public figures were relentlessly exposed, a time before presidents spoke of their boxer shorts on television. Perhaps, in our market-crazed way, we are struggling vainly to buy our way back to a world where not everything was for sale or open to public view.

thirteen

THE MARKET
FOR MERIT

As high school seniors across America ponder their choice of colleges, their parents wonder how they will pay the bill. The price of tuition, room, and board at some private colleges and universities now tops $40,000 per year. For many families, however, the actual cost is not as staggering as it seems. As with airline tickets, not everyone pays full fare. For several decades, colleges have offered financial aid to students whose families cannot afford the full price. And, in recent years, a growing number of colleges have offered merit scholarships to desirable students regardless of financial need.

The trend toward merit scholarships has been a boon for families who don't qualify for need-based financial aid, and a valuable recruiting tool for colleges eager to compete for the best students. But, from the standpoint of higher education, merit scholarships are a mixed blessing. More money for students who can afford to pay their way may mean less money for the needy. Merit-based aid increased at an annual rate of 13 percent during the 1980s (adjusting for inflation), faster than the increase in need-based aid. The effect is most dramatic among second-tier schools trying to compete with those in the top tier for the most qualified students. Private colleges and universities ranked in the top fifth of selectivity offer little merit-based aid. In contrast, at liberal arts colleges ranked in the second tier, almost half of all scholarship funds are awarded according to merit.

The strongest argument against merit scholarships is that "merit" is a euphemism for "market." According to this argument, merit scholarships represent the intrusion of market values into education. Colleges that offer top students a discount on tuition are not simply honoring high academic achievement; they are buying better students than would attend their institution if financial aid were tied to need alone.

Unlike ordinary businesses, colleges and universities do not seek to maximize profits. But they do seek to maximize qualities such as academic selectivity, excellence, and prestige, all of which cost money. The drive to compete has led many colleges to adopt market-like policies in admissions and financial aid. From the standpoint of the market, a merit scholarship, like a supersaver airfare, is a discount on a product designed to help the bottom line. Like the airlines, many colleges now employ computer-driven "enrollment management" policies that predict the "willingness to pay" of student applicants in various categories. These days the price of a seat in the freshman class may vary not only according to the financial circumstances and academic standing of the applicant, but also according to race, gender, geography, or proposed field of study. Some schools have found that those who come for a campus interview are more eager to attend and therefore more willing to accept a leaner financial package.

Whether market-like practices rationalize or corrupt college financial aid policy depends on the purpose of higher education. Insofar as education is a commodity—an investment in human capital that yields a stream of future earnings—there is a case for allocating it according to market principles. To the extent that education advances non-market ideals—the pursuit of truth, the cultivation of moral and civic sensibilities—there is reason to worry that market principles may be corrupting.

These two visions of college education clashed a few years ago in a remarkable antitrust case brought by the Justice Department against a group of elite Northeast colleges and universities. Since the late 1950s, the eight Ivy League schools and MIT had agreed to offer financial aid solely on the basis of need, as defined by a common formula. To implement their agreement, representatives of the schools met each year to compare financial aid offers and adjust for discrepancies. A student admitted to Harvard, Princeton, and Columbia, for example, would receive a comparable financial aid offer from all three.

The Justice Department brought an antitrust action against the schools, claiming the practice amounted to price-fixing. The schools replied that they were not profit-making firms but educational institutions advancing two worthy social purposes: assuring equal access for those unable to afford an elite college education, and enabling all admitted students to make their college choice untainted by financial considerations. Financial aid was not a discount on a product, they argued, but a charitable gift that schools bestowed in order to advance their educational mission.

The federal courts ultimately rejected this view. "Discounting the price of educational services for needy students is not charity when a university receives tangible benefits in exchange," stated the U.S. Court of Appeals. Those tangible benefits were not profits, but the exceptional students Ivy League schools were able to attract who would otherwise be unable to enroll. The ability to avoid competition with peer institutions in awarding financial aid also enabled Ivy League schools to set higher tuition rates than might otherwise be possible. While the Ivies can continue to share common principles for awarding aid, they can no longer compare individual cases.

Not surprisingly, the case against merit scholarships is advanced most strongly by the schools that need them least. In virtue of their prestige, the nation's most selective colleges do best in the competition for students when the financial playing field is level. One educational benefit of the merit scholarships offered by second-tier schools may be to disperse top students among a wider range of colleges rather than concentrate them among a handful of elite ones.

Still, the principled objections to merit scholarships cannot easily be waved aside. At a time when government support for education is waning, the principle of access for needy students has become difficult to sustain for all but the richest institutions. And even schools that reap a competitive benefit from the use of merit scholarships should not be lulled into ignoring the dangers of creeping commodification. The most ardent advocates of markets would still, to some degree, insulate higher education from market pressures. For example, if it is all right to offer full scholarships to attract top students, what about offering salaries? Why should the NCAA not allow open bidding for the services of star athletes? Or, if colleges find that certain courses or majors are oversubscribed, why not charge a premium for them? If an unpopular professor draws persistently low enrollments, why not offer his courses at a discount?

At a certain point, market solutions sully the character of the good they allocate, at least where higher education is concerned. The growing use of merit scholarships may be approaching that point.

SHOULD WE BUY THE
RIGHT TO POLLUTE?

At the 1997 conference on global warming in Kyoto, Japan, the United States found itself at loggerheads with developing nations on two important issues: The United States wanted those countries to commit themselves to restraints on emissions, and it wanted any agreement to include a trading scheme that would let countries buy and sell the right to pollute.

The Clinton administration was right on the first point, but wrong on the second. Creating an international market in emission credits would make it easier for us to meet our obligations under the treaty but undermine the ethic we should be trying to foster on the environment.

Indeed, China and India threatened to torpedo the talks over the issue. They were afraid that such trading would enable rich countries to buy their way out of commitments to reduce greenhouse gases. In the end, the developing nations agreed to allow some emissions trading among developed countries, with details to be negotiated the following year.

The Clinton administration made emission trading a centerpiece of its environmental policy. Creating an international market for emissions, it argues, is a more efficient way to reduce pollution than imposing fixed levels for each country.

Trading in greenhouse gases could also make compliance cheaper and less painful for the United States, which could pay to reduce some other country's carbon dioxide emissions rather than reduce its own. For example, the United States might find it cheaper (and more politically palatable) to pay to update an old coal-burning factory in a developing country than to tax gas-guzzling sports utility vehicles at home.

Since the aim is to limit the global level of these gases, one might ask, what difference does it make which places on the planet send less carbon to the sky?

It may make no difference from the standpoint of the heavens, but it does make a political difference. Despite the efficiency of international emissions trading, such a system is objectionable for three reasons.

First, it creates loopholes that could enable wealthy countries to evade their obligations. Under the Kyoto formula, for example, the United States could take advantage of the fact that Russia has already reduced its emissions 30 percent since 1990, not through energy efficiencies but through economic decline. The United States could buy excess credits from Russia, and count them toward meeting our obligations under the treaty.

Second, turning pollution into a commodity to be bought and sold removes the moral stigma that is properly associated with it. If a company or a country is fined for spewing excessive pollutants into the air, the community conveys its judgment that the polluter has done something wrong. A fee, on the other hand, makes pollution just another cost of doing business, like wages, benefits and rent.

The distinction between a fine and a fee for despoiling the environment is not one we should give up too easily. Suppose there were a $100 fine for throwing a beer can into the Grand Canyon, and a wealthy hiker decided to pay $100 for the convenience. Would there be nothing wrong in his treating the fine as if it were simply an expensive dumping charge?

Or consider the fine for parking in a place reserved for the disabled. If a busy contractor needs to park near his building site and is willing to pay the fine, is there nothing wrong with his treating that space as an expensive parking lot?

In effacing the distinction between a fine and a fee, emission trading is like a recent proposal to open carpool lanes on Los Angeles freeways to drivers without passengers who are willing to pay a fee. Such drivers are now fined for slipping into carpool lanes; under the market proposal, they would enjoy a quicker commute without opprobrium.

A third objection to emission trading among countries is that it may undermine the sense of shared responsibility that increased global cooperation requires.

Consider an illustration drawn from an autumn ritual: raking fallen leaves into great piles and lighting bonfires. Imagine a neighborhood where each family agrees to have only one small bonfire a year. But they also agree that families can buy and sell their bonfire permits as they choose.

The family in the mansion on the hill buys permits from its neighbors—paying them, in effect, to lug their leaves to the town compost heap. The market works, and pollution is reduced, but without the spirit of shared sacrifice that might have been produced had no market intervened.

Those who have sold their permits, and those who have bought them, come to regard the bonfires less as an offense against clean air than as a luxury, a status symbol that can be bought and sold. And the resentment against the family in the mansion makes future, more demanding forms of cooperation more difficult to achieve.

Of course, many countries that attended the Kyoto conference have already made cooperation elusive. They have not yet agreed to restrict their emissions at all. Their refusal undermines the prospect of a global environmental ethic as surely as does our pollution trading scheme.

But the United States would have more suasion if these developing countries could not rightly complain that trading in emissions allows wealthy nations to buy their way out of global obligations.

fifteen

HONOR AND RESENTMENT

The politics of the ancients was about virtue and honor, but we moderns are concerned with fairness and rights. There is some truth in this familiar adage, but only to a point. On the surface, our political debates make little mention of honor, a seemingly quaint concern best suited to a status-ridden world of chivalry and duels. Not far beneath the surface, however, some of our fiercest debates about fairness and rights reflect deep disagreement about the proper basis of social esteem.

Consider the fuss over Callie Smartt, a 15-year-old cheerleader at a high school in West Texas. For a year she was a popular freshman cheerleader, despite the fact that she has cerebral palsy and moves about in a wheelchair. As Sue Anne Pressley reported in the *Washington Post,* "She had plenty of school spirit to go around. . . . The fans seemed to delight in her. The football players said they loved to see her dazzling smile." But at the end of the season, Callie was kicked off the squad. Earlier this fall, she was relegated to the status of honorary cheerleader; now, even that position is being abolished. At the urging of some other cheerleaders and their parents, school officials have told Callie that, to make the squad next year, she will have to try out like anyone else, in a rigorous routine involving splits and tumbles.

The head cheerleader's father opposes Callie's participation. He claims he is only concerned for Callie's safety. If a player comes flying off the field, he worries, "the cheerleader girls who aren't handicapped could move out of the way a little faster." But Callie has never been hurt cheerleading. Her mother suspects the opposition may be motivated by resentment of the acclaim Callie has received.

But what kind of resentment might motivate the head cheerleader's father? It cannot be fear that Callie's inclusion deprives his daughter of a place; she is already on the team. Nor is it the simple envy he might feel toward a girl who outshines his daughter at tumbles and splits, which Callie, of course, does not. The resentment more likely reflects the conviction that Callie is being accorded an honor she does not deserve, in a way that mocks the pride he takes in his daughter's cheerleading prowess. If great cheerleading is something that can be done from a wheelchair, then what becomes of the honor accorded those who excel at tumbles and splits? Indignation at misplaced honor is a moral sentiment that figures prominently in our politics, complicating and sometimes inflaming arguments about fairness and rights.

Should Callie be allowed to continue on the team? Some would answer by invoking the right of nondiscrimination: provided she can perform well in the role, Callie should not be excluded from cheerleading simply because, through no fault of her own, she lacks the physical ability to perform gymnastic routines. But the nondiscrimination argument begs the question at the heart of the controversy: What does it mean to perform well in the role of cheerleader? This question, in turn, is about the virtues and excellences that the practice of cheerleading honors and rewards. The case for Callie is that, by roaring up and down the sidelines in her wheelchair, waving her pom-poms and motivating the team, she does well what cheerleaders are supposed to do: inspire school spirit.

But if Callie should be a cheerleader because she displays, despite her disability, the virtues appropriate to her role, her claim does pose a certain threat to the honor accorded the other cheerleaders. The gymnastic skills they display no longer appear essential to excellence in cheerleading, only one way among others of rousing the crowd. Ungenerous though he was, the father of the head cheerleader correctly grasped what was at stake. A social practice once taken as fixed in its purpose and in the honors it bestowed was now, thanks to Callie, redefined.

Disputes about the allocation of honor underlie other controversies about fairness and rights. Consider, for example, the debate over affirmative action in university admissions. Here too, some try to resolve the question by invoking a general argument against discrimination. Advocates of affirmative action argue it is necessary to remedy the effects of discrimination, while opponents maintain that taking race into account amounts to reverse discrimination. Again the nondiscrimination argument begs a crucial question. All admissions policies discriminate on some ground or other. The real issue is, what kind of discrimination is appropriate to the purposes universities serve? This question is contested, not only because it decides how educational opportunities are distributed but also because it determines what virtues universities define as worthy of honor.

If the sole purpose of a university were to promote scholarly excellence and intellectual virtues, then it should admit the students most likely to contribute to these ends. But if another mission of a university is to cultivate leadership for a pluralistic society, then it should seek students likely to advance civic purposes as well as intellectual ones. In a recent court case challenging its affirmative action program, the University of Texas Law School invoked its civic purpose, arguing that its minority admissions program had helped equip black and Mexican-American graduates to serve in the Texas legislature, on the federal bench and even in the president's Cabinet.

Some critics of affirmative action resent the idea that universities should honor qualities other than intellectual ones, for to do so implies that standard meritocratic virtues lack a privileged moral place. If race and ethnicity can be relevant to university admissions, then what becomes of the proud parent's conviction that his daughter is worthy of admission by virtue of her grades and test scores alone? Like the father's pride in his cheerleader daughter's tumbles and splits, it would have to be qualified by the recognition that honor is relative to social institutions, whose purposes are open to argument and revision.

Perhaps the most potent instance of the politics of honor plays itself out in debates about work. One reason many working-class voters despise welfare is not that they begrudge the money it costs but that they resent the message it conveys about what is worthy of honor and reward. Liberals who defend welfare in terms of fairness and rights often miss this point. More than an incentive to elicit effort and skills in socially useful ways, income is a measure of the things we prize. For many who "work hard and play by the rules," rewarding those who stay at home mocks the effort they expend and the pride they take in the work they do. Their resentment against welfare is not a reason to abandon the needy. But it does suggest that liberals need to articulate more convincingly the notions of virtue and honor that underlie their arguments for fairness and rights.

sixteen

ARGUING AFFIRMATIVE ACTION

Affirmative action has been the subject of recurring political and constitutional controversy since the 1970s. In 1996, California voters enacted Proposition 209, a state constitutional amendment banning preferential treatment in public education and employment. In 2003, the U.S. Supreme Court struck down an undergraduate admissions policy at the University of Michigan that used a point system to give minority applicants an advantage. But it upheld a more flexible affirmative action policy used in Michigan's law school, and ruled that race could be considered as a factor in admissions.

Some say it is all in the wording. When a 1997 referendum in Houston asked voters to end affirmative action, they refused to do so. When Proposition 209 asked California voters to end preferential treatment based on race, they obliged.

Controlling the language of a political debate is the first step toward winning it. Yet, in the case of affirmative action, the different answers reflect more than just political manipulation; they reflect a conflicted public mind. Critics of affirmative action say this is because Americans are reluctant to remedy past wrongs with new discrimination, whereas supporters say it is because of the public's lingering racism. Both are mistaken. Affirmative action is difficult to defend for a reason that has nothing to do with race. The real problem is that the best case for affirmative action challenges the sacred American myth that landing a job, or a seat in the freshman class, is a prize one deserves thanks solely to one's own efforts. Consider the two main arguments for counting race as a factor in university admissions: one argues for compensation, the other for diversity. The compensatory argument views affirmative action as a remedy for past wrongs. Minority students should be given preference now to make up for a history of discrimination that has placed them at an unfair disadvantage. This argument treats admission primarily as a benefit to the recipient and seeks to distribute the benefit in a way that compensates for past discrimination.

But the compensatory argument is the weaker of the two. As opponents of affirmative action note, those who benefit are not necessarily those who have suffered, and those who pay the compensation are seldom those responsible for the wrongs being rectified. Many beneficiaries of affirmative action are middle-class minority students who did not suffer the hardships that afflict young blacks and Hispanics from the inner city. And those who lose out under affirmative-action programs may have suffered obstacles of their own.

Those who defend affirmative action on compensatory grounds must be able to explain why otherwise qualified applicants should bear the burden of redressing the historic wrongs that minorities have suffered. Even if it can be argued that compensation should not be understood as a specific remedy for particular acts of discrimination, the compensatory rationale is too narrow to justify the range of programs advanced in the name of affirmative action.

The diversity argument is more compelling. It does not depend upon showing that the minority student given preference today actually suffered discrimination in the past. This is because it treats admission less as a reward to the recipient than as a means of advancing a socially worthy aim. The diversity argument holds that a racially mixed student body is desirable because it enables students to learn more from one another than they would if they all came from similar backgrounds. Just as a student body drawn from one part of the country would limit the range of intellectual perspectives, so would one reflecting a homogeneity of race, class, or ethnicity. Moreover, equipping disadvantaged minorities to assume positions of leadership in key public and professional roles advances the university's civic purpose and contributes to the common good.

Critics of affirmative action might concede the goal but question the means. Even if a diverse student body is desirable, isn't it unfair to exclude those who may have high enough test scores but lack, through no fault of their own, the racial or ethnic background that admissions officers need to advance their worthy purposes? Don't the students with the highest academic achievement and promise deserve to be admitted?

The honest answer to this question is: no, they don't. Here lies the far-reaching assumption underlying the diversity argument for affirmative action: admission is not an honor bestowed to reward superior virtue. Neither the student with high test scores nor the student who comes from a disadvantaged minority group morally deserves to be admitted. Provided the criteria of admission are reasonably related to a worthy social purpose, and provided applicants are admitted accordingly, no one has a right to complain.

The moral force of the diversity argument is that it detaches admissions from individual claims and connects them to considerations of the common good. But this is also the source of its political vulnerability. The belief that jobs and opportunities are rewards for those who deserve them runs deep in the American soul. Politicians constantly remind us that those who "work hard and play by the rules" deserve to get ahead, and insist that those who realize the American dream should view their success as the measure of their virtue.

The case for affirmative action and for other acts of social solidarity would be easier if the myth were weaker, if one day Americans grew skeptical of the faith that worldly success reflects moral desert. But what politician is up to the task of explaining that, even at their best, the rules of the game do not reward virtue after all, but simply call forth the qualities required, at any given moment to advance the common good?

seventeen

SHOULD VICTIMS HAVE A SAY IN SENTENCING?

Before sentencing Timothy McVeigh to death, the jury in the Oklahoma City bombing case heard heart-wrenching testimony from survivors and from victims' families. Some say that such testimony, no matter how moving, has no place in the courtroom. Whether a criminal defendant should be put to death should be decided by reasoned reflection on the facts and the law, they argue, and not by the anger and rage that the victims' families rightly feel. Others maintain that victims should have a voice in the punishment a perpetrator receives. If the punishment should fit the crime, they contend, juries must know the full measure of the victims' suffering and loss.

Judge Richard Matsch, who presided over the McVeigh trial, seemed torn between these two positions. While he allowed some victims to testify during the sentencing phase, he ruled out the use of emotionally loaded evidence like poems, wedding photographs and the testimony of a 9-year-old boy whose mother died in the bombing. He took pains to prevent testimony that might "inflame or incite the passions of the jury with respect to vengeance or . . . empathy for grief." Such emotions, he said, were "inappropriate in making a measured and deliberate moral judgment as to whether the defendant should be put to death." The judge's ambivalence reflects competing notions of the purpose of criminal punishment. Those who favor giving victims a voice in criminal sentencing rely, sometimes unwittingly, on two different arguments—one therapeutic, the other retributive. The first treats punishment as a source of solace for the victim, a cathartic expression, a moment of closure. If punishment is for the benefit of the victim, then the victim should have a say in what the punishment is. The therapeutic theory of punishment finds its clearest expression in state laws that invite victims not only to describe their pain and suffering but also to express their opinions of the defendant, making for raucous courtroom scenes resembling daytime talk shows. Texas law even allows victims or their relatives to berate the defendant in open court after sentencing.

But the therapeutic case for victim testimony is flawed. It confuses an effect of criminal punishment (that victims and their families take satisfaction in the outcome) with its primary justification—to give the perpetrator what he deserves. The most compelling reason to allow victim impact statements is a retributive one: to provide the jury with a full account of the moral gravity of the crime. Though we may be aware that 168 people died in the Oklahoma bombing, only those agonizing stories of bewildered toddlers asking plaintively for their mothers convey the full moral measure of the crime.

In the retributive view, victim impact statements are not for the sake of allowing victims to vent their emotions but rather for the sake of doing justice, of getting at the moral truth of the matter. To the extent that emotions distort rather than clarify the nature of the crime, the judge should restrain their role in sentencing.

Though the retributive argument offers the best case for victim testimony, it is open to two apparent objections. First, the use of evidence about the character of particular victims and their importance to family or community implies that some lives are worthier than others. Otherwise, what moral difference does it make whether a murderer kills a beloved parent of four children or an unmarried drifter whose death goes unmourned, a Martin Luther King Jr. or the town drunk? Unless there is some basis for judgments of this kind, it is difficult to explain the moral relevance of testimony about the life or character of particular victims.

Second, even if certain murders are morally more grievous than others, isn't it unfair to give extra punishment for aspects of a crime about which the perpetrator was unaware? If an assailant kills a stranger, should his penalty depend on whether the victim turns out to have been a sinner or a saint? The Supreme Court emphasized this objection in *Booth v. Maryland*, a 1987 case that held victim impact statements in capital cases to be unconstitutional. Allowing the jury to consider the victim's character or family circumstances "could result in imposing the death sentence because of factors about which the defendant was not aware, and that were irrelevant to the decision to kill."

The second objection is less weighty than the first. We do not punish murderers only for their "decision to kill," but also for the harm they cause. A would-be assassin whose gun fails to fire receives a lesser punishment than a successful assassin, even though both made a "decision to kill." A drunk driver who kills a pedestrian is subject to a heavier penalty than an equally drunk driver who is lucky enough to kill no one, even though neither made a "decision to kill."

The first objection, on the other hand, is not as easy to dismiss. That the retributive case for victim testimony implies a moral hierarchy among murders (and perhaps also victims) is difficult to deny. The notion of moral discrimination is at odds with the nonjudgmental instinct of our time. But that is not an argument against it. We cannot make sense of our judgments about crime and punishment without some notion of moral discrimination.

Judge Matsch is not the only one wrestling with these competing theories of punishment. The use of impact statements has burgeoned in recent years, prompted by a victims' rights movement and a 1991 Supreme Court decision, *Payne v. Tennessee,* that overruled Booth and allowed victim testimony in death penalty cases. Most states now accord victims the right to be heard, and Congress included provisions for victim testimony in the 1994 federal crime bill. In March, President Clinton signed legislation that would let victims of the Oklahoma bombing witness the trial even if they were being called to testify. "When someone is a victim, he or she should be at the center of the criminal justice process," Clinton said, "not on the outside looking in."

The increasing concern for victims' rights is a morally ambiguous tiding. It reflects the rising therapeutic impulse in American public life—a defense attorney called victim testimony "the Oprahization of sentencing"—and also the growing appeal of traditional notions of retributive justice. As the therapeutic ethic represents the flight from moral responsibility, the retributive ethic represents the yearning to recover it. The challenge is to disentangle the second impulse from the first. Victim testimony, properly controlled, can serve justice by shedding light on the moral gravity of the crime. But there is a danger in placing the victim "at the center of the criminal justice process." It is the danger, as old as the practice of private vengeance, that the psychological needs of the victim will swamp the moral imperative that the punishment fit the crime.

eighteen

CLINTON AND KANT ON LYING

Suppose, for the sake of argument, that the president was sexually involved with Monica Lewinsky. Would it be wrong for him to deny it? The obvious answer is yes—an extramarital dalliance with a White House intern is bad enough, and lying only compounds the sin. But while a public lie about private misconduct may not be a morally admirable thing, such a lie does not necessarily add to the wrong of the conduct it conceals. It might even be justified.

Consider a different case of presidential deceit—a denial of plans to lead the country into war. During the 1964 presidential campaign, Lyndon Johnson concealed his intention to escalate the war in Vietnam, much as Franklin Roosevelt had denied plans to enter World War II. "I have said this before, but I shall say it again and again and again," FDR declared during the 1940 campaign. "Your boys are not going to be sent into any foreign wars." Both presidents deceived the public—Roosevelt for the sake of a just cause, Johnson for the sake of an unjust one. The moral status of their respective deceits differs accordingly. Johnson's lie was less justified than Roosevelt's, not because it was any less truthful, but because it served an unworthy end. The Clinton case differs in that the conduct in question is not a public undertaking but an alleged private misdeed. It certainly lacks the high moral purpose of Roosevelt's cause. But there may be a case, in the name of privacy and decorum, for the president to deny a scurrilous charge even if true, provided it has no bearing on public responsibilities. The Talmud allows three exceptions to the requirement of truthfulness—involving knowledge, hospitality, and sex. A scholar who is asked whether he knows a certain passage of Talmud may say, falsely, that he does not, to avoid an immodest display of knowledge. He may also lie if asked about the quality of hospitality he has received in order to spare his host a parade of unwelcome guests. Finally, he is entitled to lie if asked about such intimate matters as the performance of his conjugal duties. (This last exemption applies only loosely to the case of Clinton. On the one hand, it suggests that the right to lie can arise from the impropriety of the question. On the other, it covers inquiries about marital relations, not alleged infidelity.)

The morality of deceit is complicated by the fact that it is possible to mislead without actually lying. Much has been made of Clinton's tendency to give carefully worded, loophole-ridden denials to embarrassing allegations. When asked, during his first presidential campaign, whether he had ever used recreational drugs, Clinton replied that he had never broken the anti-drug laws of his country or state. He later conceded that he had tried marijuana while a student in England. A close reading of his famous 1992 interview on "60 Minutes" reveals that he never actually denied an extramarital affair with Gennifer Flowers. Asked about Flowers's tabloid account of a twelve-year affair, Clinton replied, "That allegation is false." This answer is technically consistent with Clinton's reported admission in his sealed deposition in the Paula Jones case that he did have a sexual involvement with Flowers.

Is there a moral difference between an artful dodge and a bald-faced lie? No, say Clinton critics, and many ethicists as well. They argue that a misleading truth has the same purpose and, if successful, the same effect as an outright lie: to deceive the listener. One of the greatest moralists of all time, however, disagreed. Immanuel Kant, an eighteenth-century German philosopher, insisted there is all the difference in the world between a lie and a technically truthful dodge.

Kant yielded to no one in his opposition to lying. Even if a murderer came to your door looking for a person hiding in your house, Kant held, it is not morally permissible to lie. The duty to tell the truth holds irrespective of the consequences. At one point, Benjamin Constant, a French contemporary of Kant's, took issue with this uncompromising stance. The duty to tell the truth only applies, Constant argued, to those who deserve the truth, as surely the murderer does not. Kant replied that lying to a murderer is wrong, not because it harms him, but because it violates the very principle of right and offends the human dignity of the person who lies. "To be truthful (honest) in all declarations is, therefore, a sacred and unconditionally commanding law of reason that admits of no expediency whatsoever," Kant said.

Despite his categorical prohibition on lying, or perhaps because of it, Kant drew a sharp distinction between lies and statements that are misleading but not, in the formal sense, untrue. A few years before his exchange with Constant, Kant found himself in trouble with King Friedrich Wilhelm II. The King and his censors demanded that Kant refrain from any lectures or writings they deemed a distortion or depreciation of Christianity. Kant, who planned to speak and publish further on religion, responded with a carefully worded statement, promising that "as your Majesty's faithful subject, I shall in the future completely desist from all public lectures or papers concerning religion."

When the King died a few years later, Kant considered himself absolved of the promise, which bound him only as "His Majesty's faithful subject." Kant later explained that he had chosen his words "most carefully, so that I should not be deprived of my freedom . . . forever, but only so long as His Majesty was alive." By this clever evasion, the paragon of Prussian probity succeeded in misleading the censors without lying to them.

Many thought Clinton was employing a similar maneuver when, early in the scandal, he repeatedly employed the present tense to deny allegations of past impropriety, stating, "There is no sexual relationship." When journalists seized on the possible evasion, he finally issued a less equivocal denial.

If the president has shifted from a misleading truth (like Kant's) to an actual lie, there might still be a mitigating factor. Even the most righteous among us would not welcome the prying, prurient scrutiny to which public figures are exposed. Consider, again, the Talmud. It tells of a rabbinic sage so exemplary that his disciple once hid under his bed to learn the proper way to make love to one's wife. When the rabbi discovered his student's presence and asked him to leave, the disciple replied, "It is Torah and deserves to be studied." The president's popularity is unimpaired, not because the American people believe he is telling the truth, but because they have decided that his sex life is not Torah and does not deserve to be studied.

nineteen

IS THERE A RIGHT TO ASSISTED SUICIDE?

This essay was written as the Supreme Court contemplated two cases involving state laws that banned physician-assisted suicide. The Court unanimously upheld the laws and rejected the notion of a constitutional right to physician-assisted suicide.

The Supreme Court will soon decide whether terminally ill patients have a constitutional right to physician-assisted suicide. Most likely, the Court will say no. Almost every state prohibits assisted suicide, and in oral arguments earlier this year the justices voiced doubts about striking down so many state laws on so wrenching a moral issue.

If the Court rules as expected, it will not simply be overruling the two federal courts that declared suicide a constitutional right. It will also be rejecting the advice of six distinguished moral philosophers who filed a friend of the court brief. The authors of the brief comprise the Dream Team of liberal political philosophy—Ronald Dworkin (Oxford and NYU), Thomas Nagel (NYU), Robert Nozick (Harvard), John Rawls (Harvard), Thomas Scanlon (Harvard), and Judith Jarvis Thomson (MIT).[1]

At the heart of the philosophers' argument is the attractive but mistaken principle that government should be neutral on controversial moral and religious questions. Since people disagree about what gives meaning and value to life, the philosophers argue, government should not impose through law any particular answer to such questions. Instead, it should respect a person's right to live (and die) according to his own convictions about what makes life worth living. Mindful that judges are reluctant to venture onto morally contested terrain, the philosophers insist that the Court can affirm a right to assisted suicide without passing judgment on the moral status of suicide itself. "These cases do not invite or require the Court to make moral, ethical, or religious judgments about how people should approach or confront their death or about when it is ethically appropriate to hasten one's own death or to ask others for help in doing so," they write. Instead, say the philosophers, the Court should accord individuals the right to make these "grave judgments for themselves, free from the imposition of any religious or philosophical orthodoxy by court or legislature."

Despite their claim to neutrality, the philosophers' argument betrays a certain view of what makes life worth living. According to this view, the best way to live and die is to do so deliberately, autonomously, in a way that enables us to view our lives as our own creations. The best lives are led by those who see themselves not as participants in a drama larger than themselves but as authors of the drama itself "Most of us see death . . . as the final act of life's drama," the brief states, "and we want that last act to reflect our own convictions." The philosophers speak for those who would end their lives upon concluding that living on "would disfigure rather than enhance the lives they had created." Citing the Court's language in a recent abortion case, *Planned Parenthood v. Casey* (1992), the philosophers stress the individual's right to make "choices central to personal dignity and autonomy." Such freedom includes nothing less than "the right to define one's own concept of existence, of meaning, of the universe, and of the mystery of human life."

The philosophers' emphasis on autonomy and choice implies that life is the possession of the person who lives it. This ethic is at odds with a wide range of moral outlooks that view life as a gift, of which we are custodians with certain duties. Such outlooks reject the idea that a person's life is open to unlimited use, even by the person whose life it is. Far from being neutral, the ethic of autonomy invoked in the brief departs from many religious traditions and also from the views of the founders of liberal political philosophy, John Locke and Immanuel Kant. Both Locke and Kant opposed a right to suicide, and both rejected the notion that our lives are possessions to dispose of as we please.

Locke, the philosopher of consent argued for limited government on the grounds that certain rights are so profoundly ours that we cannot give them up, even by an act of consent. Since the right to life and liberty is unalienable, he maintained, we cannot sell ourselves into slavery or commit suicide: "No body can give more Power than he has himself, and he that cannot take away his own Life, cannot give another power over it."

For Kant, respect for autonomy entails duties to oneself as well as others, most notably the duty to treat humanity as an end in itself. This duty constrains the way a person can treat himself. According to Kant, murder is wrong because it uses the victim as a means rather than respects him as an end. But the same can be true of suicide. If a person "does away with himself in order to escape from a painful situation," Kant writes, "he is making use of a person merely as a means to maintain a tolerable state of affairs till the end of his life. But man is not a thing—not something to be used as a means: he must always in his actions be regarded as an end in himself." Kant concludes that a person has no more right to kill himself than to kill someone else.

The philosophers' brief assumes, contrary to Kant, that the value of a person's life is the value he or she attributes to it, provided the person is competent and fully informed. "When a competent person does want to die," the philosophers write, "it makes no sense to appeal to the patient's right not to be killed as a reason why an act designed to cause his death is impermissible." Kant would have disagreed. The fact that a person wants to die does not make it morally permissible to kill him, even if his desire is uncoerced and well-in-formed.

The philosophers might reply that permitting assisted suicide does no harm to those who find it morally objectionable; those who prefer to view their lives as episodes in a larger drama rather than as autonomous creations would remain free to do so.

But this reply overlooks the way that changes in law can bring changes in the way we understand ourselves. The philosophers rightly observe that existing laws against assisted suicide reflect and entrench certain views about what gives life meaning. But the same would be true were the Court to declare, in the name of autonomy, a right to assisted suicide. The new regime would not simply expand the range of options, but would encourage the tendency to view life less as a gift and more as a possession. It might heighten the prestige we accord autonomous, independent lives and depreciate the claims of those seen to be dependent. How this shift would affect policy toward the elderly, the disabled, the poor and the infirm, or reshape the attitudes of doctors toward their ailing patients or children toward their aging parents, remains to be seen.

To reject the autonomy argument is not necessarily to oppose assisted suicide in all cases. Even those who regard life as a sacred trust can admit that the claims of compassion may sometimes override the duty to preserve life. The challenge is to find a way to honor these claims that preserves the moral burden of hastening death, and that retains the reverence for life as something we cherish, not something we choose.

twenty

EMBRYO ETHICS
THE MORAL LOGIC OF
STEM CELL RESEARCH

At first glance, the case for federal funding of embryonic stem cell research seems too obvious to need defending. Why should the government refuse to support research that holds promise for the treatment and cure of devastating conditions such as Parkinson's disease, diabetes, and spinal cord injury? Critics of stem cell research offer two main objections: some hold that despite its worthy ends, stem cell research is wrong because it involves the destruction of human embryos; others worry that even if research on embryos is not wrong in itself, it will open the way to a slippery slope of dehumanizing practices, such as embryo farms, cloned babies, the use of fetuses for spare parts, and the commodification of human life.

Neither objection is ultimately persuasive, though each raises questions that proponents of stem cell research should take seriously. Consider the first objection. Those who make it begin by arguing, rightly, that biomedical ethics is not only about ends but also about means; even research that achieves great good is unjustified if it comes at the price of violating fundamental human rights. For example, the ghoulish experiments of Nazi doctors would not be morally justified even if they resulted in discoveries that alleviated human suffering.

Few would dispute the idea that respect for human dignity imposes certain moral constraints on medical research. The question is whether the destruction of human embryos in stem cell research amounts to the killing of human beings. The "embryo objection" insists that it does. For those who adhere to this view, extracting stem cells from a blastocyst is morally equivalent to yanking organs from a baby to save other people's lives.

Some base this conclusion on the religious belief that ensoulment occurs at conception. Others try to defend it without recourse to religion, by the following line of reasoning: Each of us began life as an embryo. If our lives are worthy of respect, and hence inviolable, simply by virtue of our humanity, one would be mistaken to think that at some younger age or earlier stage of development we were not worthy of respect. Unless we can point to a definitive moment in the passage from conception to birth that marks the emergence of the human person, this argument claims, we must regard embryos as possessing the same inviolability as fully developed human beings.

But this argument is flawed. The fact that every person began life as an embryo does not prove that embryos are persons. Consider an analogy: although every oak tree was once an acorn, it does not follow that acorns are oak trees, or that I should treat the loss of an acorn eaten by a squirrel in my front yard as the same kind of loss as the death of an oak tree felled by a storm. Despite their developmental continuity, acorns and oak trees are different kinds of things. So are human embryos and human beings. Sentient creatures make claims on us that nonsentient ones do not; beings capable of experience and consciousness make higher claims still. Human life develops by degrees.

Those who view embryos as persons often assume that the only alternative is to treat them with moral indifference. But one need not regard the embryo as a full human being in order to accord it a certain respect. To regard an embryo as a mere thing, open to any use we desire or devise, does, it seems to me, miss its significance as potential human life. Few would favor the wanton destruction of embryos or the use of embryos for the purpose of developing a new line of cosmetics. Personhood is not the only warrant for respect. For example, we consider it an act of disrespect when a hiker carves his initials in an ancient sequoia—not because we regard the sequoia as a person, but because we regard it as a natural wonder worthy of appreciation and awe. To respect the old-growth forest does not mean that no tree may ever be felled or harvested for human purposes. Respecting the forest may be consistent with using it. But the purposes should be weighty and appropriate to the wondrous nature of the thing.

The notion that an embryo in a petri dish has the same moral status as a person can be challenged on further grounds. Perhaps the best way to see its implausibility is to play out its full implications. First, if harvesting stem cells from a blastocyst were truly on a par with harvesting organs from a baby, then the morally responsible policy would be to ban it, not merely deny it federal funding. If some doctors made a practice of killing children to get organs for transplantation, no one would take the position that the infanticide should be ineligible for federal funding but allowed to continue in the private sector. If we were persuaded that embryonic stem cell research were tantamount to infanticide, we would not only ban it but treat it as a grisly form of murder and subject scientists who performed it to criminal punishment.

Second, viewing the embryo as a person rules out not only stem cell research, but all fertility treatments that involve the creation and discarding of excess embryos. In order to increase pregnancy rates and spare women the ordeal of repeated attempts, most in vitro fertilization clinics create more fertilized eggs than are ultimately implanted. Excess embryos are typically frozen indefinitely or discarded. (A small number are donated for stem cell research.) But if it is immoral to sacrifice embryos for the sake of curing or treating devastating diseases, it is also immoral to sacrifice them for the sake of treating infertility.

Third, defenders of in vitro fertilization point out that embryo loss in assisted reproduction is less frequent than in natural pregnancy, in which more than half of all fertilized eggs either fail to implant or are otherwise lost. This fact highlights a further difficulty with the view that equates embryos and persons. If natural procreation entails the loss of some embryos for every successful birth, perhaps we should worry less about the loss of embryos that occurs in in vitro fertilization and stem cell research. Those who view embryos as persons might reply that high infant mortality would not justify infanticide. But the way we respond to the natural loss of embryos suggests that we do not regard this event as the moral or religious equivalent of the death of infants. Even those religious traditions that are the most solicitous of nascent human life do not mandate the same burial rituals and mourning rites for the loss of an embryo as for the death of a child. Moreover, if the embryo loss that accompanies natural procreation were the moral equivalent of infant death, then pregnancy would have to be regarded as a public health crisis of epidemic proportions; alleviating natural embryo loss would be a more urgent moral cause than abortion, in vitro fertilization, and stem cell research combined.

Even critics of stem cell research hesitate to embrace the full implications of the embryo objection. President George W. Bush has prohibited federal funding for research on embryonic stem cell lines derived after August 9, 2001, but has not sought to ban such research, nor has he called on scientists to desist from it. And as the stem cell debate heats up in Congress, even outspoken opponents of embryo research have not mounted a national campaign to ban in vitro fertilization or to prohibit fertility clinics from creating and discarding excess embryos. This does not mean that their positions are unprincipled—only that their positions cannot rest on the principle that embryos are inviolable.

What else could justify restricting federal funding for stem cell research? It might be the worry that embryo research will lead down a slippery slope of exploitation and abuse. This objection raises legitimate concerns, but curtailing stem cell research is the wrong way to address them. Congress can stave off the slippery slope by enacting sensible regulations, beginning with a simple ban on human reproductive cloning. Following the approach adopted by the United Kingdom, Congress might also require that research embryos not be allowed to develop beyond 14 days, restrict the commodification of embryos and gametes, and establish a stem cell bank to prevent proprietary interests from monopolizing access to stem cell lines. Regulations such as these could save us from slouching toward a brave new world as we seek to redeem the great biomedical promise of our time.

twenty-one

MORAL ARGUMENT AND LIBERAL TOLERATION

ABORTION AND HOMOSEXUALITY

People defend laws against abortion and homosexual conduct in two different ways: Some argue that abortion and homosexuality are morally reprehensible and therefore worthy of prohibition; others try to avoid passing judgment on the morality of these practices, and argue instead that, in a democracy, political majorities have the right to embody in law their moral convictions.

In a similar way, arguments against antiabortion and antisodomy laws take two different forms: Some say the laws are unjust because the practices they prohibit are morally permissible, indeed sometimes desirable; others oppose these laws without reference to the moral status of the practices at issue, and argue instead that individuals have a right to choose for themselves whether to engage in them.

These two styles of argument might be called, respectively, the "naive" and the "sophisticated." The naive view holds that the justice of laws depends on the moral worth of the conduct they prohibit or protect. The sophisticated view holds that the justice of such laws depends not on a substantive moral judgment about the conduct at stake, but instead on a more general theory about the respective claims of majority rule and individual rights, of democracy on the one hand, and liberty on the other.

I shall try in this essay to bring out the truth in the naive view, which I take to be this: The justice (or injustice) of laws against abortion and homosexual conduct depends, at least in part, on the morality (or immorality) of those practices.[1] This is the claim the sophisticated view rejects. In both its majoritarian and its liberal versions, the sophisticated view tries to set aside or "bracket" controversial moral and religious conceptions for purposes of justice. It insists that the justification of laws be neutral among competing visions of the good life.

In practice, of course, these two kinds of argument can be difficult to distinguish. In the debate over cases like *Roe v. Wade*[2] and *Bowers v. Hardwick*,[3] both camps tend to advance the naive view under cover of the sophisticated. (Such is the prestige of the sophisticated way of arguing.) For example, those who would ban abortion and gay and lesbian sex out of abhorrence often argue in the name of deference to democracy and judicial restraint. Similarly, those who want permissive laws because they approve of abortion and homosexuality often argue in the name of liberal toleration.

This is not to suggest that all instances of the sophisticated argument are disingenuous attempts to promote a substantive moral conviction. Those who argue that law should be neutral among competing conceptions of the good life offer various grounds for their claim, including most prominently the following:

> (1) the *voluntarist* view holds that government should be neutral
> among conceptions of the good life in order to respect the capacity
> of persons as free citizens or autonomous agents to choose their
> conceptions for themselves; (2) the *minimalist* or pragmatic view
> says that, because people inevitably disagree about morality and re-
> ligion, government should bracket these controversies for the sake
> of political agreement and social cooperation.

In order to bring out the truth in the naive way of arguing, I look to the actual arguments judges and commentators have made in recent cases dealing with abortion and homosexuality. Their arguments, unfailingly sophisticated, illustrate the difficulty of bracketing moral judgments for purposes of law. Although much of my argument criticizes leading theories of liberal toleration, I do not think it offers any comfort to majoritarianism. The cure for liberalism is not majoritarianism, but a keener appreciation of the role of substantive moral discourse in political and constitutional argument.

PRIVACY RIGHTS: INTIMACY AND AUTONOMY

In the constitutional right of privacy, the neutral state and the voluntarist conception of the person are often joined. In the case of abortion, for example, no state may, "by adopting one theory of life,"[4] override a woman's right to decide "whether or not to terminate her pregnancy."[5] Government may not enforce a particular moral view, however widely held, for "no individual should be compelled to surrender the freedom to make that decision for herself simply because her 'value preferences' are not shared by the majority."[6]

As with religious liberty and freedom of speech, so with privacy, the ideal of neutrality often reflects a voluntarist conception of human agency. Government must be neutral among conceptions of the good life in order to respect the capacity of persons to choose their values and relationships for themselves. So close is the connection between privacy rights and the voluntarist conception of the self that commentators frequently assimilate the values of privacy and autonomy: Privacy rights are said to be "grounded in notions of individual autonomy," because "the human dignity protected by constitutional guarantees would be seriously diminished if people were not free to choose and adopt a lifestyle which allows expression of their uniqueness and individuality."[7] In "recognizing a constitutional right to privacy," the Court has given effect to the view "that persons have the capacity to live autonomously and the right to exercise that capacity."[8] Supreme Court decisions voiding laws against contraceptives "not only protect the individual who chooses not to procreate, but also the autonomy of a couple's association."[9] They protect men and women "against an unchosen commitment" to unwanted children, and "against a compelled identification with the social role of parent."[10]

In Supreme Court decisions and dissents alike, the justices have often tied privacy rights to voluntarist assumptions. The Court has thus characterized laws banning the use of contraceptives as violating "the constitutional protection of individual autonomy in matters of childbearing."[11] It has defended the right to an abortion on the grounds that few decisions are "more properly private, or more basic to individual dignity and autonomy, than a woman's decision . . . whether to end her pregnancy."[12] Justice Douglas, concurring in an abortion case, emphasized that the right of privacy protects such liberties as "the autonomous control over the development and expression of one's intellect, interests, tastes, and personality," as well as "freedom of choice in the basic decisions of one's life respecting marriage, divorce, procreation, contraception, and the education and upbringing of children."[13] And four justices would have extended privacy protection to consensual homosexual activity on the grounds that "much of the richness of a relationship will come from the freedom an individual has to *choose* the form and nature of these intensely personal bonds."[14]

Although the link between privacy and autonomy is now so familiar as to seem natural, even necessary, the right of privacy need not presuppose a voluntarist conception of the person. In fact, through most of its history in American law, the right of privacy has implied neither the ideal of the neutral state nor the ideal of a self freely choosing its aims and attachments.

Where the contemporary right of privacy is the right to engage in certain conduct without government restraint, the traditional version is the right to keep certain personal facts from public view. The new privacy protects a person's "independence in making certain kinds of important decisions," whereas the old privacy protects a person's interest "in avoiding disclosure of personal matters."[15]

The tendency to identify privacy with autonomy not only obscures these shifting understandings of privacy; it also restricts the range of reasons for protecting it. Although the new privacy typically relies on voluntarist justifications, it can also be justified in other ways. A right to be free of governmental interference in matters of marriage, for example, can be defended not only in the name of individual choice, but also in the name of the intrinsic value or social importance of the practice it protects.

FROM THE OLD PRIVACY TO THE NEW

The right to privacy first gained legal recognition in the United States as a doctrine of tort law, not constitutional law. In an influential article in 1890, Louis Brandeis, then a Boston lawyer, and his one-time law partner Samuel Warren argued that the civil law should protect "the right to privacy."[16] Far from later-day concerns with sexual freedoms, Brandeis and Warren's privacy was quaint by comparison, concerned with the publication of high society gossip by the sensationalist press, or the unauthorized use of people's portraits in advertising.[17] Gradually at first, then more frequently in the 1930s, this right to privacy gained recognition in the civil law of most states.[18] Prior to the 1960s, however, privacy received scant attention in constitutional law.

The Supreme Court first addressed the right of privacy as such in 1961 when a Connecticut pharmacist challenged the state's ban on contraceptives in *Poe v. Ullman*.[19] Although the majority dismissed the case on technical grounds,[20] Justices Douglas and Harlan dissented, arguing that the law violated the right of privacy. The privacy they defended was privacy in the traditional sense. The right at stake was not the right to use contraceptives but the right to be free of the surveillance that enforcement would require. "If we imagine a regime of full enforcement of the law," wrote Douglas, "we would reach the point where search warrants issued and officers appeared in bedrooms to find out what went on. . . . If [the State] can make this law, it can enforce it. And proof of its violation necessarily involves an inquiry into the relations between man and wife."[21] Banning the sale of contraceptives would be different from banning their use, Douglas observed. Banning the sale would restrict access to contraceptives but would not expose intimate relations to public inspection. Enforcement would take police to the drugstore, not the bedroom, and so would not offend privacy in the traditional sense.[22]

Justice Harlan also objected to the law on grounds that distinguish the old privacy from the new. He did not object that the law against contraceptives failed to be neutral among competing moral conceptions. Although Harlan acknowledged that the law was based on the belief that contraception is immoral in itself, and encourages such "dissolute action" as fornication and adultery by minimizing their "disastrous consequence,"[23] he did not find this failure of neutrality contrary to the Constitution. In a statement clearly opposed to the strictures of neutrality, Harlan argued that morality is a legitimate concern of government.

> Society is not limited in its objects only to the physical well-being of the community, but has traditionally concerned itself with the moral soundness of its people as well. Indeed to attempt a line between public behavior and that which is purely consensual or solitary would be to withdraw from community concern a range of subjects with which every society in civilized times has found it necessary to deal.[24]

Though he rejected the ideal of the neutral state, Harlan did not conclude that Connecticut could prohibit married couples from using contraceptives. Like Douglas, he reasoned that enforcing the law would intrude on the privacy essential to the prized institution of marriage. He objected to the violation of privacy in the traditional sense, to "the intrusion of the whole machinery of the criminal law into the very heart of marital privacy, requiring husband and wife to render account before a criminal tribunal of their uses of that intimacy."[25] According to Harlan, the state was entitled to embody in law the belief that contraception is immoral, but not to implement "the obnoxiously intrusive means it ha[d] chosen to effectuate that policy."[26]

Four years later, in *Griswold v. Connecticut,*[27] the dissenters prevailed. The Supreme Court invalidated Connecticut's law against contraceptives and for the first time explicitly recognized a constitutional right of privacy. Although the right was located in the Constitution rather than tort law, it remained tied to the traditional notion of privacy as the interest in keeping intimate affairs from public view. The violation of privacy consisted in the intrusion required to enforce the law, not the restriction on the freedom to use contraceptives. "Would we allow the police to search the sacred precincts of marital bedrooms for telltale signs of the use of contraceptives?" wrote Justice Douglas for the Court. "The very idea is repulsive to the notions of privacy surrounding the marriage relationship."[28]

The justification for the right was not voluntarist but based on a substantive moral judgment; the privacy the Court vindicated was not for the sake of letting people lead their sexual lives as they choose, but rather for the sake of affirming and protecting the social institution of marriage.

> Marriage is a coming together for better or for worse, hopefully enduring, and intimate to the degree of being sacred. It is an association that promotes a way of life, . . . a harmony in living, . . . a bilateral loyalty. . . . [I]t is an association for as noble a purpose as any involved in our prior decisions.[29]

Although commentators and judges often view *Griswold* as a dramatic constitutional departure, the privacy right it proclaimed was consistent with traditional notions of privacy going back to the turn of the century. From the standpoint of shifting privacy conceptions, the more decisive turn came seven years later in *Eisenstadt v. Baird,*[30] a seemingly similar case. Like *Griswold,* it involved a state law restricting contraceptives. In *Eisenstadt,* however, the challenged law restricted the distribution of contraceptives, not their use. While it therefore limited access to contraceptives, its enforcement could not be said to require governmental surveillance of intimate activities. It did not violate privacy in the traditional sense.[31] Furthermore, the law prohibited distributing contraceptives only to unmarried persons, and so did not burden the institution of marriage as the Connecticut law did.

Despite these differences, the Supreme Court struck down the law with only a single dissent. Its decision involved two innovations, one explicit, the other unacknowledged. The explicit innovation redescribed the bearers of privacy rights from persons *qua* participants in the social institution of marriage to persons *qua* individuals, independent of their roles or attachments. As the Court explained, "It is true that in *Griswold* the right of privacy in question inhered in the marital relationship. Yet the marital couple is not an independent entity with a mind and heart of its own, but an association of two individuals each with a separate intellectual and emotional makeup."[32]

The subtler, though no less fateful change in *Eisenstadt* was in the shift from the old privacy to the new. Rather than conceiving privacy as freedom from surveillance or disclosure of intimate affairs, the Court found that the right to privacy now protected the freedom to engage in certain activities without governmental restriction. Although privacy in *Griswold* prevented intrusion into "the sacred precincts of marital bedrooms,"[33] privacy in *Eisenstadt* prevented intrusion into *decisions* of certain kinds. Moreover, as the meaning of privacy changed, so did its justification. The Court protected privacy in *Eisenstadt* not for the social practices it promoted but for the individual choice it secured. "If the right of privacy means anything, it is the right of the *individual,* married or single, to be free from unwarranted governmental intrusion into matters so fundamentally affecting a person as the decision whether to bear or beget a child."[34]

One year later, in *Roe v. Wade*,[35] the Supreme Court gave the new privacy its most controversial application by striking down a Texas law against abortion and extending privacy to "encompass a woman's decision whether or not to terminate her pregnancy."[36] First with contraception, then with abortion, the right of privacy had become the right to make certain sorts of choices, free of interference by the state.

The voluntarist grounds of the new privacy found explicit statement in a 1977 case invalidating a New York law prohibiting the sale of contraceptives to minors under age sixteen.[37] For the first time, the Court used the language of autonomy to describe the interest privacy protects, and argued openly for the shift from the old privacy to the new. Writing for the Court in *Carey v. Population Services International*, Justice Brennan admitted that *Griswold* focused on the fact that a law forbidding the *use* of contraceptives can bring the police into marital bedrooms.[38] "But subsequent decisions have made clear that the constitutional protection of individual autonomy in matters of childbearing is not dependent on that element."[39] Surveying the previous cases, he emphasized that *Eisenstadt* protected the "*decision* whether to bear or beget a child,"[40] and *Roe* protected "a woman's *decision* whether or not to terminate her pregnancy."[41] He concluded that "the teaching of *Griswold* is that the Constitution protects individual decisions in matters of childbearing from unjustified intrusion by the State."[42]

Given the voluntarist interpretation of privacy, restricting the *sale* of contraceptives violates privacy as harshly as banning their *use;* the one limits choice as surely as the other. "Indeed, in practice," Brennan observed, "a prohibition against all sales, since more easily and less offensively enforced, might have an even more devastating effect upon the freedom to choose contraception."[43] Ironically, the very fact that a ban on sales does *not* threaten the old privacy makes it a greater threat to the new.

Later decisions upholding abortion rights also used the language of autonomy to describe the privacy interest at stake. "Few decisions are . . . more properly private, or more basic to individual dignity and autonomy," held the Court in one such case, "than a woman's decision . . . whether to end her pregnancy. A woman's right to make that choice freely is surely fundamental."[44] The notion of privacy as autonomy found perhaps its fullest expression in a 1992 abortion rights opinion authored by Justices Sandra Day O'Connor, Anthony Kennedy, and David Souter. Privacy rights protect "the most intimate and personal choices a person may make in a lifetime, choices central to personal dignity and autonomy." The justices went on to draw an explicit connection between privacy as autonomy and the voluntarist conception of the person: "At the heart of liberty is the right to define one's own concept of existence, of meaning, of the universe, and of the mystery of human life. Beliefs about these matters could not define the attributes of personhood were they formed under compulsion of the State."[45]

Despite its increasing tendency to identify privacy with autonomy, the Court refused, in a 5–4 decision, to extend privacy protection to consensual homosexual activity. Writing for the majority, Justice White emphasized that the Court's previous privacy cases protected choice only with respect to child rearing and education, family relationships, procreation, marriage, contraception, and abortion. "We think it evident," he held, "that none of the rights announced in those cases bears any resemblance to the claimed constitutional right of homosexuals to engage in acts of sodomy."[46] He also rejected the claim that Georgia's citizens could not embody in law their belief "that homosexual sodomy is immoral and unacceptable."[47] Neutrality to the contrary, "the law . . . is constantly based on notions of morality, and if all laws representing essentially moral choices are to be invalidated under the Due Process Clause, the courts will be very busy indeed."[48]

Writing for the four dissenters, Justice Blackmun argued that the Court's previous privacy decisions did not depend on the virtue of the practices they protected but on the principle of free individual choice in intimate matters. "We protect those rights not because they contribute . . . to the general public welfare, but because they form so central a part of an individual's life. 'The concept of privacy embodies the "moral fact that a person belongs to himself and not others nor to society as a whole."'"[49]

Blackmun argued for the application of earlier privacy rulings in the considerations of homosexual practices by casting the Court's concern for conventional family ties in individualist terms: "We protect the decision whether to have a child because parenthood alters so dramatically an individual's self-definition . . . And we protect the family because it contributes so powerfully to the happiness of individuals, not because of a preference for stereotypical households."[50] Because the right of privacy in sexual relationships protects "the freedom an individual has to *choose* the form and nature of these intensely personal bonds,"[51] it protects homosexual activity no less than other intimate choices.

Defending the ideal of the neutral state, Blackmun added that traditional religious condemnations of homosexuality "give the State no license to impose their judgments on the entire citizenry."[52] To the contrary, the State's appeal to religious teachings against homosexuality undermines its claim that the law "represents a legitimate use of secular coercive power."[53]

Despite the Court's reluctance to extend privacy rights to homosexuals, the privacy cases of the last twenty-five years offer ample evidence of assumptions drawn from the liberal conception of the person. They also raise two questions about the liberalism they reflect: First, whether bracketing controversial moral issues is even possible;

and second, whether the voluntarist conception of privacy limits the range of reasons for protecting privacy.

THE MINIMALIST CASE FOR TOLERATION: ABORTION

Unlike the voluntarist grounds for the neutral state, minimalist liberalism seeks a conception of justice that is political not philosophical, that does not presuppose any particular conception of the person, autonomous or otherwise. It proposes bracketing controversial moral and religious issues for the sake of securing social cooperation in the face of disagreement about ends, not for the sake of such "comprehensive" liberal ideals as autonomy or individuality.[54] One objection to minimalist liberalism is that the case for bracketing a particular moral or religious controversy may partly depend on an implicit answer to the controversy it purports to bracket. In the case of abortion, for example, the more confident we are that fetuses are, in the relevant moral sense, different from babies, the more confident we can be in bracketing the question about the moral status of fetuses for political purposes.

The Court's argument in *Roe v. Wade*[55] illustrates the difficulty of deciding constitutional cases by bracketing controversial moral and religious issues. Although the Court claimed to be neutral on the question of when life begins, its decision presupposes a particular answer to that question. The Court began by observing that Texas's law against abortion rests upon a particular theory of when life begins. "Texas urges that . . . life begins at conception and is present throughout pregnancy, and that, therefore, the State has a compelling interest in protecting that life from and after conception."[56]

The Court then claimed to be neutral on that question: "We need not resolve the difficult question of when life begins. When those trained in the respective disciplines of medicine, philosophy, and theology are unable to arrive at any consensus, the judiciary . . . is not in a position to speculate as to the answer."[57] It then noted "the wide divergence of thinking on this most sensitive and difficult question," throughout the western tradition and in the law of various American states.[58]

From this survey, the Court concluded that "the unborn have never been recognized in the law as persons in the whole sense."[59] Accordingly, it argued that Texas was wrong to embody in law a particular theory of life. Since no theory was conclusive, it held that Texas erred in "adopting one theory of life . . . [which would] override the rights of the pregnant woman that are at stake."[60]

However, contrary to its professions of neutrality, the Court's decision presupposed a particular answer to the question it claimed to bracket.

> With respect to the State's important and legitimate interest in potential life, the "compelling" point is at viability. This is so because the fetus then presumably has the capability of meaningful life outside the mother's womb. State regulation protective of fetal life after viability thus has both logical and biological justifications.[61]

That the Court's decision in *Roe* presupposes a particular answer to the question it purports to bracket is no argument against its decision, only an argument against its claim to have bracketed the controversial question of when life begins. It does not replace Texas's theory of life with a neutral stance, but with a different theory of its own.

The minimalist case for neutrality is subject to a further difficulty: Even given an agreement to bracket controversial moral and religious issues for the sake of social cooperation, it may be controversial what counts as bracketing; and this controversy may require for its solution either a substantive evaluation of the interests at stake, or the autonomous conception of agency that minimalist liberalism resolves to avoid. *Thornburgh v. American College of Obstetri-*

cians & Gynecologists,[62] a 1986 abortion case upholding *Roe,* offers an example of this difficulty.

Writing in dissent, Justice White urged the Court in *Thornburgh* to overrule *Roe v. Wade* and "return the issue to the people."[63] He agreed that abortion was a controversial moral issue, but argued that the best way for the Court to bracket this controversy was to let each state decide the question for itself. He proposed, in effect, to bracket the intractable controversy over abortion as Stephen Douglas proposed to bracket the intractable controversy over slavery—by refusing to impose a single answer on the country as a whole. "Abortion is a hotly contested moral and political issue," White wrote. "Such issues, in our society, are to be resolved by the will of the people, either as expressed through legislation or through the general principles they have already incorporated into the Constitution they have adopted."[64] For the Court to do otherwise is not to be neutral but to "impose its own controversial choices of value upon the people."[65]

Justice Stevens responded to White by arguing for a different way of bracketing. Given the controversial moral issues at stake, he urged that individual women, not legislatures, should decide the question for themselves. For the Court to insist that women be free to choose for themselves is not to impose the *Court's* values, but simply to prevent local majorities from imposing *their* values on individuals. "No individual should be compelled to surrender the freedom to make that decision for herself simply because her 'value preferences' are not shared by the majority."[66] For Stevens, the basic question is not which theory of life is true, but "whether the 'abortion decision' should be made by the individual or by the majority 'in the unrestrained imposition of its own, extraconstitutional value preferences.'"[67]

What is striking is that both ways of bracketing are in principle consistent with minimalist liberalism: The practical interest in social cooperation under conditions of disagreement about the good offers no grounds for choosing one over the other. Even given agreement to bracket an intractable moral or religious controversy for the sake of social cooperation, it may still be unclear what counts as bracketing. Moreover, resolving that question—deciding between White's position and Stevens'—requires either a substantive view about the moral and religious interests at stake or an autonomous conception of the person such as the voluntarist view affirms. Both solutions, however, would deny minimalist liberalism its minimalism; each would implicate its putatively political conception of justice in precisely the moral and philosophical commitments that it seeks to avoid.

THE VOLUNTARIST CASE FOR TOLERATION: HOMOSEXUALITY

The dissenters' argument for toleration in *Bowers v. Hardwick*[68] illustrates the difficulties with the version of liberalism that ties toleration to autonomy rights alone. In refusing to extend the right of privacy to homosexuals, the majority in *Bowers* declared that none of the rights announced in earlier privacy cases resembled the rights homosexuals were seeking: "No connection between family, marriage, or procreation on the one hand and homosexual activity on the other has been demonstrated."[69] Any reply to the Court's position would have to show some connection between the practices already subject to privacy protection and the homosexual practices not yet protected. What then is the resemblance between heterosexual intimacies on the one hand, and homosexual intimacies on the other, such that both are entitled to a constitutional right of privacy?

This question might be answered in at least two different ways—one voluntarist, the other substantive. The first argues from the autonomy the practices reflect, whereas the second appeals to the human goods the practices realize. The voluntarist answer holds that people should be free to choose their intimate associations for themselves, regardless of the virtue or popularity of the practices they choose so long as they do not harm others. In this view, homosexual relationships resemble the heterosexual relationships the Court has already protected in that all reflect the choices of autonomous selves.

By contrast, the substantive answer claims that much that is valuable in conventional marriage is also present in homosexual unions. In this view, the connection between heterosexual and homosexual relations is not that both result from individual choice but that both realize important human goods. Rather than rely on autonomy alone, this second line of reply articulates the virtues homosexual intimacy may share with heterosexual intimacy, along with any distinctive virtues of its own. It defends homosexual privacy the way *Griswold* defended marital privacy, by arguing that, like marriage, homosexual union may also be "intimate to the degree of being sacred . . . a harmony in living . . . a bilateral loyalty," an association for a "noble . . . purpose."[70]

Of these two possible replies, the dissenters in *Bowers* relied wholly on the first. Rather than protect homosexual intimacies for the human goods they share with intimacies the Court already protects, Justice Blackmun cast the Court's earlier cases in individualist terms, and found their reading applied equally to homosexuality because "much of the richness of a relationship will come from the freedom an individual has to *choose* the form and nature of these intensely personal bonds."[71] At issue was not homosexuality as such but respect for the fact that "different individuals will make different choices" in deciding how to conduct their lives.[72]

Justice Stevens, in a separate dissent, also avoided referring to the values homosexual intimacy may share with heterosexual love. Instead, he wrote broadly of "'the individual's right to make certain unusually important decisions'" and "'respect for the dignity of individual choice,'"[73] rejecting the notion that such liberty belongs to heterosexuals alone. "From the standpoint of the individual, the homosexual and the heterosexual have the same interest in deciding how he will live his own life, and, more narrowly, how he will conduct himself in his personal and voluntary associations with his companions."[74]

The voluntarist argument so dominates the *Bowers* dissents that it seems difficult to imagine a judicial rendering of the substantive view. But a glimmer of this view can be found in the appeals court opinion in the same case.[75] The United States Court of Appeals had ruled in Hardwick's favor and had struck down the law under which he was convicted. Like Blackmun and Stevens, the appeals court constructed an analogy between privacy in marriage and privacy in homosexual relations. But unlike the Supreme Court dissenters, it did not rest the analogy on voluntarist grounds alone. It argued instead that both practices may realize important human goods.

The marital relationship is significant, wrote the court of appeals, not only because of its procreative purpose but also "because of the unsurpassed opportunity for mutual support and self-expression that it provides."[76] It recalled the Supreme Court's observation in *Griswold* that "marriage is a coming together for better or for worse, hopefully enduring, and intimate to the degree of being sacred."[77] And it went on to suggest that the qualities the Court so prized in *Griswold* could be present in homosexual unions as well: "For some, the sexual activity in question here serves the same purpose as the intimacy of marriage."[78]

Ironically, this way of extending privacy rights to homosexuals depends on an "old-fashioned" reading of *Griswold* as protecting the human goods realized in marriage, a reading the Court has long since renounced in favor of an individualist reading.[79] By drawing on the aspect of *Griswold* that affirms certain values and ends, the substantive case for homosexual privacy offends the liberalism that insists on neutrality. It grounds the right of privacy on the good of the practice it would protect, and so fails to be neutral among conceptions of the good.

The more frequently employed precedent for homosexual rights is not *Griswold* but *Stanley v. Georgia*,[80] which upheld the right to possess obscene materials in the privacy of one's home. *Stanley* did not hold that the obscene films found in the defendant's bedroom served a "noble purpose," only that he had a right to view them in private. The toleration *Stanley* defended was wholly independent of the value or importance of the thing being tolerated.[81]

In the 1980 case of *People v. Onofre*,[82] the New York Court of Appeals vindicated privacy rights for homosexuals on precisely these grounds. The court reasoned that if, following *Stanley*, there is a right to the "satisfaction of sexual desires by resort to material condemned as obscene," there should also be a right "to seek sexual gratification from what at least once was commonly regarded as 'deviant' conduct," so long as it is private and consensual.[83] The court emphasized its neutrality toward the conduct it protected: "We express no view as to any theological, moral or psychological evaluation of consensual sodomy. These are aspects of the issue on which informed, competent authorities and individuals may and do differ."[84] The court's role was simply to ensure that the State bracketed these competing moral views, rather than embodying any one of them in law.[85]

The case for toleration that brackets the morality of homosexuality has a powerful appeal. In the face of deep disagreement about values, it seems to ask the least of the contending parties. It offers social peace and respect for rights without the need for moral conversion. Those who view sodomy as sin need not be persuaded to change their minds, only to tolerate those who practice it in private. By insisting only that each respect the freedom of others to live the lives they choose, this toleration promises a basis for political agreement that does not await shared conceptions of morality.

Despite its promise, however, the neutral case for toleration is subject to two related difficulties. First, as a practical matter, it is by no means clear that social cooperation can be secured on the strength of autonomy rights alone, absent some measure of agreement on the moral permissibility of the practices at issue. It may not be accidental that the first practices subject to the right of privacy were accorded constitutional protection in cases that spoke of the sanctity of marriage and procreation. Only later did the Court abstract privacy rights from these practices and protect them without reference to the human goods they were once thought to make possible. This suggests that the voluntarist justification of privacy rights is dependent—politically as well as philosophically—on some measure of agreement that the practices protected are morally permissible.

A second difficulty with the voluntarist case for toleration concerns the quality of respect it secures. As the New York case suggests, the analogy with *Stanley* tolerates homosexuality at the price of demeaning it; it puts homosexual intimacy on a par with obscenity—a base thing that should nonetheless be tolerated so long as it takes place in private. If *Stanley* rather than *Griswold* is the relevant analogy, the interest at stake is bound to be reduced, as the New York court reduced it, to "sexual gratification." (The only intimate relationship at stake in *Stanley* was between a man and his pornography.)

The majority in *Bowers* exploited this assumption by ridiculing the notion of a "fundamental right to engage in homosexual sodomy."[86] The obvious reply is that *Bowers* is no more about a right to homosexual sodomy than *Griswold* was about a right to heterosexual intercourse. But by refusing to articulate the human goods that homosexual intimacy may share with heterosexual unions, the voluntarist case for toleration forfeits the analogy with *Griswold* and makes the ridicule difficult to refute.

The problem with the neutral case for toleration is the opposite side of its appeal; it leaves wholly unchallenged the adverse views of homosexuality itself. Unless those views can be plausibly addressed, even a Court ruling in their favor is unlikely to win for homosexuals more than a thin and fragile toleration. A fuller respect would require, if not admiration, at least some appreciation of the lives homosexuals live. Such appreciation, however, is unlikely to be cultivated by a legal and political discourse conducted in terms of autonomy rights alone.

The liberal may reply that autonomy arguments in court need not foreclose more substantive, affirmative arguments elsewhere; bracketing moral argument for constitutional purposes does not mean bracketing moral argument altogether. Once their freedom of choice in sexual practice is secured, homosexuals can seek, by argument and example, to win from their fellow citizens a deeper respect than autonomy can supply.

The liberal reply, however, underestimates the extent to which constitutional discourse has come to constitute the terms of political discourse in American public life. While most at home in constitutional law, the main motifs of contemporary liberalism—rights as trumps, the neutral state, and the unencumbered self—figure with increasing prominence in our moral and political culture. Assumptions drawn from constitutional discourse increasingly set the terms of political debate in general.

Admittedly, the tendency to bracket substantive moral questions makes it difficult to argue for toleration in the language of the good. Defining privacy rights by defending the practices privacy protects seems either reckless or quaint; reckless because it rests so much on moral argument, quaint because it recalls the traditional view that ties the case for privacy to the merits of the conduct privacy protects. But as the abortion and sodomy cases illustrate, the attempt to bracket moral questions faces difficulties of its own. They suggest the truth in the "naive" view, that the justice or injustice of laws against abortion and homosexual conduct may have something to do with the morality or immorality of these practices after all.

EPILOGUE

Since this essay was written, the U.S. Supreme Court, in the case of *Lawrence v. Texas* (2003),[87] reversed *Bowers v. Hardwick,* and struck down a law that criminalized so-called "deviate sexual intercourse" between persons of the same sex. The Court's opinion, written by Justice Anthony Kennedy, drew to some extent on the autonomy-based, nonjudgmental line of reasoning I have criticized: "Liberty presumes an autonomy of self that includes freedom of thought, belief, expression, and certain intimate conduct."[88] And it cited with approval the extravagant statement of the voluntarist conception of the person announced in *Casey:* "At the heart of liberty is the right to define one's own concept of existence, of meaning, of the universe, and of the mystery of human life. Beliefs about these matters could not define the attributes of personhood were they formed under compulsion of the State."[89]

But despite its rhetoric of autonomy and choice, Justice Kennedy's opinion also gestured toward a different, more substantive reason for striking down the Texas law—that it wrongly demeaned a morally legitimate mode of life. First, the opinion pointed out that *Bowers* was no more about a right to homosexual sodomy than *Griswold* was about a right to heterosexual intercourse: "To say that the issue in *Bowers* was simply the right to engage in certain sexual conduct demeans the claim the individual put forward, just as it would demean a married couple were it to be said marriage is simply about the right to have sexual intercourse." Privacy rights should protect the sexual intimacy of gays and straights alike, not because sex reflects autonomy and choice, but because it expresses an important human good. "When sexuality finds overt expression in intimate conduct with another person, the conduct can be but one element in a personal bond that is more enduring."[90]

Second, the Court insisted on reversing *Bowers,* even though it could have ruled more narrowly and invalidated the Texas law on equal protection grounds. (Unlike the law in *Bowers,* the law in *Lawrence* banned sodomy by same-sex but not opposite-sex couples.) "If protected conduct is made criminal and the law which does so remains unexamined for its substantive validity, its stigma might remain even if it were not enforceable as drawn for equal protection reasons." In seeking to remove the stigma that antisodomy laws attach to gay sexual intimacy, the Court went beyond liberal toleration to affirm the moral legitimacy of homosexuality. To allow *Bowers* to stand as precedent would "demean[] the lives of homosexual persons."[91]

Justice Antonin Scalia saw the moral stakes clearly. In a biting dissent, he castigated the Court for signing on to "the agenda promoted by some homosexual activists directed at eliminating the moral opprobrium that has traditionally attached to homosexual conduct," and for "tak[ing] sides in the culture war."[92] Grasping the moral logic of *Lawrence,* he worried that once the Court rejected "moral disapprobation of homosexual conduct" as a legitimate state interest for purposes of criminal law, it would be difficult to justify prohibitions on same-sex marriage.[93]

Scalia did not argue openly for preserving the moral disapproval of homosexuality. He claimed, for his part, to take no side in the culture war. Rather than defend the antisodomy law on its merits, he supported it in the name of majoritarianism. The "promotion of majoritarian sexual morality" was a legitimate state interest, and the Court's role was simply to assure, "as neutral observer, that the democratic rules of engagement" were observed.[94] But Scalia's confidence that stigmatizing homosexual conduct is a legitimate state interest seems to depend on more than a value-neutral commitment to majoritarianism. (His own moral view can be glimpsed in the analogy he draws between Texas's antisodomy law and laws banning bestiality and incest.) At the very least, the case for letting majorities ban homosexual intimacy is far stronger if homosexuality is immoral than if it is morally permissible.

Ironically, just as the liberals in *Lawrence* were freeing themselves from the assumption that privacy rights can be adjudicated without reference to the moral status of the practices that rights protect, the conservatives were embracing it. But neither liberal toleration nor deference to majoritarianism can avoid the need for substantive moral argument. Scalia's dissent in *Lawrence* and Justice Blackmun's opinion in *Roe v. Wade* have this in common: Both illustrate the difficulty of bracketing moral judgment, whether in the name of respecting individual choice or deferring to majoritarian sentiment.

Part III

LIBERALISM, PLURALISM, AND COMMUNITY

The essays in this section explore the varieties of liberalism prominent in contemporary political philosophy, and the encounter between liberalism and its critics. They develop two lines of criticism: First, given liberalism's emphasis on individual choice, it does not offer an adequate account of community, solidarity, and membership. Second, given its emphasis on the fact that people in pluralist societies often hold conflicting visions of the good life, liberalism wrongly insists that citizens relegate their moral and religious convictions to the private realm, or at least set them aside for political purposes.

In Chapters 22 ("Morality and the Liberal Ideal") and 23 ("The Procedural Republic and the Unencumbered Self") I argue that the liberalism of Immanuel Kant and John Rawls is more persuasive than the utilitarianism they reject. Their conception of the person as a freely choosing, independent self offers a powerful corrective to the utilitarian idea that we are simply the sum of our preferences and desires. But the Kantian and Rawlsian self raises problems of its own; we cannot conceive ourselves as "unencumbered selves" without cost to those loyalties and traditions that situate us in the world and give our lives their moral particularity.

Chapters 24–26 take up several non-Kantian varieties of liberalism. Chapter 24, "Justice as Membership," discusses Michael Walzer's *Spheres of Justice,* an important contribution to what came to be known as the communitarian critique of liberalism. Chapter 25, "The Peril of Extinction," responds to the ardent individualism of George Kateb, who argued that the moral peril of nuclear war consists in its threat to individual rights. Chapter 26, "Dewey's Liberalism and Ours," recalls the liberalism of America's leading public philosopher of the early twentieth century, John Dewey. Richard Rorty has tried to appropriate Dewey for the liberalism that asserts the priority of the right over the good. But Dewey was not a Kantian or a rights-based liberal. To the contrary, his concern with cultivating a public realm that draws on the moral and spiritual energies of citizens actually makes him a more natural ally of today's communitarians.

Liberals often worry about religion in politics because they associate religion with intolerance. The resolve to avoid wars of religion has shaped much liberal political thought. In recent years, Christian, Jewish, and Islamic theologians have wrestled with sources of intolerance to be found in the teachings and traditions of their faiths. Chapter 27, "Mastery and Hubris in Judaism," examines the quest of Rabbi David Hartman, one of the foremost Jewish thinkers of our time, to articulate a pluralist ethic from within the Jewish tradition. I include the essay here in hopes of showing how religious and theological reflections can illuminate contemporary moral and political questions, even for those who may not share the faith from which those reflections derive.

By the 1990s, the debate between utilitarians and Kantian liberals had largely given way to the "liberal-communitarian" debate. In 1993 John Rawls published *Political Liberalism*, a book that recast the version of liberalism he presented in his classic work, *A Theory of Justice* (1971). Chapter 28, "Political Liberalism," examines Rawls's revised view. Chapter 29, "Remembering Rawls," is a memorial to Rawls on the occasion of his death in 2002. Chapter 30, "The Limits of Communitarianism," looks back on the liberal-communitarian debate and explains why some of those labeled "communitarians" (including me) are reluctant to embrace the term.

twenty-two

MORALITY AND THE LIBERAL IDEAL

Liberals often take pride in defending what they oppose—pornography, for example, or unpopular views. They say the state should not impose on its citizens a preferred way of life, but should leave them as free as possible to choose their own values and ends, consistent with a similar liberty for others. This commitment to freedom of choice requires liberals constantly to distinguish between permission and praise, between allowing a practice and endorsing it. It is one thing to allow pornography, they argue, something else to affirm it.

Conservatives sometimes exploit this distinction by ignoring it. They charge that those who would allow abortions favor abortion, that opponents of school prayer oppose prayer, that those who defend the rights of Communists sympathize with their cause. And in a pattern of argument familiar in our politics, liberals reply by invoking higher principles; it is not that they dislike pornography less, but rather that they value toleration, or freedom of choice, or fair procedures more.

But in contemporary debate, the liberal rejoinder seems increasingly fragile, its moral basis increasingly unclear. Why should toleration and freedom of choice prevail when other important values are also at stake? Too often the answer implies some version of moral relativism, the idea that it is wrong to "legislate morality" because all morality is merely subjective. "Who is to say what is literature and what is filth? That is a value judgment, and whose values should decide?"

Relativism usually appears less as a claim than as a question. "Who is to judge?" But it is a question that can also be asked of the values that liberals defend. Toleration and freedom and fairness are values too, and they can hardly be defended by the claim that no values can be defended. So it is a mistake to affirm liberal values by arguing that all values are merely subjective. The relativist defense of liberalism is no defense at all.

What, then, can be the moral basis of the higher principles the liberal invokes? Recent political philosophy has offered two main alternatives—one utilitarian, the other Kantian. The utilitarian view, following John Stuart Mill, defends liberal principles in the name of maximizing the general welfare. The state should not impose on its citizens a preferred way of life, even for their own good, because doing so will reduce the sum of human happiness, at least in the long run; better that people choose for themselves, even if, on occasion, they get it wrong. "The only freedom which deserves the name," writes Mill in *On Liberty*, "is that of pursuing our own good in our own way, so long as we do not attempt to deprive others of theirs, or impede their efforts to obtain it." He adds that his argument does not depend on any notion of abstract right, only on the principle of the greatest good for the greatest number. "I regard utility as the ultimate appeal on all ethical questions; but it must be utility in the largest sense, grounded on the permanent interests of man as a progressive being."

Many objections have been raised against utilitarianism as a general doctrine of moral philosophy. Some have questioned the concept of utility, and the assumption that all human goods are in principle commensurable. Others have objected that by reducing all values to preferences and desires, utilitarians are unable to admit qualitative distinctions of worth, unable to distinguish noble desires from base ones. But most recent debate has focused on whether utilitarianism offers a convincing basis for liberal principles, including respect for individual rights.

In one respect, utilitarianism would seem well suited to liberal purposes. Seeking to maximize overall happiness does not require judging people's values, only aggregating them. And the willingness to aggregate preferences without judging them suggests a tolerant spirit, even a democratic one. When people go to the polls we count their votes, whatever they are.

But the utilitarian calculus is not always as liberal as it first appears. If enough cheering Romans pack the Colosseum to watch the lion devour the Christian, the collective pleasure of the Romans will surely outweigh the pain of the Christian, intense though it be. Or if a big majority abhors a small religion and wants it banned, the balance of preferences will favor suppression, not toleration. Utilitarians sometimes defend individual rights on the grounds that respecting them now will serve utility in the long run. But this calculation is precarious and contingent. It hardly secures the liberal promise not to impose on some the values of others. As the majority will is an inadequate instrument of liberal politics—by itself it fails to secure individual rights—so the utilitarian philosophy is an inadequate foundation for liberal principles.

The case against utilitarianism was made most powerfully by Immanuel Kant. He argued that empirical principles, such as utility, were unfit to serve as basis for the moral law. A wholly instrumental defense of freedom and rights not only leaves rights vulnerable, but fails to respect the inherent dignity of persons. The utilitarian calculus treats people as means to the happiness of others, not as ends in themselves, worthy of respect.

Contemporary liberals extend Kant's argument with the claim that utilitarianism fails to take seriously the distinction between persons. In seeking above all to maximize the general welfare, the utilitarian treats society as a whole as if it were a single person; it conflates our many, diverse desires into a single system of desires. It is indifferent to the distribution of satisfactions among persons, except insofar as this may affect the overall sum. But this fails to respect our plurality and distinctness. It uses some as means to the happiness of all, and so fails to respect each as an end in himself.

In the view of modern-day Kantians, certain rights are so fundamental that even the general welfare cannot override them. As John Rawls writes in his important work, *A Theory of Justice*, "Each person possesses an inviolability founded on justice that even the welfare of society as a whole cannot override. . . . The rights secured by justice are not subject to political bargaining or to the calculus of social interests."

So Kantian liberals need an account of rights that does not depend on utilitarian considerations. More than this, they need an account that does not depend on any particular conception of the good, that does not presuppose the superiority of one way of life over others. Only a justification neutral about ends could preserve the liberal resolve not to favor any particular ends, or to impose on its citizens a preferred way of life. But what sort of justification could this be? How is it possible to affirm certain liberties and rights as fundamental without embracing some vision of the good life, without endorsing some ends over others? It would seem we are back to the relativist predicament—to affirm liberal principles without embracing any particular ends.

The solution proposed by Kantian liberals is to draw a distinction between the "right" and the "good"—between a framework of basic rights and liberties, and the conceptions of the good that people may choose to pursue within the framework. It is one thing for the state to support a fair framework, they argue, something else to affirm some particular ends. For example, it is one thing to defend the right to free speech so that people may be free to form their own opinions and choose their own ends, but something else to support it on the grounds that a life of political discussion is inherently worthier than a life unconcerned with public affairs, or on the grounds that free speech will increase the general welfare. Only the first defense is available in the Kantian view, resting as it does on the ideal of a neutral framework.

Now, the commitment to a framework neutral with respect to ends can be seen as a kind of value—in this sense the Kantian liberal is no relativist—but its value consists precisely in its refusal to affirm a preferred way of life or conception of the good. For Kantian liberals, then, the right is prior to the good, and in two senses. First, individual rights cannot be sacrificed for the sake of the general good; and second, the principles of justice that specify these rights cannot be premised on any particular vision of the good life. What justifies the rights is not that they maximize the general welfare or otherwise promote the good, but rather that they comprise a fair framework within which individuals and groups can choose their own values and ends, consistent with a similar liberty for others.

Of course, proponents of the rights-based ethic notoriously disagree about what rights are fundamental, and about what political arrangements the ideal of the neutral framework requires. Egalitarian liberals support the welfare state, and favor a scheme of civil liberties together with certain social and economic rights—rights to welfare, education, health care, and so on. Libertarian liberals defend the market economy, and claim that redistributive policies violate peoples' rights; they favor a scheme of civil liberties combined with a strict regime of private property rights. But whether egalitarian or libertarian, rights-based liberalism begins with the claim that we are separate, individual persons, each with our own aims, interests, and conceptions of the good; it seeks a framework of rights that will enable us to realize our capacity as free moral agents, consistent with a similar liberty for others.

Within academic philosophy, the last decade or so has seen the ascendance of the rights-based ethic over the utilitarian one, due in large part to the influence of Rawls's *A Theory of Justice.* The legal philosopher H. L. A. Hart recently described the shift from "the old faith that some form of utilitarianism must capture the essence of political morality" to the new faith that "the truth must lie with a doctrine of basic human rights, protecting specific basic liberties and interests of individuals. . . . Whereas not so long ago great energy and much ingenuity of many philosophers were devoted to making some form of utilitarianism work, latterly such energies and ingenuity have been devoted to the articulation of theories of basic rights."

But in philosophy as in life, the new faith becomes the old orthodoxy before long. Even as it has come to prevail over its utilitarian rival, the rights-based ethic has recently faced a growing challenge from a different direction, from a view that gives fuller expression to the claims of citizenship and community than the liberal vision allows. The communitarian critics, unlike modern liberals, make the case for a politics of the common good. Recalling the arguments of Hegel against Kant, they question the liberal claim for the priority of the right over the good, and the picture of the freely choosing individual it embodies. Following Aristotle, they argue that we cannot justify political arrangements without reference to common purposes and ends, and that we cannot conceive of ourselves without reference to our role as citizens, as participants in a common life.

This debate reflects two contrasting pictures of the self. The rights-based ethic, and the conception of the person it embodies, were shaped in large part in the encounter with utilitarianism. Where utilitarians conflate our many desires into a single system of desire, Kantians insist on the separateness of persons. Where the utilitarian self is simply defined as the sum of its desires, the Kantian self is a choosing self, independent of the desires and ends it may have at any moment. As Rawls writes, "The self is prior to the ends which are affirmed by it; even a dominant end must be chosen from among numerous possibilities."

The priority of the self over its ends means I am never defined by my aims and attachments, but always capable of standing back to survey and assess and possibly to revise them. This is what it means to be a free and independent self, capable of choice. And this is the vision of the self that finds expression in the ideal of the state as a neutral framework. On the rights-based ethic, it is precisely because we are essentially separate, independent selves that we need a neutral framework, a framework of rights that refuses to choose among competing purposes and ends. If the self is prior to its ends, then the right must be prior to the good.

Communitarian critics of rights-based liberalism say we cannot conceive ourselves as independent in this way, as bearers of selves wholly detached from our aims and attachments. They say that certain of our roles are partly constitutive of the persons we are—as citizens of a country, or members of a movement, or partisans of a cause. But if we are partly defined by the communities we inhabit, then we must also be implicated in the purposes and ends characteristic of those communities. As Alasdair MacIntyre writes in his book, *After Virtue,* "What is good for me has to be the good for one who inhabits these roles." Open-ended though it be, the story of my life is always embedded in the story of those communities from which I derive my identity—whether family or city, tribe or nation, party or cause. In the communitarian view, these stories make a moral difference, not only a psychological one. They situate us in the world and give our lives their moral particularity.

What is at stake for politics in the debate between unencumbered selves and situated ones? What are the practical differences between a politics of rights and a politics of the common good? On some issues, the two theories may produce different arguments for similar policies. For example, the civil rights movement of the 1960s might be justified by liberals in the name of human dignity and respect for persons, and by communitarians in the name of recognizing the full membership of fellow citizens wrongly excluded from the common life of the nation. And where liberals might support public education in hopes of equipping students to become autonomous individuals, capable of choosing their own ends and pursuing them effectively, communitarians might support public education in hopes of equipping students to become good citizens, capable of contributing meaningfully to public deliberations and pursuits.

On other issues, the two ethics might lead to different policies. Communitarians would be more likely than liberals to allow a town to ban pornographic bookstores, on the grounds that pornography offends its way of life and the values that sustain it. But a politics of civic virtue does not always part company with liberalism in favor of conservative policies. For example, communitarians would be more willing than some rights-oriented liberals to see states enact laws regulating plant closings, to protect their communities from the disruptive effects of capital mobility and sudden industrial change. More generally, where the liberal regards the expansion of individual rights and entitlements as unqualified moral and political progress, the communitarian is troubled by the tendency of liberal programs to displace politics from smaller forms of association to more comprehensive ones. Where libertarian liberals defend the private economy and egalitarian liberals defend the welfare state, communitarians worry about the concentration of power in both the corporate economy and the bureaucratic state, and the erosion of those intermediate forms of community that have at times sustained a more vital public life.

Liberals often argue that a politics of the common good, drawing as it must on particular loyalties, obligations, and traditions, opens the way to prejudice and intolerance. The modern nation-state is not the Athenian polis, they point out; the scale and diversity of modern life have rendered the Aristotelian political ethic nostalgic at best and dangerous at worst. Any attempt to govern by a vision of the good is likely to lead to a slippery slope of totalitarian temptations.

*   *   *

Communitarians reply, rightly in my view, that intolerance flourishes most where forms of life are dislocated, roots unsettled, traditions undone. In our day, the totalitarian impulse has sprung less from the convictions of confidently situated selves than from the confusions of atomized, dislocated, frustrated selves, at sea in a world where common meanings have lost their force. As Hannah Arendt has written, "What makes mass society so difficult to bear is not the number of people involved, or at least not primarily, but the fact that the world between them has lost its power to gather them together, to relate and to separate them." Insofar as our public life has withered, our sense of common involvement diminished, we lie vulnerable to the mass politics of totalitarian solutions. So responds the party of the common good to the party of rights. If the party of the common good is right, our most pressing moral and political project is to revitalize those civic republican possibilities implicit in our tradition but fading in our time.

twenty-three

THE PROCEDURAL REPUBLIC AND THE UNENCUMBERED SELF

Political philosophy seems often to reside at a distance from the world. Principles are one thing, politics another, and even our best efforts to "live up" to our ideals typically founder on the gap between theory and practice.[1]

But if political philosophy is unrealizable in one sense, it is unavoidable in another. This is the sense in which philosophy inhabits the world from the start; our practices and institutions are embodiments of theory. To engage in a political practice is already to stand in relation to theory.[2] For all our uncertainties about ultimate questions of political philosophy—of justice and value and the nature of the good life—the one thing we know is that we live *some* answer all the time.

In this essay I will try to explore the answer we live now, in contemporary America. What is the political philosophy implicit in our practices and institutions? How does it stand, as philosophy? And how do tensions in the philosophy find expression in our present political condition?

It may be objected that it is a mistake to look for a single philosophy, that we live no "answer," only answers. But a plurality of answers is itself a kind of answer. And the political theory that affirms this plurality is the theory I propose to explore.

THE RIGHT AND THE GOOD

We might begin by considering a certain moral and political vision. It is a liberal vision, and like most liberal visions gives pride of place to justice, fairness, and individual rights. Its core thesis is this: a just society seeks not to promote any particular ends, but enables its citizens to pursue their own ends, consistent with a similar liberty for all; it therefore must govern by principles that do not presuppose any particular conception of the good. What justifies these regulative principles above all is not that they maximize the general welfare, or cultivate virtue, or otherwise promote the good, but rather that they conform to the concept of *right*, a moral category given prior to the good, and independent of it.

This liberalism says, in other words, that what makes the just society just is not the *telos* or purpose or end at which it aims, but precisely its refusal to choose in advance among competing purposes and ends. In its constitution and its laws, the just society seeks to provide a framework within which its citizens can pursue their own values and ends, consistent with a similar liberty for others.

The ideal I've described might be summed up in the claim that the right is prior to the good, and in two senses: the priority of the right means first, that individual rights cannot be sacrificed for the sake of the general good (in this it opposes utilitarianism), and second, that the principles of justice that specify these rights cannot be premised on any particular vision of the good life. (In this it opposes teleological conceptions in general.)

This is the liberalism of much contemporary moral and political philosophy, most fully elaborated by Rawls, and indebted to Kant for its philosophical foundations.[3] But I am concerned here less with the lineage of this vision than with what seem to me three striking facts about it.

First, it has a deep and powerful philosophical appeal. Second, despite its philosophical force, the claim for the priority of the right over the good ultimately fails. And third, despite its philosophical failure, this liberal vision is the one by which we live. For us in late twentieth-century America, it is our vision, the theory most thoroughly embodied in the practices and institutions most central to our public life. And seeing how it goes wrong as philosophy may help us to diagnose our present political condition. So first, its philosophical power; second, its philosophical failure; and third, however briefly, its uneasy embodiment in the world.

But before taking up these three claims, it is worth pointing out a central theme that connects them. And that is a certain conception of the person, of what it is to be a moral agent. Like all political theories, the liberal theory I have described is something more than a set of regulative principles. It is also a view about the way the world is, and the way we move within it. At the heart of this ethic lies a vision of the person that both inspires and undoes it. As I will try to argue now, what make this ethic so compelling, but also, finally, vulnerable, are the promise and the failure of the unencumbered self.

KANTIAN FOUNDATIONS

The liberal ethic asserts the priority of right, and seeks principles of justice that do not presuppose any particular conception of the good.[4] This is what Kant means by the supremacy of the moral law, and what Rawls means when he writes that "justice is the first virtue of social institutions."[5] Justice is more than just another value. It provides the framework that *regulates* the play of competing values and ends; it must therefore have a sanction independent of those ends. But it is not obvious where such a sanction could be found.

Theories of justice, and for that matter, ethics, have typically founded their claims on one or another conception of human purposes and ends. Thus Aristotle said the measure of a polis is the good at which it aims, and even J. S. Mill, who in the nineteenth century called "justice the chief part, and incomparably the most binding part of all morality," made justice an instrument of utilitarian ends.[6]

This is the solution Kant's ethic rejects. Different persons typically have different desires and ends, and so any principle derived from them can only be contingent. But the moral law needs a *categorical* foundation, not a contingent one. Even so universal a desire as happiness will not do. People still differ in what happiness consists of, and to install any particular conception as regulative would impose on some the conceptions of others, and so deny at least to some the freedom to choose their *own* conceptions. In any case, to govern ourselves in conformity with desires and inclinations, given as they are by nature or circumstance, is not really to be *self*-governing at all. It is rather a refusal of freedom, a capitulation to determinations given outside us.

According to Kant, the right is "derived entirely from the concept of freedom in the external relationships of human beings, and has nothing to do with the end which all men have by nature [i.e., the aim of achieving happiness] or with the recognized means of attaining this end."[7] As such, it must have a basis prior to all empirical ends. Only when I am governed by principles that do not presuppose any particular ends am I free to pursue my own ends consistent with a similar freedom for all.

But this still leaves the question of what the basis of the right could possibly be. If it must be a basis prior to all purposes and ends, unconditioned even by what Kant calls "the special circumstances of human nature,"[8] where could such a basis conceivably be found? Given the stringent demands of the Kantian ethic, the moral law would seem almost to require a foundation in nothing, for any empirical precondition would undermine its priority. "Duty!" asks Kant at his most lyrical, "What origin is there worthy of thee, and where is to be found the root of thy noble descent which proudly rejects all kinship with the inclinations?"[9]

His answer is that the basis of the moral law is to be found in the *subject,* not the object of practical reason, a subject capable of an autonomous will. No empirical end, but rather "a subject of ends, namely a rational being himself, must be made the ground for all maxims of action."[10] Nothing other than what Kant calls "the subject of all possible ends himself" can give rise to the right, for only this subject is also the subject of an autonomous will. Only this subject could be that "something which elevates man above himself as part of the world of sense" and enables him to participate in an ideal, unconditioned realm wholly independent of our social and psychological inclinations. And only this thoroughgoing independence can afford us the detachment we need if we are ever freely to choose for ourselves, unconditioned by the vagaries of circumstance.[11]

Who or what exactly *is* this subject? It is, in a certain sense, *us.* The moral law, after all, is a law we give *ourselves;* we don't *find* it, we *will* it. That is how it (and we) escape the reign of nature and circumstance and merely empirical ends. But what is important to see is that the "we" who do the willing are not "we" *qua* particular persons, you and me, each for ourselves—the moral law is not up to us as individuals—but "we" *qua* participants in what Kant calls "pure practical reason," "we" *qua* participants in a transcendental subject.

Now what is to guarantee that I *am* a subject of this kind, capable of exercising pure practical reason? Well, strictly speaking, there *is* no guarantee; the transcendental subject is only a possibility. But it is a possibility I must *presuppose* if I am to think of myself as a free moral agent. Were I wholly an empirical being, I would not be capable of freedom, for every exercise of will would be conditioned by the desire for some object. All choice would be heteronomous choice, governed by the pursuit of some end. My will could never be a first cause, only the effect of some prior cause, the instrument of one or another impulse or inclination. "When we think of ourselves as free," writes Kant, "we transfer ourselves into the intelligible world as members and recognize the autonomy of the will."[12] And so the notion of a subject prior to and independent of experience, such as the Kantian ethic requires, appears not only possible but indispensible, a necessary presupposition of the possibility of freedom.

How does all of this come back to politics? As the subject is prior to its ends, so the right is prior to the good. Society is best arranged when it is governed by principles that do not presuppose any particular conception of the good, for any other arrangement would fail to respect persons as being capable of choice; it would treat them as objects rather than subjects, as means rather than ends in themselves.

We can see in this way how Kant's notion of the subject is bound up with the claim for the priority of right. But for those in the Anglo-American tradition, the transcendental subject will seem a strange foundation for a familiar ethic. Surely, one may think, we can take rights seriously and affirm the primacy of justice without embracing the *Critique of Pure Reason*. This, in any case, is the project of Rawls.

He wants to save the priority of right from the obscurity of the transcendental subject. Kant's idealist metaphysic, for all its moral and political advantage, cedes too much to the transcendent, and wins for justice its primacy only by denying it its human situation. "To develop a viable Kantian conception of justice," Rawls writes, "the force and content of Kant's doctrine must be detached from its background in transcendental idealism" and recast within the "canons of a reasonable empiricism."[13] And so Rawls's project is to preserve Kant's moral and political teaching by replacing Germanic obscurities with a domesticated metaphysic more congenial to the Anglo-American temper. This is the role of the original position.

FROM TRANSCENDENTAL SUBJECT TO UNENCUMBERED SELF

The original position tries to provide what Kant's transcendental argument cannot—a foundation for the right that is prior to the good, but still situated in the world. Sparing all but essentials, the original position works like this: it invites us to imagine the principles we would choose to govern our society if we were to choose them in advance, before we knew the particular persons we would be—whether rich or poor, strong or weak, lucky or unlucky—before we knew even our interests or aims or conceptions of the good. These principles—the ones we would choose in that imaginary situation—are the principles of justice. What is more, if it works, they are principles that do not presuppose any particular ends.

What they *do* presuppose is a certain picture of the person, of the way we must be if we are beings for whom justice is the first virtue. This is the picture of the unencumbered self, a self understood as prior to and independent of its purposes and ends.

Now the unencumbered self describes first of all the way we stand toward the things we have, or want, or seek. It means there is always a distinction between the values I *have* and the person I *am*. To identify any characteristics as *my* aims, ambitions, desires, and so on, is always to imply some subject "me" standing behind them, at a certain distance, and the shape of this "me" must be given prior to any of the aims or attributes I bear. One consequence of this distance is to put the self *itself* beyond the reach of its experience, to secure its identity once and for all. Or to put the point another way, it rules out the possibility of what we might call *constitutive* ends. No role or commitment could define me so completely that I could not understand myself without it. No project could be so essential that turning away from it would call into question the person I am.

For the unencumbered self, what matters above all, what is most essential to our personhood, are not the ends we choose but our capacity to choose them. The original position sums up this central claim about us. "It is not our aims that primarily reveal our nature," writes Rawls, "but rather the principles that we would acknowledge to govern the background conditions under which these aims are to be formed . . . We should therefore reverse the relation between the right and the good proposed by teleological doctrines and view the right as prior."[14]

Only if the self is prior to its ends can the right be prior to the good. Only if my identity is never tied to the aims and interests I may have at any moment can I think of myself as a free and independent agent, capable of choice.

This notion of independence carries consequences for the kind of community of which we are capable. Understood as unencumbered selves, we are of course free to join in voluntary association with others, and so are capable of community in the cooperative sense. What is denied to the unencumbered self is the possibility of membership in any community bound by moral ties antecedent to choice; he cannot belong to any community where the self *itself* could be at stake. Such a community—call it constitutive as against merely cooperative—would engage the identity as well as the interests of the participants, and so implicate its members in a citizenship more thoroughgoing than the unencumbered self can know.

For justice to be primary, then, we must be creatures of a certain kind, related to human circumstance in a certain way. We must stand to our circumstance always at a certain distance, whether as transcendental subject in the case of Kant, or as unencumbered selves in the case of Rawls. Only in this way can we view ourselves as subjects as well as objects of experience, as agents and not just instruments of the purposes we pursue.

The unencumbered self and the ethic it inspires, taken together, hold out a liberating vision. Freed from the dictates of nature and the sanction of social roles, the human subject is installed as sovereign, cast as the author of the only moral meanings there are. As participants in pure practical reason, or as parties to the original position, we are free to construct principles of justice unconstrained by an order of value antecedently given. And as actual, individual selves, we are free to choose our purposes and ends unbound by such an order, or by custom or tradition or inherited status. So long as they are not unjust, our conceptions of the good carry weight, whatever they are, simply in virtue of our having chosen them. We are, in Rawls's words, "self-originating sources of valid claims."[15]

This is an exhilarating promise, and the liberalism it animates is perhaps the fullest expression of the Enlightenment's quest for the self-defining subject. But is it true? Can we make sense of our moral and political life by the light of the self-image it requires? I do not think we can, and I will try to show why not by arguing first within the liberal project, then beyond it.

JUSTICE AND COMMUNITY

We have focused so far on the foundations of the liberal vision, on the way it derives the principles it defends. Let us turn briefly now to the substance of those principles, using Rawls as our example. Sparing all but essentials once again, Rawls's two principles of justice are these: first, equal basic liberties for all, and second, only those social and economic inequalities that benefit the least-advantaged members of society (the difference principle).

In arguing for these principles, Rawls argues against two familiar alternatives—utilitarianism and libertarianism. He argues against utilitarianism that it fails to take seriously the distinction between persons. In seeking to maximize the general welfare, the utilitarian treats society as whole as if it were a single person; it conflates our many, diverse desires into a single system of desires, and tries to maximize. It is indifferent to the distribution of satisfactions among persons, except insofar as this may affect the overall sum. But this fails to respect our plurality and distinctness. It uses some as means to the happiness of all, and so fails to respect each as an end in himself. While utilitarians may sometimes defend individual rights, their defense must rest on the calculation that respecting those rights will serve utility in the long run. But this calculation is contingent and uncertain. So long as utility is what Mill said it is, "the ultimate appeal on all ethical questions,"[16] individual rights can never be secure. To avoid the danger that their life prospects might one day be sacrificed for the greater good of others, the parties to the original position therefore insist on certain basic liberties for all, and make those liberties prior.

If utilitarians fail to take seriously the distinctness of persons, libertarians go wrong by failing to acknowledge the arbitrariness of fortune. They define as just whatever distribution results from an efficient market economy, and oppose all redistribution on the grounds that people are entitled to whatever they get, so long as they do not cheat or steal or otherwise violate someone's rights in getting it. Rawls opposes this principle on the ground that the distribution of talents and assets and even efforts by which some get more and others get less is arbitrary from a moral point of view, a matter of good luck. To distribute the good things in life on the basis of these differences is not to do justice, but simply to carry over into human arrangements the arbitrariness of social and natural contingency. We deserve, as individuals, neither the talents our good fortune may have brought, nor the benefits that flow from them. We should therefore regard these talents as common assets, and regard one another as common beneficiaries of the rewards they bring. "Those who have been favored by nature, whoever they are, may gain from their good fortune only on terms that improve the situation of those who have lost out . . . In justice as fairness, men agree to share one another's fate."[17]

This is the reasoning that leads to the difference principle. Notice how it reveals, in yet another guise, the logic of the unencumbered self. I cannot be said to deserve the benefits that flow from, say, my fine physique and good looks, because they are only accidental, not essential facts about me. They describe attributes I *have,* not the person I *am,* and so cannot give rise to a claim of desert. Being an unencumbered self, this is true of *everything* about me. And so I cannot, as an individual, deserve anything at all.

However jarring to our ordinary understandings this argument may be, the picture so far remains intact; the priority of right, the denial of desert, and the unencumbered self all hang impressively together.

But the difference principle requires more, and it is here that the argument comes undone. The difference principle begins with the thought, congenial to the unencumbered self, that the assets I have are only accidentally mine. But it ends by assuming that these assets are therefore *common* assets and that society has a prior claim on the fruits of their exercise. But this assumption is without warrant. Simply because I, as an individual, do not have a privileged claim on the assets accidentally residing "here," it does not follow that everyone in the world collectively does. For there is no reason to think that their location in society's province or, for that matter, within the province of humankind, is any *less* arbitrary from a moral point of view. And if their arbitrariness within *me* makes them ineligible to serve *my* ends, there seems no obvious reason why their arbitrariness within any particular society should not make them ineligible to serve that society's ends as well.

To put the point another way, the difference principle, like utilitarianism, is a principle of sharing. As such, it must presuppose some prior moral tie among those whose assets it would deploy and whose efforts it would enlist in a common endeavor. Otherwise, it is simply a formula for using some as means to others' ends, a formula this liberalism is committed to reject.

But on the cooperative vision of community alone, it is unclear what the moral basis for this sharing could be. Short of the constitutive conception, deploying an individual's assets for the sake of the common good would seem an offense against the "plurality and distinctness" of individuals this liberalism seeks above all to secure.

If those whose fate I am required to share really are, morally speaking, *others,* rather than fellow participants in a way of life with which my identity is bound, the difference principle falls prey to the same objections as utilitarianism. Its claim on me is not the claim of a constitutive community whose attachments I acknowledge, but rather the claim of a concatenated collectivity whose entanglements I confront.

What the difference principle requires, but cannot provide, is some way of identifying those *among* whom the assets I bear are properly regarded as common, some way of seeing ourselves as mutually indebted and morally engaged to begin with. But as we have seen, the constitutive aims and attachments that would save and situate the difference principle are precisely the ones denied to the liberal self; the moral encumbrances and antecedent obligations they imply would undercut the priority of right.

What, then, of those encumbrances? The point so far is that we cannot be persons for whom justice is primary, and also be persons for whom the difference principle is a principle of justice. But which must give way? Can we view ourselves as independent selves, independent in the sense that our identity is never tied to our aims and attachments?

I do not think we can, at least not without cost to those loyalties and convictions whose moral force consists partly in the fact that living by them is inseparable from understanding ourselves as the particular persons we are—as members of this family or community or nation or people, as bearers of that history, as citizens of this republic. Allegiances such as these are more than values I happen to have, and to hold, at a certain distance. They go beyond the obligations I voluntarily incur and the "natural duties" I owe to human beings as such. They allow that to some I owe more than justice requires or even permits, not by reason of agreements I have made but instead in virtue of those more or less enduring attachments and commitments that, taken together, partly define the person I am.

To imagine a person incapable of constitutive attachments such as these is not to conceive an ideally free and rational agent, but to imagine a person wholly without character, without moral depth.

For to have character is to know that I move in a history I neither summon nor command, which carries consequences nonetheless for my choices and conduct. It draws me closer to some and more distant from others; it makes some aims more appropriate, others less so. As a self-interpreting being, I am able to reflect on my history and in this sense to distance myself from it, but the distance is always precarious and provisional, the point of reflection never finally secured outside the history itself. But the liberal ethic puts the self beyond the reach of its experience, beyond deliberation and reflection. Denied the expansive self-understandings that could shape a common life, the liberal self is left to lurch between detachment on the one hand, and entanglement on the other. Such is the fate of the unencumbered self, and its liberating promise.

THE PROCEDURAL REPUBLIC

But before my case can be complete, I need to consider one powerful reply. While it comes from a liberal direction, its spirit is more practical than philosophical. It says, in short, that I am asking too much. It is one thing to seek constitutive attachments in our private lives; among families and friends, and certain tightly knit groups, there may be found a common good that makes justice and rights less pressing. But with public life—at least today, and probably always—it is different. So long as the nation-state is the primary form of political association, talk of constitutive community too easily suggests a darker politics rather than a brighter one; amid echoes of the Moral Majority, the priority of right, for all its philosophical faults, still seems the safer hope.

This is a challenging rejoinder, and no account of political community in the twentieth century can fail to take it seriously. It is challenging not least because it calls into question the status of political philosophy and its relation to the world. For if my argument is correct, if the liberal vision we have considered is not morally self-sufficient but parasitic on a notion of community it officially rejects, then we should expect to find that the political practice that embodies this vision is not *practically* self-sufficient either—that it must draw on a sense of community it cannot supply and may even undermine. But is that so far from the circumstance we face today? Could it be that through the original position darkly, on the far side of the veil of ignorance, we may glimpse an intimation of our predicament, a refracted vision of ourselves?

How does the liberal vision—and its failure—help us make sense of our public life and its predicament? Consider, to begin, the following paradox in the citizen's relation to the modern welfare state. In many ways, we stand near the completion of a liberal project that has run its course from the New Deal through the Great Society and into the present. But notwithstanding the extension of the franchise and the expansion on individual rights and entitlements in recent decades, there is a widespread sense that, individually and collectively, our control over the forces that govern our lives is receding rather than increasing. This sense is deepened by what appear simultaneously as the power and the powerlessness of the nation-state. On the one hand, increasing numbers of citizens view the state as an overly intrusive presence, more likely to frustrate their purposes than advance them. And yet, despite its unprecedented role in the economy and society, the modern state seems itself disempowered, unable effectively to control the domestic economy, to respond to persisting social ills, or to work America's will in the world.

This is a paradox that has fed the appeals of recent politicians (including Carter and Reagan), even as it has frustrated their attempts to govern. To sort it out, we need to identify the public philosophy implicit in our political practice, and to reconstruct its arrival. We need to trace the advent of the procedural republic, by which I mean a public life animated by the liberal vision and self-image we've considered.

The story of the procedural republic goes back in some ways to the founding of the republic, but its central drama begins to unfold around the turn of the century. As national markets and large-scale enterprise displaced a decentralized economy, the decentralized political forms of the early republic became outmoded as well. If democracy was to survive, the concentration of economic power would have to be met by a similar concentration of political power. But the Progressives understood, or some of them did, that the success of democracy required more than the centralization of government; it also required the nationalization of politics. The primary form of political community had to be recast on a national scale. For Herbert Croly, writing in 1909, the "nationalizing of American political, economic, and social life" was "an essentially formative and enlightening political transformation." We would become more of a democracy only as we became "more of a nation . . . in ideas, in institutions, and in spirit."[18]

This nationalizing project would be consummated in the New Deal, but for the democratic tradition in America, the embrace of the nation was a decisive departure. From Jefferson to the populists, the party of democracy in American political debate had been, roughly speaking, the party of the provinces, of decentralized power, of small-town and small-scale America. And against them had stood the party of the nation—first Federalists, then Whigs, then the Republicans of Lincoln—a party that spoke for the consolidation of the union. It was thus the historic achievement of the New Deal to unite, in a single party and political program, what Samuel Beer has called "liberalism and the national idea."[19]

What matters for our purpose is that, in the twentieth century, liberalism made its peace with concentrated power. But it was understood at the start that the terms of this peace required a strong sense of national community, morally and politically to underwrite the extended involvements of a modern industrial order. If a virtuous republic of small-scale, democratic communities was no longer a possibility, a national republic seemed democracy's next best hope. This was still, in principle at least, a politics of the common good. It looked to the nation, not as a neutral framework for the play of competing interests, but rather as a formative community, concerned to shape a common life suited to the scale of modern social and economic forms.

But this project failed. By the mid- or late twentieth century, the national republic had run its course. Except for extraordinary moments, such as war, the nation proved too vast a scale across which to cultivate the shared self-understandings necessary to community in the formative, or constitutive sense. And so the gradual shift, in our practices and institutions, from a public philosophy of common purposes to one of fair procedures, from a politics of good to a politics of right, from the national republic to the procedural republic.

OUR PRESENT PREDICAMENT

A full account of this transition would take a detailed look at the changing shape of political institutions, constitutional interpretation, and the terms of political discourse in the broadest sense. But I suspect we would find in the *practice* of the procedural republic two broad tendencies foreshadowed by its philosophy: first, a tendency to crowd out democratic possibilities; second, a tendency to undercut the kind of community on which it nonetheless depends.

Where liberty in the early republic was understood as a function of democratic institutions and dispersed power,[20] liberty in the procedural republic is defined in opposition to democracy, as an individual's guarantee against what the majority might will. I am free insofar as I am the bearer of rights, where rights are trumps.[21] Unlike the liberty of the early republic, the modern version permits—in fact even requires—concentrated power. This has to do with the universalizing logic of rights. Insofar as I have a right, whether to free speech or a minimum income, its provision cannot be left to the vagaries of local preferences but must be assured at the most comprehensive level of political association. It cannot be one thing in New York and another in Alabama. As rights and entitlements expand, politics is therefore displaced from smaller forms of association and relocated at the most universal form—in our case, the nation. And even as politics flows to the nation, power shifts away from democratic institutions (such as legislatures and political parties) and toward institutions designed to be insulated from democratic pressures, and hence better equipped to dispense and defend individual rights (notably the judiciary and bureaucracy).

These institutional developments may begin to account for the sense of powerlessness that the welfare state fails to address and in some ways doubtless deepens. But it seems to me a further clue to our condition recalls even more directly the predicament of the unencumbered self—lurching, as we left it, between detachment on the one hand, entanglement on the other. For it is a striking feature of the welfare state that it offers a powerful promise of individual rights, and also demands of its citizens a high measure of mutual engagement. But the self-image that attends the rights cannot sustain the engagement.

As bearers of rights, where rights are trumps, we think of ourselves as freely choosing, individual selves, unbound by obligations antecedent to rights, or to the agreements we make. And yet, as citizens of the procedural republic that secures these rights, we find ourselves implicated willy-nilly in a formidable array of dependencies and expectations we did not choose and increasingly reject.

In our public life, we are more entangled, but less attached, than ever before. It is as though the unencumbered self presupposed by the liberal ethic had begun to come true—less liberated than disempowered, entangled in a network of obligations and involvements unassociated with any act of will, and yet unmediated by those common identifications or expansive self-definitions that would make them tolerable. As the scale of social and political organization has become more comprehensive, the terms of our collective identity have become more fragmented, and the forms of political life have outrun the common purpose needed to sustain them.

Something like this, it seems to me, has been unfolding in America for the past half-century or so. I hope I have said at least enough to suggest the shape a fuller story might take. And I hope in any case to have conveyed a certain view about politics and philosophy and the relation between them—that our practices and institutions are themselves embodiments of theory, and to unravel their predicament is, at least in part, to seek after the self-image of the age.

twenty-four

JUSTICE AS MEMBERSHIP

There are some things money can't buy and other things it tries to buy but shouldn't—elections, for example, or in an earlier day, salvation. But the sale of elections, like the sale of indulgences, usually brings a demand for reform. What is wrong with buying these things? And where else should money's writ not rule? How the good things in life should be distributed is the subject of Michael Walzer's book *Spheres of Justice,* which offers an imaginative alternative to the ongoing debate over distributive justice.

The debate is typically carried on between libertarians on the one hand and egalitarians on the other. Libertarians argue that money, the medium of free exchange, should buy whatever those who possess it want; people should be free to use their money as they choose. Egalitarians reply that money could be a fair instrument of distribution only if everyone had the same amount. So long as some have more and others less, some will deal from strength, others from weakness, and the so-called free market can hardly be fair. But critics of the egalitarian approach respond that even if all wealth were equally distributed, the equality would end when the dealing began. Those favorably endowed by fortune or circumstance would do well; those less favorably endowed less well. So long as people have different abilities and desires the reign of perfect equality can never last for long.

Walzer rescues the case for equality from its critics and defenders alike, by shifting the ground of the libertarian-egalitarian debate. The key to his solution is to worry less about the distribution of money and more about limiting the things that money can buy. This is the point of talking about spheres of justice. He maintains that different goods occupy different spheres, which are properly governed by different principles—welfare to the needy, honors to the deserving, political power to the persuasive, offices to the qualified, luxuries to those able and willing to pay for them, divine grace to the pious, and so on.

For Walzer, the injustice of unequal wealth lies not in the yachts and gourmet dinners that money commands but in money's power to dominate in spheres where it does not belong, as when it buys political influence. And while money may be the worst offender, it is not the only currency that wrongly rules beyond its own sphere. For example, when an office is obtained by kinship instead of ability, that is nepotism. Nepotism and bribery are easy to condemn because they result in goods being distributed by principles alien to their spheres.

But as Walzer acknowledges, the idea of spheres, taken alone, does not tell us how to distribute this or that good. Most of our political arguments arise over precisely what goods belong to what spheres. What sort of goods, for example, are health care and housing and education? Should we regard them as basic needs to be publicly provided as required or as goods and services to be sold in the market? Or, to take a different sort of example, in what sphere does sex belong? Should sexual pleasure be "distributed" only on the basis of love and commitment or also in exchange for cash or other goods?

Whether we are debating the welfare state or sexual mores, we need some way of deciding which goods fit which distributive principles. One way of deciding, perhaps the most familiar way, is to try to identify certain universal natural or human rights and to deduce from these whatever particular rights may follow—the right to housing or health care or the right to engage in prostitution, as the case may be.

Walzer rejects the appeal to rights and adopts in its place a conception of membership in a community, a conception that poses a powerful challenge to political theories that put rights first. For him, distributive justice must begin with such membership because we are all members of political communities before we are bearers of rights. Whether we have a right to a particular good depends on the role that good plays in our communal life and on its importance to us as members.

Walzer illustrates this point with an argument for greater public provision of medical care, an argument that appeals not to a universal "right to treatment," but instead to the character of contemporary American life and the shared understandings that define it. What the care of souls meant to the medieval Christians, he argues, the cure of bodies means to us. For them, eternity was a socially recognized need—"hence, a church in every parish, regular services, catechism for the young, compulsory communion, and so on." For us, a long and healthy life is a socially recognized need—"hence, doctors and hospitals in every district, regular checkups, health education for the young, compulsory vaccination, and so on." Medical care becomes a matter of membership in the society. To be cut off from it is "not only dangerous but degrading," a kind of excommunication.

In Walzer's conception, then, the case for equality is tied to the case for membership. Different communities invest different goods with different meanings and values, which give rise, in turn, to different understandings of membership. For example, Walzer reminds us that in different times and places, bread has been "the staff of life, the body of Christ, the symbol of the Sabbath, the means of hospitality and so on." What matters is that each community be faithful to its shared understandings and open to political debate about what those understandings require.

This is a humane and hopeful vision, and Walzer conveys it with a wry and gentle grace. His book is laced with specific illustrations and historical examples, designed to bring out our own understanding of social goods—of offices and honors, security and welfare, work and leisure, schooling and dating, property and power—often by contrast with other cultures and traditions. If his approach is at times more evocative than systematic, this is in keeping with his purpose—to resist the universalizing impulse of philosophy, to affirm the rich particularity of our moral lives.

Some may take issue with this purpose on the grounds that it is essentially conservative and uncritical. Societies faithful to the shared understandings of their members do not make for just societies, it may be said, only consistent ones. If the notion of justice is to have any critical force, one can further argue, it must be based on standards independent of any particular society; otherwise justice is left hostage to the very values it must judge. Walzer sometimes seems vulnerable to this challenge, as when he doubts that we can ever judge the meanings of communities other than our own.

But I don't think his pluralism requires that kind of moral relativism. Walzer's relativist voice is in tension with a more affirmative voice that gives his case its moral force. Implicit in his argument is a particular vision of community, the kind that cultivates the common life we share as members.

One expression of the kind of community Walzer has in mind is the public holiday, an institution that he contrasts with the modern vacation. Whereas vacations are private occasions, free of obligations, a time to "go away" from our usual place, holidays are public occasions (sometimes religious, sometimes civic), that we celebrate together. In our own time, those holidays that survive are increasingly attached to long weekends, to our private vacations.

He uses the history of the word "vacation" to show how far we have come from the communal life: "In Ancient Rome, the days on which there were no religious festivals or public games were called dies vacantes, 'empty days.' The holidays, by contrast, were full—full of obligation but also of celebration, full of things to do, feasting and dancing, rituals and plays. This was when time ripened to produce the social goods of shared solemnity and revelry. Who would give up days like that? But we have lost that sense of fullness; and the days we crave are the empty ones, which we can fill by ourselves as we please."

Though Walzer leaves little doubt which form of rest makes for the richer common life, he concludes nonetheless (in his relativist voice) that justice doesn't choose between holidays and vacations but simply requires public support for whichever form happens to prevail. But this is at odds with the deeper suggestion implicit in his account that a community that values vacations over holidays not only lacks a certain fullness but is unlikely to sustain the sense of belonging necessary if the community is to provide for such holidays.

It is one thing to expect a community to share the expenses of public celebrations and another to demand that it subsidize private vacations. The eclipse of holidays by vacations suggests the weakening of those moral ties that any case for public provision must presuppose. This seems to me the larger force of Walzer's claim. Where justice begins with membership, it cannot be concerned with distribution alone; it must also attend to the moral conditions that cultivate membership.

twenty-five

THE PERIL OF
EXTINCTION

There are many things wrong with destroying humankind—the lives lost, the suffering and pain, the futures denied. But these terrible things are also wrong with wars that spare the species. What makes the nuclear nightmare different is not simply the scale of suffering or the number of deaths, but the possibility that human history could come to an end. Unlike other instruments of destruction, nuclear war introduces the possibility of extinction, and this possibility makes a moral difference. But what does this difference consist in? What is the moral difference between the loss of human lives and the end of human life?

Such speculation may seem as idle as it is grim. But as George Kateb rightly insists, policy must answer to philosophy, even a policy so powerfully governed by military and technological imperatives as nuclear deterrence. What is puzzling is not his enterprise but his answer. According to Kateb, the moral crux of the nuclear peril consists in the fact that nuclear war violates individual rights. If this seems a small complaint for so fateful an event, Kateb claims nonetheless that the doctrine of individualism is "the most adequate idealism" for the nuclear age, the moral philosophy best suited "to see the nuclear predicament truly and to protest and resist its perpetuation."[1]

Kateb believes that individualist principles rule out the use of "any nuclear weapon, of any size, for any purpose, by any country." This he calls "the no-use doctrine." Since the only end of legitimate government is to protect individual rights, and since nuclear war violates those rights, no use of nuclear weapons is morally permissible. Those who use nuclear weapons forfeit their right to govern, and can justifiably be overthrown, by violence if need be, by their fellow citizens or others. Indeed, even the threat to use nuclear weapons, implicit in the doctrine of deterrence, is at odds with legitimate government, and gives rise to the right to resist.

Kateb's hard line against nuclear war seems to offer a firmness appropriate to the peril. And as Kateb reminds us, it is the peril of extinction that makes the nuclear world "utterly distinct." But why, from the standpoint of individualism, *is* the destruction of humankind a loss beyond the loss of lives? Why should we worry about the survival of the world, apart from the reasons we have to worry about the survival of the millions who comprise it? By tying his case to an individualistic ethic, Kateb obscures the distinctness of the peril he would confront; he makes it difficult to see how extinction could be, so to speak, a fate worse than death.

There are at least two ways of accounting for the special loss of extinction; neither fits well with the individualism Kateb defends. The first appeals to the common world we share as human beings. As Hannah Arendt writes,

> The common world is what we enter when we are born and what we leave behind when we die. It is what we have in common not only with those who live with us, but also with those who were here before and with those who will come after us.

According to Arendt, the permanence of the common world is essential to the possibility of human meaning. Only by engaging in significant action can mere mortals aspire to an "earthly immortality." But to escape the ruin of time, such acts must be remembered; meaning depends on memory. As the common world is the carrier of memory, no less than the possibility of human meaning depends on its survival. It is from this point of view that Jonathan Schell describes the nuclear predicament as "a crisis of life in the common world."

A second case against extinction appeals to those particular common worlds defined by peoples and nations, cultures and communities. The memories they bear draw their resonance from local references and traditions. The events they recall have meaning for their members even when they lack universal significance. To care for the fate of a community is to care for a way of life more enduring than an individual life, but less expansive than humanity in general.

This explains why genocide is a crime more heinous than the many murders it entails. To destroy not only persons but also a people is to extinguish a language and culture, a distinctive way of being. By destroying a world, even one more bounded than the world of humankind, genocide intimates the ultimate extinction. It diminishes our humanity by effacing one of its distinctive expressions.

The idea that we should cherish the common worlds we inhabit draws Kateb's emphatic rebuke. "Such a way of conceiving a people does not answer to the American experience." It is alien, "Old World," "folk-mystique," a piece of superstition. Far from an argument against annihilation, the conviction that cultures and peoples are worth preserving "constitutes a fertile source of the possibility of extinction." Once we believe that a people outlives the individuals who at any moment comprise it, we are more likely to prefer our own kind, to fight for abstractions, to travel down the road of massive ruin. "The idea of a people is a pernicious atavism," the very thing modern individualism is meant to cure.

Those who prize communal ties need to guard against the decay of pride into chauvinism, especially where the community commands, as it sometimes does, the power of a state. The suggestion that solidarity as such is a slippery slope to statism, however, is a caricature of vast proportions. Nor does Kateb say enough about his individualistic alternative to show whether it can overcome such familiar difficulties as sustaining a scheme of rights without appealing to a sense of community beyond the social contract. But leaving aside these broader questions of political theory, the question remains how Kateb can cast extinction as a special kind of peril, while at the same time denying any notion of a common world worth preserving. If individualism teaches us to outgrow all solidarities, what reason does it leave to love the world? And if we have no reason, why worry so about extinction?

The nuclear peril is different because it threatens us whole; it threatens the continuities that situate us in the world. In the individualist view, the extinction of the species can only be another case, a bigger case, of murder. Kateb seems to concede as much when he writes, "The emphasis is on the death of millions of individuals." But this denies our sense that the loss of the world is a loss beyond the loss of lives. The language of individual rights does not help us say what is wrong with nuclear war. Without some kind of communal language, the distinctness of the nuclear age is likely to defy description.

twenty-six

DEWEY'S LIBERALISM
AND OURS

1.

In the first half of the twentieth century, John Dewey was America's most celebrated philosopher. More than a philosopher, he was a public intellectual who wrote about politics and education, science and faith, for an audience beyond the academy. When Dewey died in 1952, at age ninety-three, Henry Commager described him as "the guide, the mentor, and the conscience of the American people; it is scarcely an exaggeration to say that for a generation no issue was clarified until Dewey had spoken."

In the decades following his death, however, Dewey's work was largely ignored. Academic philosophy became increasingly technical and regarded Dewey's broad speculations as fuzzy and old-fashioned. Even moral and political philosophers, embroiled in debates about utilitarian versus Kantian ethics, found little reason to turn to Dewey. Except in schools of education, where his influence persisted, few students read his books. Meanwhile, the central political debates of the day—about the scope of rights and entitlements, about the relation between government and the economy—had little to do, or so it seemed, with Dewey's political teaching.

In recent years, Dewey has made a comeback. Why this is so, and whether the Dewey revival holds promise for contemporary philosophy and politics, are among the questions that Alan Ryan poses in

John Dewey and the High Tide of American Liberalism (1995). Ryan's book is itself an expression of the Dewey revival it describes. It follows the publication a few years ago of Robert Westbrook's excellent biography, *John Dewey and American Democracy,* and coincides with the appearance of other books and articles on aspects of Dewey's thought.[1] Ryan, a political theorist who teaches at Oxford, is a spirited and sympathetic guide to Dewey's life and thought. He describes his book less as a full-fledged biography than as "a friendly but critical tour of the ideas that established Dewey's astonishing hold over the educated American public of his day." In this aim, Ryan admirably succeeds.

If the narrative occasionally flags, the fault lies less with the author than with his subject. Rarely has so eventful a life been led by so colorless a figure. Like few philosophers of his day or ours, Dewey lived a life of public engagement. A leading voice of Progressive reform, he founded an experimental school in Chicago, worked with the social reformer Jane Addams at Hull House, and supported women's suffrage and Margaret Sanger's birth control movement. He became the nation's foremost apostle of what came to be called progressive education and a hero to school teachers. He helped to establish the American Association of University Professors, the New School for Social Research, and the American Civil Liberties Union. He traveled to Japan, China, Turkey, Mexico, and the Soviet Union to lecture and advise on educational reform, and chaired an unsuccessful attempt to form a new political party based on social democratic principles. At the age of seventy-eight, Dewey led a commission of inquiry that cleared Leon Trotsky of Stalin's charge, made at the Moscow trials of 1936, that Trotsky had committed sabotage and treason against the Soviet regime. Notwithstanding this remarkable variety of activities, Dewey found time to write more than a thousand essays and books, many for a general audience, which have recently been gathered in thirty-seven volumes of collected works.[2]

*   *   *

But Dewey himself was scarcely as imposing a person as his activism and influence might suggest. He was a shy, impassive man, an awkward writer, and a poor public speaker. Even when writing for a general audience, he was not particularly adept at making complex ideas accessible. Sidney Hook, one of Dewey's greatest admirers, acknowledged that America's greatest philosopher of education was not impressive as a classroom teacher:

> He made no attempt to motivate or arouse the interest of his auditors, to relate problems to their own experiences, to use graphic, concrete illustrations in order to give point to abstract and abstruse positions. He rarely provoked a lively participation and response from students . . . Dewey spoke in a husky monotone . . . His discourse was far from fluent. There were pauses and sometimes long lapses as he gazed out of the window or above the heads of his audience.

Dewey's lack of presence as a writer, speaker, or personality makes his popular appeal something of a mystery. The mystery is compounded by the fact that the political positions he espoused were often at odds with conventional opinion. A non-Marxist critic of capitalism, he voted for Eugene Debs over Woodrow Wilson in 1912, opposed the New Deal as too tepid a response to the crisis of industrial capitalism, and always voted for Norman Thomas over Franklin Roosevelt. What was it then, that won Dewey so broad an audience for half a century?

The answer, Ryan persuasively suggests, is that Dewey's philosophy helped Americans make their peace with the modern world. It did so by easing the seemingly stark alternatives that confronted Americans in the early twentieth century—between science and faith, individualism and community, democracy and expertise. Dewey's philosophy blurred these familiar distinctions. Science, he wrote, was not necessarily opposed to faith, but another way of making sense of the world as we experience it. Individualism, properly understood, was not the rampant pursuit of self-interest but the un-folding of a person's distinctive capacities in a "common life" that calls them forth. Democracy was not simply a matter of counting up people's preferences, however irrational, but a way of life that edu-cates citizens to be capable of "intelligent action."

Dewey argued, in short, that Americans could embrace the mod-ern world without forsaking some of their most cherished alle-giances. Raised in Vermont as a Congregationalist, a member of the first generation of university teachers of philosophy who were not clergymen, Dewey was not aggressively secular. He retained the vo-cabulary of faith, of moral and religious uplift, and applied it to de-mocracy and education. This position, as Ryan argues, appealed to people who were seeking moral and religious ideals and ways to ex-press them that were compatible with the assumptions of secular so-ciety. During a century of wars, vast social and economic changes, and widespread anxiety about them, Dewey offered a reassuring message, even a consoling one.

Dewey's tendency to blur distinctions, the subject of much annoy-ance among his critics, did not spring simply from a desire to soothe the anxieties of his readers. It reflected the two central tenets of his philosophy; pragmatism and liberalism. Recent debates about Dewey's work have concentrated on these two doctrines and on the relation between them. Since pragmatism and liberalism are often used in ways at odds with Dewey's meaning, it is important to see how he understood them.

In common usage, pragmatism describes a merely expedient ap-proach to things, ungoverned by moral principle. But this is not what Dewey meant by it. For him, pragmatism described a challenge to the way philosophers understood the search for truth. Since the time of the Greeks, philosophers had assumed that the quest for truth was a quest for knowledge of an ultimate reality, or metaphysical order, in-dependent of our perceptions and beliefs. Philosophers disagreed among themselves about whether the meaning of this ultimate reality was something we supply or something we discover; they disagreed as well about the nature of relations between mind and body, subject and object, and between the ideal and the real. But they shared the assumption that the test of truth is the correspondence between our thoughts about the world and the world as it really is. Dewey rejected this assumption. At the heart of his pragmatism was the notion that the truth of a statement or belief depends on its usefulness in making sense of experience and guiding action, not on its correspondence to an ultimate reality that exists outside or beyond our experience. According to Dewey, philosophy should "surrender all pretension to be peculiarly concerned with ultimate reality" and accept the pragmatic notion that "no theory of Reality in general, *Uberhaupt,* is possible or needed."[3]

If Dewey is right, important consequences follow for philosophers. If philosophy lacks a distinctive subject matter, if the validity of a belief can only be determined by testing it in experience, then conventional distinctions between thought and action, knowing and doing, must be reconsidered. The process of knowing does not consist in grasping something accurately from the outside; it involves taking part in events in a purposive, intelligent way. Philosophers should give up their search for conditions of knowledge in general and attend to the particular problems for thought and action that arise in everyday life. "Philosophy," Dewey writes, "recovers itself when it ceases to be a device for dealing with the problems of philosophers and becomes a method, cultivated by philosophers, for dealing with the problems of men."[4]

The idea of philosophy as unavoidably practical and experimental suggests that the philosopher must respond to the events of his or her time not only as a concerned citizen but also as a philosopher. It therefore suggests a closer connection between philosophy and democracy than most philosophers would accept. As Ryan observes,

"Dewey came to think that every aspect of philosophy was an aspect of understanding a modern democratic society." So close a link between philosophy and democracy runs counter to the familiar contrast between philosophy, understood as the pursuit of truth, and democracy, understood as a way of representing opinions and interests. But Dewey viewed philosophy as less detached and democracy as more elevated than the familiar contrast assumes. More than a system of majority rule, democracy was, for Dewey, a way of life that fosters communication and deliberation among citizens, deliberation that issues in intelligent collective action.

Ardent democrat though he was, Dewey did not defend democracy as founded in consent or the general will. Instead, he viewed democracy as the political expression of an experimental, pragmatic attitude to the world. Dewey's pragmatism led him to celebrate democracy for much the same reasons that he celebrated science. Ryan explains the parallel between democracy and science in Dewey's thought as follows:

> There is no truth legitimating the observations and experiments of scientists and no will legitimating democratic decision making . . . [Dewey] eschewed any suggestion that "democracy" was uniquely legitimate either because it was government by the general will or because it was uniquely apt to uncover the truth. The nearest he got to a single account of democracy's virtues was that they were like those of science: It excluded the fewest alternatives, allowed all ideas a fair shot at being tried out, encouraged progress, and did not rely on authority.

Dewey's pragmatism gave his liberalism a distinctive, and in some ways unfamiliar, cast. Most versions of liberal political theory rest on moral and metaphysical assumptions at odds with Dewey's pragmatism. John Locke held that legitimate government is limited by natural, inalienable rights; Immanuel Kant argued that no policy, however popular or conducive to utility, may violate principles of justice and right that are not derived from experience but are prior to it; even John Stuart Mill, who based justice and rights on "utility," broadly conceived, relied on a strong distinction between public and private spheres of action.

Dewey rejected all of these versions of liberalism, for they rested on moral or metaphysical foundations that were held to be prior to politics and prior to experience. Unlike these classical liberals and many contemporary ones, Dewey did not base his political theory on the existence of fundamental rights or a social contract. Although he favored civil liberties, he was not primarily concerned with defining the rights that limit majority rule; nor did he try to derive principles of justice that would govern the basic structure of society, or to identify a realm of privacy free from government intrusion.

Central to Dewey's liberalism was the idea that freedom consists in participating in a common life that enables individuals to realize their distinctive capacities. The problem of freedom is not how to balance individual rights against the claims of community, but how, as he put it to establish "an entire social order, possessed of a spiritual authority that would nurture and direct the inner as well as the outer life of individuals."[5] Civil liberties are vital for such a society, not because they enable individuals to pursue their own ends but because they make possible the social communication, the free inquiry and debate, that democratic life requires.

The overriding importance of democracy for Dewey is not that it provides a mechanism for weighing everyone's preferences equally, but that it provides a "form of social organization, extending to all the areas and ways of living," in which the full powers of individuals can be "fed, sustained and directed."[6] For Dewey, the "first object of a renascent liberalism" was not justice or rights but education, the task of "producing the habits of mind and character, the intellectual and moral patterns," that suited citizens to the mutual responsibilities of a shared public life.[7] Democratic education of this kind, he stressed, was not only a matter of schooling but the essential task of liberal social and political institutions as well. Schools would be small communities that would prepare children to engage in a democratic public life, which would in turn educate citizens to advance the common good.

2.

Ryan's observation that Dewey's life and thought represent the "high tide of American liberalism" raises the question of Dewey's relevance today. Does the marked difference, in argument and emphasis, between Dewey's liberalism and ours reflect the obsolescence of his liberalism or the inadequacy of our own? Ryan himself seems divided about this question. On the one hand, he is wary of Dewey's view that freedom is bound up with membership in a community, a view that reflects Dewey's debt to Hegel. Dewey's "urge to close the gap between what we desire for ourselves and what we want for other people," Ryan writes, "contains more wishful thinking than is decent in a philosophical theory." On the other hand, Ryan describes Dewey's liberalism as a desirable corrective to the preoccupation with rights that characterizes much liberal political theory and practice today. "Rights-obsessed liberalism is only one liberalism," Ryan writes, "and not the most persuasive."

In the end, Ryan suggests, a liberalism grounded in rights and Dewey's more communitarian version of liberalism may not differ as sharply in practice as they do in theory. Despite Dewey's rejection of natural rights, for example, he endorsed traditional liberal rights on other grounds—as a necessary condition for a democratic community hospitable to communication, intelligent action, and the full realization of human capacities. "The traditional political liberties remain firmly in place" in Dewey's liberalism, Ryan observes,

> not because they are "natural rights"—there are no natural rights—
> or because there is a chronic problem of defending each individual

in a democracy from the potential ill will of a majority. They remain in place as part of the machinery that allows a truly democratic public to form . . . The diehard rights-obsessed liberal will not be persuaded by this, but Dewey would not be persuaded by him. Nor does this matter as much as it may seem. Dewey was quite ready to agree that the full battery of *legal* rights that the liberal traditionally demands are the indispensable way to institutionalize the ground rules of a democratic community.

While it is true that Dewey's liberalism and the contemporary version of liberalism associated with such theorists as John Rawls and Ronald Dworkin both affirm a familiar range of rights, the differences between the two are not without consequence for politics. This can be seen by considering the attempt by Richard Rorty to enlist Dewey's pragmatism in the service of his own version of contemporary liberalism, which holds that political argument should be detached from moral and religious argument. In a number of influential works, Rorty has praised Dewey's attempt to set epistemology aside and abandon the idea that philosophy can provide a foundation for knowledge.[8]

More recently, in an article entitled "The Priority of Democracy to Philosophy," Rorty has sought to show that Dewey's pragmatism can provide support for the kind of liberalism he favors. Just as philosophy should set aside the search for knowledge of an ultimate reality beyond experience, Rorty argues, so politics should set aside competing visions of morality and religion. Politics should not aim at any particular conception of the good life, but should settle for a society in which people tolerate one another in public and pursue their moral and religious ideals in private. A liberal democracy should not only avoid legislating morality, Rorty maintains; it should also banish moral and religious argument from political discourse. "Such a society will become accustomed to the thought that social policy needs no more authority than successful accommodation among individuals."

Rorty acknowledges that encouraging citizens to set aside their moral convictions for political purposes is likely to make them philosophically "light-minded" and lead to a spiritual "disenchantment" of public life. People will gradually give up the tendency to view politics as the appropriate vehicle for the expression of moral and spiritual ideals. But Rorty argues that such a result is precisely the wisdom of the pragmatic liberalism that he and, allegedly, Dewey endorse. "For Dewey, communal and public disenchantment is the price we pay for individual and private spiritual liberation."[9]

It is a measure of Rorty's philosophical ingenuity that he derives from Dewey's pragmatism a political theory sharply at odds with the one that Dewey himself affirmed. Dewey rejected the notion that government should be neutral among conceptions of the good life. He lamented rather than celebrated the moral and spiritual disenchantment of public life. He rejected a sharp distinction between public and private life and defended the view, derived from Hegel and the British idealist philosopher T. H. Green, that individual freedom can only be realized as part of a social life that cultivates the moral and civic character of citizens and inspires a commitment to the common good.

Rorty sets aside the communal aspect of Dewey's thought. Drawing instead on Dewey's pragmatism, he constructs a liberalism that renounces moral or philosophical foundations. Rorty argues that pragmatism teaches us to abandon the idea that philosophy supplies the foundations of knowledge; similarly, liberalism teaches us to abandon the idea that moral and religious ideals supply the justifications for political arrangements. Rorty's liberalism asserts that democracy takes precedence over philosophy in the sense that the case for democracy need not presuppose any particular vision of the good life. Rorty's creative rewriting (some would say hijacking) of Dewey's liberalism helps to clarify what is at stake in the contrast between

Dewey's communitarian liberalism and the rights-based liberalism more familiar in our time.

For Dewey, the primary problem with American democracy in his day was not an insufficient emphasis on justice and rights, but the impoverished character of public life. The source of this impoverishment was the discrepancy between the impersonal and organized character of modern economic life and the ways Americans conceived of themselves. Americans of the early twentieth century increasingly thought of themselves as freely choosing individuals, even as the huge scale of economic life dominated by large corporations undermined their capacity to direct their own lives. Paradoxically, Dewey observed, people clung to an individualistic philosophy "at just the time when the individual was counting for less in the direction of social affairs, at a time when mechanical forces and vast impersonal organizations were determining the frame of things."[10]

Central among the mechanical forces were steam, electricity, and railroads. Their effect was to dissolve the local forms of community that had prevailed in American life through much of the nineteenth century without substituting a new form of political community. As Dewey wrote, "The machine age in developing the Great Society has invaded and partially disintegrated the small communities of former times without generating a Great Community."[11] The erosion of traditional forms of community and authority at the hands of commerce and industry seemed at first a source of individual liberation. But Americans soon discovered that the loss of community had very different effects. Although the new forms of communication and technology brought a new, more extensive interdependence, they did not bring a sense of engagement in common purposes and pursuits. "Vast currents are running which bring men together," Dewey wrote, but these currents did nothing to build a new kind of political community. As Dewey stressed, "No amount of aggregated collective action of itself constitutes a community." In spite of the increasing use of railroads, telegraph wires, and the increasingly complex division of labor, or perhaps because of them, "the Public seems to be lost."[12] The new national economy had "no political agencies worthy of it," leaving the democratic public atomized, inchoate, and unorganized.[13] According to Dewey, the revival of democracy awaited the recovery of a shared public life, which depended in turn on creating new communitarian institutions, especially schools, that could equip citizens to act effectively within the modern economy. "Till the Great Society is converted into a Great Community, the Public will remain in eclipse."[14]

Like many liberals of his day and since, Dewey assumed that the Great Community would take the form of a national community; American democracy would flourish insofar as it managed to inspire a sense of mutual responsibility and allegiance to the nation as a whole. Since the economy was now national in scale, political institutions had to become national as well, if only to keep up. National markets called forth big government, which required in turn a strong sense of national community to sustain it.

From the Progressive era to the New Deal to the Great Society, American liberalism sought to cultivate a deeper sense of national community and civic engagement, but with only mixed success. Except in extraordinary moments, such as war, the nation proved too vast for anything resembling a Great Community to be formed, too disparate to serve as a forum for the public deliberation Dewey rightly prized. Partly as a result, American liberals in the postwar years gradually turned their attention from the character of public life to the expansion of both rights against the government and entitlements backed by the government. By the 1980s and 1990s, however, the liberalism of rights and entitlements was in retreat, having lost much of its moral energy and political appeal.

As in Dewey's day, there is today a widespread fear that citizens are losing control of the forces that govern their lives, that people are turning away from public responsibilities, and that the politicians and parties lack the moral or civic imagination to respond. Once again there is reason to worry that the "Public," as Dewey conceived it, is in eclipse, while the play of powerful interests and the din of strident voices leave little room for reasoned public discourse. Now as then it could be said, with Dewey, that "the political elements in the constitution of the human being, those having to do with citizenship, are crowded to one side."[15] Now, however, it is conservatives, rather than liberals, who speak most explicitly of citizenship, community, and the moral prerequisites of a shared public life. Although the conservatives' conception of community is often narrow and ungenerous, liberals often lack the moral resources to mount a convincing reply. What Ryan calls the "rights-obsessed liberalism" familiar in our time insists that government must be neutral on questions of the good life, that it must avoid taking sides on moral and religious controversies. The great service of Ryan's book is to remind us that liberalism was not always reluctant to speak the language of morality, community, and religion. "Deweyan liberalism," he writes,

> is different. It is a genuine liberalism, unequivocally committed to progress and the expansion of human tastes, needs, and interests . . . Nonetheless, it comes complete with a contentious world view and a contentious view of what constitutes a good life; it takes sides on questions of religion, and it is not obsessed with the defense of rights . . . The individual it celebrates is someone who is thoroughly engaged with his or her work, family, local community and its politics, who has not been coerced, bullied, or dragged into these interests but sees them as fields for a self-expression quite consistent with losing himself or herself in the task at hand.

At a time when the liberalism of rights and entitlements finds itself at low ebb, we might do well to recall the more robust civic liberalism for which Dewey spoke.

twenty-seven

MASTERY AND HUBRIS
IN JUDAISM
WHAT'S WRONG WITH
PLAYING GOD?

David Hartman, one of the leading religious thinkers of our time, is also our most important Jewish public philosopher. In his teachings and writings, he has fostered a rich encounter between the Jewish tradition and modern moral and political philosophy. As Maimonides drew Aristotle into conversation with Moses and Rabbi Akiva, so Hartman has renovated Jewish thought by bringing the liberal sensibilities of Immanuel Kant and John Stuart Mill to bear on Talmudic argument.

Much of Hartman's work is devoted to showing that it is possible to reconcile halakhic Judaism with modern pluralism.[1] The pluralism he defends is not simply a pragmatic response to the moral and religious disagreements that abound in modern societies, a compromise for the sake of peace. To the contrary, Hartman's pluralism has its source in his theology, in his distinctive vision of covenantal Judaism.

PLURALISM: ETHICAL AND INTERPRETIVE

At the heart of Hartman's theology is the notion of God as a self-limiting being who restrains himself in order to make room for human freedom and responsibility. The notion of divine self-limitation is first intimated in the biblical account of creation. God creates human beings in his own image, but as distinct from himself, as free and independent creatures, capable of violating his commands (as Adam shows when he eats from the tree of knowledge), and also of arguing with him (as Abraham does before the destruction of Sodom).

But for Hartman, the fullest expression of God's self-limitation is the Sinai covenant. In giving the Torah to the Jewish people at Sinai, God enlists human beings as partners in his project for history. Rather than achieve his purposes directly, through miraculous intervention or prophetic revelation, God ties his hopes to a community that undertakes to live by his commandments. But the Torah he hands down at Sinai is not transparent or self-interpreting. God leaves it to human beings—the scholars and rabbis—to determine the meaning of his law. Here is a further sense in which God limits himself and makes room for human initiative. "God's self-limiting love for human beings is expressed in His entrusting the elaboration and expansion of the Torah to rabbinic scholars."[2] The successive elaborations, embodied in Talmud and Midrash, become constitutive of the Torah revealed at Sinai. "With the development of the oral tradition, Israel became a partner in the development of revelation; revelation ceased being the divine Word completely given at Sinai and became an open-ended Word creatively elaborated by countless generations of students."[3]

Hartman argues for two forms of pluralism—one interpretive, the other ethical. His interpretive pluralism emerges directly from his covenantal theology and reflects the open-ended character of Talmudic argument. Different rabbis, however learned, can come to different conclusions. Even God cannot intervene to resolve a Talmudic dispute, as a well-known *midrash* attests. ("It is not in heaven.") Minority opinions are not condemned as heretical but are legitimized and preserved. The open-ended character of interpretation makes room for pluralism within halakhic Judaism.

But Hartman also defends a more far-reaching, ethical pluralism that takes seriously the ethical systems of other faiths, and of secular morality. According to Hartman, God's covenant with the Jewish people does not mean that Judaism is the only authentic way to worship God. Nor must a system of ethics be founded on divine revelation.[4] Hartman rejects the notion that, without revelation, there can be no rational grounding of ethical norms. "Human history has shown that individuals are capable of developing viable ethical systems not rooted in divine authority. God's revelation of the ethical is not meant to compensate for a presumed inability of human reason to formulate an ethical system."[5] Unlike many religious thinkers, Hartman maintains that "secular humanism is a viable and morally coherent position."[6]

Hartman does not claim that ethical pluralism is mandated by biblical and Talmudic Judaism, only that it is a possible interpretation. He acknowledges that some aspects of the tradition are at odds with pluralism. Hartman's claim might prompt one to ask which interpretation is truest to the Jewish tradition taken as a whole—the pluralist reading or the exclusivist one? But Hartman does not focus on this question, and I will not pursue it here. Instead, I would like to explore a different issue raised by Hartman's ethical pluralism: If people can reason their way to morality without divine revelation, then what is religion for? Or, to put the question another way: Why does the possibility of a valid secular morality pose no threat to halakhic Judaism as Hartman understands it? In support of his own willingness to accept secular ethics as legitimate, Hartman cites Maimonides, who drew freely on Aristotle's ethics: "Maimonides demonstrated that covenantal halakhic spirituality is in no way threatened or undermined by admitting the validity of ethical norms whose source is independent of the notion of revelation."[7]

Many people with strong religious convictions believe they have a stake in denying the adequacy of secular morality. That Hartman, as a halakhic Jew, has no such stake reflects more than a tolerant stance toward the beliefs of others. It also reflects a deep conviction that religion is about more than grounding moral principles. Notwithstanding the importance of the ethical *mitzvot*, Hartman is critical of those who identify Judaism with certain ethical precepts said to be unique or distinctive to Jews. "In order to appreciate the seriousness with which Judaism takes the ethical mitzvoth, it is not necessary to claim some special Jewish ethical sensibility or to adduce the moral genius of the Hebrew prophets."[8] To identify Judaism with the ethical not only fails to notice similar ethical norms in many other traditions; it also reflects an impoverished understanding of Jewish religious and spiritual life.

RELIGIOUS ANTHROPOLOGY

For Hartman, religion is about more than ethical precepts, more than ritual and celebration. It is also a way of making sense of our relation to God, nature, and the cosmos, and of determining the mode of being appropriate to that relation. At the heart of Hartman's covenantal theology lie fundamental questions of religious anthropology: What does it mean for a human being to live in the presence of God? What dispositions, sensibilities, and stance toward the world does a religious person have? Is he humble and submissive, or assertive and bold? What sort of religious personality does halakhic Judaism, properly understood, cultivate and affirm? What limits on human powers, if any, should we recognize and observe?

As these questions suggest, religious anthropology is at once metaphysical and normative. It is metaphysical in that it seeks an account of the universe, and of the place of human beings within it. It is normative in that any account of our relation to God and nature carries implications for the way we should be and the lives we should live. Those who insist on a purely formal or positivist view of law might deny that any such account carries normative weight; whatever the law prohibits may not be done, and whatever the law does not prohibit is permissible. But if Hartman is right that halakhah is open to competing interpretations, the best interpretation may be the one that fits with the larger theological picture. In this way, Hartman's religious anthropology informs his understanding of ethics and law.

In order to illustrate the importance of Hartman's religious anthropology, I would like to consider a set of moral and political questions, increasingly prominent in contemporary public discourse, that cannot be resolved by invoking familiar moral principles or ethical precepts alone. Although Hartman has not addressed these questions directly, his religious anthropology provides a fruitful way of thinking about them, and a language in which to do so.

BIOTECHNOLOGY: PLAYING GOD?

Many of the most difficult issues we face in the modern world concern the proper use of our growing technological power to remake nature, including human nature. Arguments about the limits, if any, of human dominion over nature have figured in debates about environmental policy for some time. Recent advances in biotechnology have sharpened the question, as illustrated by debates over genetically modified food, the bioengineering of animals, human cloning, new reproductive technologies, and other techniques that give human beings the power to choose or change their children's (or their own) genetic characteristics. While few object to the cloning of Dolly the sheep, many are troubled by the prospect of cloning human beings or using genetic technologies that would enable parents to create "designer babies" by specifying in advance the sex, height, eye color, athletic prowess, musical ability, or IQ of their children.

Troubling though these scenarios are, it is not easy to say exactly what is wrong with them. There is, of course, the safety objection: attempting such practices prematurely poses grave risk of genetic abnormalities and other medical harms. But even assuming the medical risks can eventually be overcome, there remains a lingering unease. The standard lexicon of ethical principles—utility, rights, and informed consent—does not capture the features of genetic engineering that trouble us most deeply. And so those who worry about these practices—including those who otherwise argue within secular moral frameworks—find themselves invoking the idea that human beings shouldn't "play God." By this they suggest that certain human interventions in nature represent a kind of "hubris," a drive to mastery and dominion that exceeds the bounds of properly human endeavor. Whether or not the "playing God" objection to genetic engineering is decisive, it prompts us to consider the proper relation of human beings to God and nature. It forces us onto the terrain of religious anthropology.

Judaism is more permissive than many traditions with respect to human dominion over nature. As Hartman points out, the God of creation is not one with nature, as in pantheistic conceptions, nor embodied in nature, as in pagan cosmologies, but a transcendent being whose existence is prior to nature. So if human intervention in nature is subject to certain limits, these limits do not arise from the idea that nature is enchanted or sacred as such, as some "deep green" ecologists believe. The limits on the exercise of human powers over nature arise not from nature itself but from a proper understanding of the relation between human beings and God. If it is wrong to clone ourselves in a quest for immortality, or to genetically alter our children so that they will better fulfill our ambitions and desires, the sin is not the desecration of nature but the deification of ourselves.

But at what point does the exercise of scientific or technological power amount to deification, or a hubristic quest to usurp God's role? In rabbinic times, some saw the physician's practice of medicine as a failure of faith, as an illegitimate intrusion on God's role as healer of the sick. But the Talmud rejects this view, and teaches that "permission has been given to the physician to heal" (*Berakhot* 60a).

A midrashic story explains the permission to heal by comparing it to the permission given the farmer to rework nature in planting and cultivating crops:

> R. Ishmael and R. Akiva were strolling in the streets of Jerusalem accompanied by another person. They were met by a sick person. He said to them, "My masters, tell me by what means I may be Healed." They told him, "Do thus and so and be healed." He asked them, "And who afflicted me?" They replied, "The Holy One, blessed be He." [The sick person] responded, "You intrude in a realm which is not yours; He has afflicted and you heal! Are you not transgressing His will?"
>
> They asked him, "What is your occupation?" He answered, "I am a tiller of the soil and here is the sickle in my hand." They asked him, "Who created the orchard?" He answered, "The Holy One, blessed be He." Said they, "You too intrude in a realm which is not yours. [God] created it and you cut away its fruit!" He said to them, "Do you not see the sickle in my hand? If I did not plow, sow, fertilize and weed it, nothing would grow." They said to him, "Oh you fool! Does your occupation not teach you this, as Scripture says 'as for man, his days are as grass: as grass of the field, so he flourishes' (Psalms 103:15). Just as a tree, without weeding, fertilizing, and plowing will not grow; and even if it grows, then without irrigation and fertilizing it will not live but will surely die—so it is with regard to the body. Drugs and medical procedures are the fertilizer, and the physician is the tiller of the soil."[9]

The permission of the physician to heal the sick does not resolve the question of whether certain forms of genetic engineering wrongly intrude in God's realm. Many uses of the new biotechnology, such as choosing to have a boy rather than a girl, or gaining a competitive edge in sports through the use of performance-enhancing drugs or genetic alteration, have nothing to do with healing the sick or curing disease. My inability to run a three-minute mile or hit seventy home runs, however disappointing, is not a disease; my doctor has no obligation to provide me with a cure. But it is a further question whether there is anything wrong with using science and technology to acquire these powers.

THE PROMETHEAN SPIRIT

Hartman's teacher, Rabbi Joseph Soloveitchik, accords human beings almost boundless scope for the exercise of their powers. For Soloveitchik, man's creation in the image of God implies that human beings have a divine mandate to participate in the act of creation itself. He argues that God deliberately created an imperfect universe so that human beings would be empowered to improve it. "The most fervent desire of halakhic man is to behold the replenishment in the deficiency in creation," Soloveitchik writes. "The dream of creation is the central idea in the halakhic consciousness—the idea of the importance of man as a partner of the Almighty in the act of creation, man as creator of worlds."[10]

According to Soloveitchik, the incompleteness of creation was an expression of God's love for humankind. "The Creator of the world diminished the image and stature of creation in order to leave something for man, the work of his hands, to do, in order to adorn man with the crown of creator and maker." Soloveitchik includes in the mandate of creativity the project of self-creation. "Herein is embodied the entire task of creation and the obligation to participate in the renewal of the cosmos. The most fundamental principle of all is that man must create himself. It is this idea that Judaism introduced into the world."[11]

The Promethean spirit of Soloveitchik's religious anthropology would seem to sanction a boundless human dominion over nature. It is hard to imagine a scientific pursuit he would condemn as hubristic. He might even sympathize with James Watson's famous reply to those who criticized modern scientists for playing God. "If we don't play God," Watson is reported to have said, "who will?" As

Hartman observes, Soloveitchik's vision of Jewish spirituality supports "the whole modern technological spirit, which has often been viewed as a threat to the religious quest."[12]

What then becomes of religious humility? What prevents so empowered and autonomous a human being from mistaking himself for God? Soloveitchik answers this question by attributing to halakhic man a second mandate—to imitate not only the creativity of God but also His withdrawal from the world, and His acceptance of defeat. "Jewish ethics, then, requires man, in certain situations, to withdraw. Man must not always be a victor."[13] The majesty of human mastery and dominion is reined in by an obligation of sacrifice and submission to the ultimately inscrutable will of God, as exemplified by Abraham's willingness to sacrifice his son. For Soloveitchik, the religious personality, riven by contrasting orientations to life, is bound to oscillate between two radically different spiritual sensibilities: Facing nature, he displays a heady sense of mastery and dominion; facing God, his sense of agency gives way to the unquestioning sacrifice and utter submission of the *Akedah.*

Hartman rejects Soloveitchik's religious anthropology on two grounds. First, Hartman does not believe that a wrenching oscillation between radical polarities of assertiveness and submissiveness is true to human experience, either spiritually or psychologically. Second, his covenantal theology moderates the polarities from the start. Without the Promethean vision of human mastery and dominion, the temptation to hubris can be contained without recourse to what Hartman calls "the ultimate principle of authoritarian religion," the claim that God's will is inscrutable.[14]

> The enormous elation that [Soloveitchik's] halakhic man feels in exercising his creative powers in the majestic gesture of subduing nature must be counteracted by the move of sacrificial surrender based on the *Akedah.* I would argue, however, that this drastic cure

is unnecessary because the disease need not arise in the first place. Judaism contains its own internal corrective mechanisms, which can protect against any inclination to hubris.[15]

RESTRAINING HUBRIS: AFFIRMING FINITUDE

I would like to bring out the features of Hartman's religious anthropology that stave off the temptation to hubris even while affirming human adequacy and dignity. Hartman acknowledges the tension, running throughout the rabbinic tradition, between self-assertion and submission. Since his primary aim, at least in *A Living Covenant*, is to reconcile halakhic Judaism with modernity, he begins by emphasizing the openness of the tradition to human initiative, creativity, and freedom. His primary target is the image of the halakhic Jew as passive and submissive, bound by the yoke of the law to the authoritative teachings of the past. Against this image, Hartman offers a covenantal anthropology that makes room for human adequacy and dignity. Given his target, he emphasizes the creative, autonomous spirit of rabbinic Judaism. But his appeal to the Sinai covenant as the warrant for human initiative also implies certain restraints on the human drive for mastery and dominion. If applied to contemporary debates about genetic engineering, these restraints might help articulate the "hubris objection," and offer a corrective to the drift to deification.

The sources of restraint can be glimpsed in three themes of Hartman's religious anthropology: (1) human finitude, (2) Shabbat, and (3) idolatry. For Hartman, the celebration of human finitude means that a religious life can affirm and embrace the limits and imperfections of the world. Notwithstanding the messianic yearning that runs through the Jewish tradition, "the vitality of the covenant does not presuppose belief in messianic redemption, the immortality of the soul, or the resurrection of the dead."[16] Hartman acknowledges the perspective within Judaism that views death and suffering as a punishment for sin. From such a perspective, observing the *mitzvot* and living according to halakhah will prepare the way for divine deliverance from suffering and affliction. "Even the body's vulnerability to disease will ultimately be eliminated."[17]

Hartman does not rule out the possibility of messianic redemption, but he argues that covenantal Judaism does not require it. Moreover, he suggests that human finitude can be affirmed as an expression of the irreducible difference between God and the world. "Finite human beings who accept their creatureliness know that they remain separate from their Creator," Hartman writes. Although the human intellect may be tempted to believe that it can "be freed from finitude, and think the thoughts of God," this is an illusion that has led to dogmatism and wars in the name of truth. Our embodiment restrains this impulse and recalls us to our human situation. "Rooted in our bodies, we are always reminded of the limited, fragile, but dignified quality of human finitude."[18] A "religious sensibility that celebrates finitude and creatureliness as permanent features of covenantal life"[19] is one of the restraints internal to Hartman's vision that reins in the tendency to hubris.

SHABBAT AND SLEEP

A second theme of restraint in Hartman's religious anthropology is the Sabbath. Like the celebration of human finitude, the obligation to keep the Sabbath serves to check our drive to dominion. "On the Sabbath, Jews celebrate God as the Creator . . . Awe, wonder, and humility are expressed by giving up mastery and control over the world for a day. Nature is not our absolute possession."[20] Sabbath observance restrains the human tendency to self-deification by releasing us from the activities of mastery and control that prevail during the rest of the week. "On the Sabbath, a person may not stand over and against the universe as a Promethean figure . . . The halakhic notion of the holiness of the Sabbath aims at controlling the human impulse to mastery by setting limits to human dominance of nature."[21] When the sun sets and the Sabbath arrives, nature ceases to be a mere instrument to human purposes:

> Halakhah prohibits my plucking a flower from my garden or doing with it as I please. At sunset the flower becomes a "thou" with a right to existence irrespective of its instrumental value for me. I stand silently before nature as before a fellow creature and not as before an object of my control. By forcing us to experience the meaning of being creatures of God, the Sabbath aims at healing the human grandiosity of technological arrogance.[22]

What are the implications of Shabbat for genetic engineering and other feats of biotechnology? Hartman's account can be interpreted in two ways—one permissive, the other restrictive: The permissive interpretation holds that nature becomes a "thou" only one day in seven, and remains a mere instrument of human desires the rest of the week. The restrictive interpretation, by contrast, would carry something of Shabbat into our everyday stance toward the natural world, and impose some limits on the project of mastery.

Of the two interpretations, the second seems more plausible, and truer to Hartman's concern with the way halakhah shapes religious character. Since the point of Shabbat is to cultivate a certain humility toward God's creation, shouldn't that humility inform our orientation to the world when our work resumes? Although Hartman does not elaborate an ethic of nature and human dominion, he clearly implies that the experience of Shabbat should shape our behavior and check our hubris throughout the week: "The Sabbath develops the characteristic of gratitude, the sense that life is a gift, and the need to give up the longing for absolute power."[23]

Even if I am right that Hartman's Shabbat teaching implies an ethic of restraint in our everyday dealings with nature, it is difficult to know which transformations of the world and of ourselves carry the risk of self-deification. One way of thinking about this question is to ask what projects of bioengineering, if successfully carried out and practiced on a wide scale, would erode our appreciation of life as a gift.

Consider a small but suggestive example: the case of sleep. Sleep is a biological necessity, not a disease in need of a cure. But suppose we devised a way of banishing sleep, or radically reducing our need for it. The possibility is not entirely hypothetical. A new drug, invented to treat narcolepsy (excessive sleepiness), is increasingly popular among people who want to stay awake for extended periods of time. Without the side effects of caffeine or other stimulants, it enables people to think and work effectively without sleep. In military use, it has enabled soldiers to function well for 40 hours, and then, after 8 hours of sleep, to fight for another 40 hours without rest.[24] Suppose such a drug were safe, and imagine that an improved version of it enabled people to forgo sleep for a week, or a month, or even a year. At what point, if any, would the use of this drug become ethically troubling? And on what grounds? From the standpoint of utility, it would surely lead to greater productivity and wealth. Worries about unfairness could be met, in principle at least, by making the drug accessible to all. And assuming its use were voluntary, no one could claim that it violated people's rights. If we would still find it troubling, it must be for reasons connected to the "hubris objection," which takes us back to Hartman's themes of Shabbat and the affirmation of human finitude.

In explaining the meaning of Shabbat, Hartman cites a *midrash* about the danger of human self-deification: When God created Adam, the angels mistook him for a divine being. "What did the Holy One, blessed be He, do? He caused sleep to fall upon him and thus all knew he was a human being."[25] Hartman reads this *midrash* as responding to the tendency of human power to blur the gap between God and human beings, a theological problem for which sleep provides the solution. "Sleep . . . destroys the illusion of omnipotence, forcing us to recognize our humanity. Sleep symbolizes a state of consciousness in which human beings give up mastery and control." He compares Adam's sleep in the *midrash* to "the restful joy of 'Sabbath sleep.'"[26] Sleep, like Shabbat, recalls us to human limits by regulating our lives according to a rhythm of rest beyond our control. To rid ourselves, by technological means, of the need for sleep would deprive us of a feature of human life that checks our impulse to mastery and dominion.

IDOLATRY

A third source of restraint in Hartman's religious anthropology is the rejection of idolatry. He cites Maimonides' view that rejecting idolatry is central to halakhic Judaism. "Whoever denies idolatry," Maimonides writes in the *Mishneh Torah,* "confesses his faith in the whole Torah, in all the prophets and all that the prophets were commanded, from Adam to the end of time. And this is the fundamental principle of all commandments."[27]

Hartman points out that the prohibition of idolatry does not only apply to the ancient idols of pagan worship. If idolatry had no broader meaning, it would pose no threat in the modern world, and the struggle against it would be of merely antiquarian interest. The rejection of idolatry depends for its normative significance on the enduring presence of false gods, objects or pursuits that exert an appeal sufficiently seductive to inspire misplaced worship and allegiance.

What form does idolatry take in the modern world? In Talmudic times, the rabbis worried most about the worship of emperors and kings, whose sovereignty and power posed the most potent rival to religious commitment. Hartman observes that the idolatry of absolute power persists in our time in "the demand for total and uncritical allegiance to a political state."[28] This was certainly true of the great tyrannies of the twentieth century, as in the notorious cases of

Hitler's Germany and Stalin's Soviet Union. But with the fall of Communism, the locus of idolatry may have shifted. Although local tyrants and charismatic rulers still hold sway in various places, political rule today does not rivet the attention or absorb the energies or inspire the allegiance that render it a rival good to God. This is not to claim that liberal democracy has triumphed throughout the world; it is only to suggest that, in liberal and illiberal societies alike, the pull of the political is less compelling, less seductive, and therefore less capable of stirring idolatrous passions.

In the contemporary world, the idolatrous temptation has migrated from politics to other domains—consumerism, entertainment, and technology. The obsession with consumption in affluent market societies erodes the sacred by turning everything into a commodity. The entertainment industry, now global in its reach, makes idols of celebrities and promotes their worship on a scale that Roman emperors would have envied. Finally, biotechnology in the age of the genome promises not only to remedy devastating diseases but also to empower us to choose our genetic characteristics and those of our progeny. It is difficult to imagine a more exhilarating prospect, or a more demanding test of human humility and restraint. If idolatry is the ultimate sin, if arrogance and hubris are the dispositions most at odds with religious character, then the ancient struggle against self-deification is likely to find renewed occasion in our time.

POLITICAL LIBERALISM

Rare is the work of political philosophy that provokes sustained debate. It is a measure of its greatness that John Rawls's *A Theory of Justice*[1] inspired not one debate, but three.

The first, by now a starting point for students of moral and political philosophy, is the argument between utilitarians and rights-oriented liberals. Should justice be founded on utility, as Jeremy Bentham and John Stuart Mill argue, or does respect for individual rights require a basis for justice independent of utilitarian considerations, as Kant and Rawls maintain? Before Rawls wrote, utilitarianism was the dominant view within Anglo-American moral and political philosophy. Since *A Theory of Justice*, rights-oriented liberalism has come to predominate.[2]

The second debate inspired by Rawls's work is an argument within rights-oriented liberalism. If certain individual rights are so important that even considerations of the general welfare cannot override them, it remains to ask which rights these are. Libertarian liberals, like Robert Nozick and Friedrich Hayek, argue that government should respect basic civil and political liberties, and also the right to the fruits of our labor as conferred by the market economy; redistributive policies that tax the rich to help the poor thus violate our rights.[3] Egalitarian liberals like Rawls disagree. They argue that we cannot meaningfully exercise our civil and political liberties without the provision of basic social and economic needs; government should therefore assure each person, as a matter of right, a decent level of such goods as education, income, housing, health care, and the like. The debate between the libertarian and egalitarian versions of rights-oriented liberalism, which flourished in the academy in the 1970s, corresponds roughly to the debate in American politics, familiar since the New Deal, between defenders of the market economy and advocates of the welfare state.

The third debate prompted by Rawls's work centers on an assumption shared by libertarian and egalitarian liberals alike. This is the idea that government should be neutral among competing conceptions of the good life. Despite their various accounts of what rights we have, rights-oriented liberals agree that the principles of justice that specify our rights should not depend for their justification on any particular conception of the good life.[4] This idea, central to the liberalism of Kant, Rawls, and many contemporary liberals, is summed up in the claim that the right is prior to the good.[5]

CONTESTING THE PRIORITY OF THE RIGHT OVER THE GOOD

For Rawls, as for Kant, the right is prior to the good in two respects, and it is important to distinguish them. First, the right is prior to the good in the sense that certain individual rights "trump," or outweigh, considerations of the common good. Second, the right is prior to the good in that the principles of justice that specify our rights do not depend for their justification on any particular conception of the good life. It is this second claim for the priority of the right that prompted the most recent wave of debate about Rawlsian liberalism, an argument that has flourished in the last decade under the somewhat misleading label of the "liberal-communitarian debate."

A number of political philosophers writing in the 1980s took issue with the notion that justice can be detached from considerations of the good. Challenges to contemporary rights-oriented liberalism found in the writings of Alasdair MacIntyre,[6] Charles Taylor,[7] Michael Walzer,[8] and also in my own work,[9] are sometimes described as the "communitarian" critique of liberalism. The term "communitarian" is misleading, however, insofar as it implies that rights should rest on the values or preferences that prevail in any given community at any given time. Few, if any, of those who have challenged the priority of the right are communitarians in this sense.[10] The question is not whether rights should be respected, but whether rights can be identified and justified in a way that does not presuppose any particular conception of the good. At issue in the third wave of debate about Rawls's liberalism is not the relative weight of individual and communal claims, but the terms of relation between the right and the good.[11] Those who dispute the priority of the right argue that justice is relative to the good, not independent of it. As a philosophical matter, our reflections about justice cannot reasonably be detached from our reflections about the nature of the good life and the highest human ends. As a political matter, our deliberations about justice and rights cannot proceed without reference to the conceptions of the good that find expression in the many cultures and traditions within which those deliberations take place.

Much of the debate about the priority of the right has focused on competing conceptions of the person and of how we should understand our relation to our ends. Are we, as moral agents, bound only by the ends and roles we choose for ourselves, or can we sometimes be obligated to fulfill certain ends we have not chosen—ends given by nature or God, for example, or by our identities as members of families, peoples, cultures, or traditions? In various ways, those who have criticized the priority of right have resisted the notion that we can make sense of our moral and political obligations in wholly voluntarist or contractual terms.

In *A Theory of Justice*, Rawls linked the priority of the right to a voluntarist, or broadly Kantian, conception of the person. According to this conception, we are not simply defined as the sum of our desires, as utilitarians assume, nor are we beings whose perfection consists in realizing certain purposes or ends given by nature, as Aristotle held. Rather, we are free and independent selves, unbound by antecedent moral ties, capable of choosing our ends for ourselves. This is the conception of the person that finds expression in the ideal of the state as a neutral framework. It is precisely because we are free and independent selves, capable of choosing our own ends, that we need a framework of rights that is neutral among ends. To base rights on some conception of the good would impose on some the values of others and so fail to respect each person's capacity to choose his or her own ends.

This conception of the person, and its link to the case for the priority of the right, are expressed throughout *A Theory of Justice.* Its most explicit statement comes toward the end of the book, in Rawls's account of "the good of justice." There Rawls argues, following Kant, that teleological doctrines are "radically misconceived" because they relate the right and the good in the wrong way:

> We should not attempt to give form to our life by first looking to the good independently defined. It is not our aims that primarily reveal our nature but rather the principles that we would acknowledge to govern the background conditions under which these aims are to be formed and the manner in which they are to be pursued. For the self is prior to the ends which are affirmed by it; even a dominant end must be chosen from among numerous possibilities ... We should therefore reverse the relation between the right and the good proposed by teleological doctrines and view the right as prior.[12]

In *A Theory of Justice,* the priority of the self to its ends supports the priority of the right to the good. "A moral person is a subject with ends he has chosen, and his fundamental preference is for conditions that enable him to frame a mode of life that expresses his nature as a free and equal rational being as fully as circumstances permit."[13] The notion that we are free and independent selves, unclaimed by prior moral ties, assures that considerations of justice will always outweigh other, more particular aims. In an eloquent expression of Kantian liberalism, Rawls explains the moral importance of the priority of the right in the following terms:

> The desire to express our nature as a free and equal rational being can be fulfilled only by acting on the principles of right and justice as having first priority . . . It is acting from this precedence that expresses our freedom from contingency and happenstance. Therefore in order to realize our nature we have no alternative but to plan to preserve our sense of justice as governing our other aims. This sentiment cannot be fulfilled if it is compromised and balanced against other ends as but one desire among the rest . . . How far we succeed in expressing our nature depends upon how consistently we act from our sense of justice as finally regulative. What we cannot do is express our nature by following a plan that views the sense of justice as but one desire to be weighed against others. For this sentiment reveals what the person is, and to compromise it is not to achieve for the self free reign but to give way to the contingencies and accidents of the world.[14]

In different ways, those who disputed the priority of the right took issue with Rawls's conception of the person as a free and independent self, unencumbered by prior moral ties.[15] They argued that a conception of the self given prior to its aims and attachments could not make sense of certain important aspects of our moral and political experience. Certain moral and political obligations that we commonly recognize—such as obligations of solidarity, for example, or religious duties—may claim us for reasons unrelated to a choice. Such obligations are difficult to dismiss as merely confused, and yet difficult to account for if we understand ourselves as free and independent selves, unbound by moral ties we have not chosen.[16]

DEFENDING THE PRIORITY OF THE RIGHT OVER THE GOOD

In *Political Liberalism,* Rawls defends the priority of the right over the good. He sets aside, for the most part, issues raised in the first two waves of debate, about utility versus rights and libertarian versus egalitarian notions of distributive justice. *Political Liberalism* focuses instead on issues posed by the third wave of debate, about the priority of the right.

Given the controversy over the Kantian conception of the person that supports the priority of the right, at least two lines of reply are possible. One is to defend liberalism by defending the Kantian conception of the person; the other is to defend liberalism by detaching it from the Kantian conception. In *Political Liberalism,* Rawls adopts the second course. Rather than defend the Kantian conception of the person as a moral ideal, he argues that liberalism as he conceives it does not depend on that conception of the person after all. The priority of the right over the good does not presuppose any particular conception of the person, not even the one advanced in Part III of *A Theory of Justice.*

Political Versus Comprehensive Liberalism

The case for liberalism, Rawls now argues, is political, not philosophical or metaphysical, and so does not depend on controversial claims about the nature of the self (pp. 29–35). The priority of the right over the good is not the application to politics of Kantian moral philosophy, but a practical response to the familiar fact that people in modern democratic societies typically disagree about the good. Because people's moral and religious convictions are unlikely to converge, it is more reasonable to seek agreement on principles of justice that are neutral with respect to those controversies (pp. xvi–xvii).

Central to Rawls's revised view is the distinction between political liberalism and liberalism as part of a comprehensive moral doctrine (pp. 154–158). Comprehensive liberalism affirms liberal political arrangements in the name of certain moral ideals, such as autonomy or individuality or self-reliance. Examples of liberalism as a comprehensive moral doctrine include the liberal visions of Kant and John Stuart Mill.[17] As Rawls acknowledges, the version of liberalism presented in *A Theory of Justice* is also an instance of comprehensive liberalism. "An essential feature of a well-ordered society associated with justice as fairness is that all its citizens endorse this conception on the basis of what I now call a comprehensive philosophical doctrine" (p. xvi). It is this feature that Rawls now revises, by recasting his theory as a "political conception of justice" (p. xvi).

Unlike comprehensive liberalism, political liberalism refuses to take sides in the moral and religious controversies that arise from comprehensive doctrines, including controversies about conceptions of the self. "Which moral judgments are true, all things considered, is not a matter for political liberalism" (p. xx). "To maintain impartiality between comprehensive doctrines, it does not specifically address the moral topics on which those doctrines divide" (p. xxviii). Given the difficulty of securing agreement on any comprehensive conception, it is unreasonable to expect that, even in a well-ordered society, all people will support liberal institutions for the same reason—as expressing the priority of the self to its ends, for example. Political liberalism abandons this hope as unrealistic and contrary to the aim of basing justice on principles that adherents of various moral and religious conceptions can accept. Rather than seek a philosophical foundation for principles of justice, political liberalism seeks the support of an "overlapping consensus" (p. 134). This means that different people can be persuaded to endorse liberal political arrangements, such as equal basic liberties, for different reasons, reflecting the various comprehensive moral and religious conceptions they espouse. Because political liberalism does not depend for its justification on any one of those moral or religious conceptions, it is presented as a "freestanding" view; it "applies the principle of toleration to philosophy itself" (p. 10).

Although political liberalism renounces reliance on the Kantian conception of the person, it does not do without a conception of the person altogether. As Rawls acknowledges, some such conception is necessary to the idea of the original position, the hypothetical social contract that gives rise to the principles of justice. The way to think about justice, Rawls argued in *A Theory of Justice,* is to ask which principles would be agreed to by persons who found themselves gathered in an initial situation of equality, each in temporary ignorance of his or her race and class, religion and gender, aims and attachments.[18] But in order for this way of thinking about justice to carry weight, the design of the original position must reflect something about the sort of persons we actually are, or would be in a just society.

One way of justifying the design of the original position would be to appeal to the Kantian conception of the person that Rawls advanced in Part III of *A Theory of Justice.* If our capacity to choose our ends is more fundamental to our nature as moral persons than are the particular ends we choose, if "it is not our aims that primarily reveal our nature but rather the principles that we would acknowledge to govern the background conditions under which these aims are to be formed,"[19] if "the self is prior to the ends which are affirmed by it,"[20] then it makes sense to think about justice from the standpoint of persons deliberating prior to any knowledge of the ends they will pursue. If "a moral person is a subject with ends he has chosen, and his fundamental preference is for conditions that enable him to frame a mode of life that expresses his nature as a free and equal rational being as fully as circumstances permit,"[21] then the original position can be justified as an expression of our moral personality and the "fundamental preference" that flows from it.

Once Rawls disavows reliance on the Kantian conception of the person, however, this way of justifying the original position is no longer available. But this raises a difficult question: what reason remains for insisting that our reflections about justice should proceed without reference to our purposes and ends? Why must we "bracket," or set aside, our moral and religious convictions, our conceptions of the good life? Why should we not base the principles of justice that govern the basic structure of society on our best understanding of the highest human ends?

The Political Conception of the Person

Political liberalism replies as follows: the reason we should think about justice from the standpoint of persons who abstract from their ends is not that this procedure expresses our nature as free and independent selves given prior to our ends. Rather, this way of thinking about justice is warranted by the fact that, for *political* purposes, though not necessarily for all moral purposes, we should think of ourselves as free and independent citizens, unclaimed by prior duties or obligations (pp. 29–35). For political liberalism, what justifies the design of the original position is a "political conception of the person" (p. 29). The political conception of the person embodied in the original position closely parallels the Kantian conception of the person, with the important difference that its scope is limited to our public identity, our identity as citizens. Thus, for example, our freedom as citizens means that our public identity is not claimed or defined by the ends we espouse at any given time. As free persons, citizens view themselves "as independent from and not identified with any particular such conception with its scheme of final ends" (p. 30). Our public identity is not affected by changes over time in our conceptions of the good.

In our personal or nonpublic identity, Rawls allows, we may regard our "ends and attachments very differently from the way the political conception supposes" (p. 31). There, persons may find themselves claimed by loyalties and commitments "they believe they would not, indeed could and should not, stand apart from and evaluate objectively. They may regard it as simply unthinkable to view themselves apart from certain religious, philosophical, and moral convictions, or from certain enduring attachments and loyalties" (p. 31). But however encumbered we may be in our personal identities, however claimed by moral or religious convictions, we must bracket our encumbrances in public, and regard ourselves, *qua* public selves, as independent of any particular loyalties or attachments or conceptions of the good (p. 31).

A related feature of the political conception of the person is that we are "self-authenticating sources of valid claims" (p. 32). The claims we make as citizens carry weight, whatever they are, simply by virtue of our making them (provided they are not unjust). That some claims may reflect high moral or religious ideals, or notions of patriotism and the common good, while others express mere interests or preferences, is not relevant from the standpoint of political liberalism. From a political point of view, claims founded on duties and obligations of citizenship or solidarity or religious faith are just things people want—nothing more, nothing less. Their validity as political claims has nothing to do with the moral importance of the goods they affirm, but consists solely in the fact that someone asserts them. Even divine commandments and imperatives of conscience count as "self-authenticating" claims, politically speaking.[22] This ensures that even those who regard themselves as claimed by moral or religious or communal obligations are nonetheless, for political purposes, unencumbered selves.

This political conception of the person explains why, according to political liberalism, we should reflect about justice as the original position invites us to do, in abstraction from our ends. But this raises a further question: why should we adopt the standpoint of the political conception of the person in the first place? Why should our political identities not express the moral and religious and communal convictions we affirm in our personal lives? Why insist on the separation between our identity as citizens and our identity as moral persons more broadly conceived? Why, in deliberating about justice, should we set aside the moral judgments that inform the rest of our lives?

Rawls's answer is that this separation or "dualism" between our identity as citizens and our identity as persons "originates in the special nature of democratic political culture" (p. xxi). In traditional societies, people sought to shape political life in the image of their comprehensive moral and religious ideals. But in a modern democratic society like our own, marked as it is by a plurality of moral and religious views, we typically distinguish between our public and personal identities. Confident though I may be of the truth of the moral and religious ideals I espouse, I do not insist that these ideals be reflected in the basic structure of society. Like other aspects of political liberalism, the political conception of the person as a free and independent self is "implicit in the public political culture of a democratic society" (p. 13).

But suppose Rawls is right, and the liberal self-image he attributes to us is implicit in our political culture. Would this provide sufficient grounds for affirming it, and for adopting the conception of justice it supports? Some have read Rawls's recent writings as suggesting that justice as fairness, being a political conception of justice, requires no moral or philosophical justification apart from an appeal to the shared understandings implicit in our political culture. Rawls seemed to invite this interpretation when he wrote, in an article published after *A Theory of Justice* but before *Political Liberalism*, as follows:

> What justifies a conception of justice is not its being true to an order antecedent to and given to us, but its congruence with our deeper understanding of ourselves and our aspirations, and our realization that, given our history and the traditions embedded in our public life, it is the most reasonable doctrine for us.[23]

Richard Rorty, in an insightful article, interprets (and welcomes) Rawls's revised view as "thoroughly historicist and antiuniversalist."[24] Although *A Theory of Justice* seemed to base justice on a Kantian conception of the person, Rorty writes, Rawls's liberalism "no longer seems committed to a philosophical account of the human self, but only to a historico-sociological description of the way we live now."[25] On this view, Rawls is not "supplying philosophical foundations for democratic institutions, but simply trying to systematize the principles and intuitions typical of American liberals."[26] Rorty endorses what he takes to be Rawls's pragmatic turn, a turn away from the notion that liberal political arrangements require a philosophical justification, or "extrapolitical grounding" in a theory of the human subject. "Insofar as justice becomes the first virtue of a society," Rorty writes, "the need for such legitimation may gradually cease to be felt. Such a society will become accustomed to the thought that social policy needs no more authority than successful accommodation among individuals, individuals who find themselves heir to the same historical traditions and faced with the same problems."[27]

In *Political Liberalism,* Rawls pulls back from this purely pragmatic account. Although justice as fairness begins "by looking to the public culture itself as the shared fund of implicitly recognized basic ideas and principles" (p. 8), it does not affirm these principles simply on the grounds that they are widely shared. Though Rawls argues that his principles of justice could gain the support of an overlapping consensus, the overlapping consensus he seeks "is not a mere modus vivendi" (p. 147), or compromise among conflicting views. Adherents of different moral and religious conceptions begin by endorsing the principles of justice for reasons drawn from within their own conceptions. But, if all goes well, they come to support those principles as expressing important political values. As people learn to live in a pluralist society governed by liberal institutions, they acquire virtues that strengthen their commitment to liberal principles.

> The virtues of political cooperation that make a constitutional regime possible are . . . very great virtues. I mean, for example, the virtues of tolerance and being ready to meet others halfway, and the virtue of reasonableness and the sense of fairness. When these vir-

tues are widespread in society and sustain its political conception of justice, they constitute a very great public good. (p. 157)

Rawls emphasizes that affirming liberal virtues as a great public good and encouraging their cultivation is not the same as endorsing a perfectionist state based on a comprehensive moral conception. It does not contradict the priority of the right over the good. The reason is that political liberalism affirms liberal virtues for political purposes only—for their role in supporting a constitutional regime that protects people's rights. Whether and to what extent these virtues should figure in people's moral lives generally is a question that political liberalism does not claim to answer (pp. 194–195).

ASSESSING POLITICAL LIBERALISM

If *Political Liberalism* defends the priority of right by detaching it from the Kantian conception of the person, how convincing is its defense? As I shall try to argue, *Political Liberalism* rescues the priority of the right from controversies about the nature of the self only at the cost of rendering it vulnerable on other grounds. Specifically, I shall try to show that liberalism conceived as a political conception of justice is open to three objections.

First, notwithstanding the importance of the "political values" to which Rawls appeals, it is not always reasonable to bracket, or set aside for political purposes, claims arising from within comprehensive moral and religious doctrines. Where grave moral questions are concerned, whether it is reasonable to bracket moral and religious controversies for the sake of political agreement partly depends on which of the contending moral or religious doctrines is true.

Second, for political liberalism, the case for the priority of the right over the good depends on the claim that modern democratic societies are characterized by a "fact of reasonable pluralism" about the good (p. xvii). Though it is certainly true that people in modern democratic societies hold a variety of conflicting moral and religious views, it cannot be said that there is a "fact of reasonable pluralism" about morality and religion that does not also apply to questions of justice.

Third, according to the ideal of public reason advanced by political liberalism, citizens may not legitimately discuss fundamental political and constitutional questions with reference to their moral and religious ideals. But this is an unduly severe restriction that would impoverish political discourse and rule out important dimensions of public deliberation.

Bracketing Grave Moral Questions

Political liberalism insists on bracketing our comprehensive moral and religious ideals for political purposes, and on separating our political from our personal identities. The reason is this: in modern democratic societies like ours, where people typically disagree about the good life, bracketing our moral and religious convictions is necessary if we are to secure social cooperation on the basis of mutual respect. But this raises a question that political liberalism cannot answer within its own terms. Even granting the importance of securing social cooperation on the basis of mutual respect, what is to guarantee that this interest is always so important as to outweigh any competing interest that could arise from within a comprehensive moral or religious view?

One way of assuring the priority of the political conception of justice (and hence the priority of the right) is to deny that any of the moral or religious conceptions it brackets could be true.[28] But this would implicate political liberalism in precisely the sort of philosophical claim it seeks to avoid. Time and again Rawls emphasizes that political liberalism does not depend on skepticism about the claims of comprehensive moral and religious doctrines. If political liberalism therefore allows that some such doctrines might be true, then what is to assure that none can generate values sufficiently compelling to burst the brackets, so to speak, and morally outweigh the political values of toleration, fairness, and social cooperation based on mutual respect?

One might reply that political values and values arising from within comprehensive moral and religious doctrines address different subjects. Political values, one might say, apply to the basic structure of society and to constitutional essentials, whereas moral and religious values apply to the conduct of personal life and voluntary associations. But if it were simply a difference of subject matter, no conflict between political values and moral and religious values could ever arise, and there would be no need to assert, as Rawls repeatedly does, that in a constitutional democracy governed by political liberalism, "political values normally outweigh whatever nonpolitical values conflict with them" (p. 146).

The difficulty of asserting the priority of "political values" without reference to the claims of morality and religion can be seen by considering two political controversies that bear on grave moral and religious questions. One is the contemporary debate about abortion rights. The other is the famous debate between Abraham Lincoln and Stephen Douglas over popular sovereignty and slavery.

Given the intense disagreement over the moral permissibility of abortion, the case for seeking a political solution that brackets the contending moral and religious issues—that is neutral with respect to them—would seem especially strong. But whether it is reasonable to bracket, for political purposes, the comprehensive moral and religious doctrines at stake largely depends on which of those doctrines is true. If the doctrine of the Catholic Church is true, if human life in the relevant moral sense does begin at conception, then bracketing the moral-theological question when human life begins is far less reasonable than it would be on rival moral and religious assumptions. The more confident we are that fetuses are, in the relevant moral sense, different from babies, the more confident we can be in affirming a political conception of justice that sets aside the controversy about the moral status of fetuses.

The political liberal might reply that the political values of toleration and equal citizenship for women are sufficient grounds for concluding that women should be free to choose for themselves whether to have an abortion; government should not take sides on the moral and religious controversy over when human life begins.[29] But if the Catholic Church is right about the moral status of the fetus, if abortion is morally tantamount to murder, then it is not clear why the political values of toleration and women's equality, important though they are, should prevail. If the Catholic doctrine is true, the political liberal's case for the priority of political values must become an instance of just-war theory; he or she would have to show why these values should prevail even at the cost of some 1.5 million civilian deaths each year.

Of course, to suggest the impossibility of bracketing the moral-theological question of when human life begins is not to argue against a right to abortion. It is simply to show that the case for abortion rights cannot be neutral with respect to that moral and religious controversy. It must engage rather than avoid the comprehensive moral and religious doctrines at stake. Liberals often resist this engagement because it violates the priority of the right over the good. But the abortion debate shows that this priority cannot be sustained. The case for respecting a woman's right to decide for herself whether to have an abortion depends on showing—as I believe can be shown—that there is a relevant moral difference between aborting a fetus at a relatively early stage of development and killing a child.

A second illustration of the difficulty with a political conception of justice that tries to bracket controversial moral questions is offered by the 1858 debates between Abraham Lincoln and Stephen Douglas. Douglas's argument for the doctrine of popular sovereignty is perhaps the most famous case in American history for bracketing a controversial moral question for the sake of political agreement. Because people were bound to disagree about the morality of slavery, Douglas argued, national policy should be neutral on that question. The doctrine of popular sovereignty he defended did not judge slavery right or wrong, but left the people of each territory free to make their own judgments. "To throw the weight of federal power into the scale, either in favor of the free or the slave states," would violate the fundamental principles of the Constitution and run the risk of civil war. The only hope of holding the country together, he argued, was to agree to disagree, to bracket the moral controversy over slavery and respect "the right of each state and each territory to decide these questions for themselves."[30]

Lincoln argued against Douglas's case for a political conception of justice. Policy should express rather than avoid a substantive moral judgment about slavery. Though Lincoln was not an abolitionist, he believed government should treat slavery as the moral wrong that it was, and prohibit its extension to the territories. "The real issue in this controversy—the one pressing upon every mind—is the sentiment on the part of one class that looks upon the institution of slavery *as a wrong,* and of another class that *does not* look upon it as a wrong."[31] Lincoln and the Republican party viewed slavery as a wrong and insisted that it *"be treated* as a wrong, and one of the methods of treating it as a wrong is to *make provision that it shall grow no larger."*[32]

Whatever his personal moral views, Douglas claimed that, for political purposes at least, he was agnostic on the question of slavery; he did not care whether slavery was "voted up or voted down."[33] Lincoln replied that it was reasonable to bracket the question of the morality of slavery only on the assumption that it was not the moral evil he regarded it to be. Any man can advocate political neutrality

who does not see anything wrong in slavery, but no man can logically say it who does see a wrong in it; because no man can logically say he don't care whether a wrong is voted up or voted down. He may say he don't care whether an indifferent thing is voted up or down, but he must logically have a choice between a right thing and a wrong thing. He contends that whatever community wants slaves has a right to have them. So they have if it is not a wrong. But if it is a wrong, he cannot say people have a right to do wrong.[34]

The debate between Lincoln and Douglas was not primarily about the morality of slavery, but about whether to bracket a moral controversy for the sake of political agreement. In this respect, their debate over popular sovereignty is analogous to the contemporary debate over abortion rights. As some contemporary liberals argue that government should not take a stand one way or the other on the morality of abortion, but let each woman decide the question for herself, so Douglas argued that national policy should not take a stand one way or the other on the morality of slavery, but let each territory decide the question for itself. There is of course the difference that in the case of abortion rights, those who would bracket the substantive moral question typically leave the choice to the individual, while in the case of slavery, Douglas's way of bracketing was to leave the choice to the territories.

But Lincoln's argument against Douglas was an argument against bracketing as such, at least where grave moral questions are at stake. Lincoln's point was that the political conception of justice defended by Douglas depended for its plausibility on a particular answer to the substantive moral question it claimed to bracket. This point applies with equal force to those arguments for abortion rights that claim to take no side in the controversy over the moral status of the fetus. Even in the face of so dire a threat to social cooperation as the prospect of civil war, Lincoln argued that it made neither moral nor political sense to bracket the most divisive moral controversy of the day.

I say, where is the philosophy or the statesmanship based on the assumption that we are to quit talking about it . . . and that the public

mind is all at once to cease being agitated by it? Yet this is the policy
. . . that Douglas is advocating—that we are to care nothing about
it! I ask you if it is not a false philosophy? Is it not a false statesmanship that undertakes to build up a system of policy upon the basis
of caring nothing about *the very thing that every body does care the
most about?*[35]

Present-day liberals will surely resist the company of Douglas and
want national policy to oppose slavery, presumably on the grounds
that slavery violates people's rights. The question is whether liberalism conceived as a political conception of justice can make this claim
consistent with its own strictures against appeals to comprehensive
moral ideals. For example, a Kantian liberal can oppose slavery as a
failure to treat persons as ends in themselves, worthy of respect. But
this argument, resting as it does on a Kantian conception of the person, is unavailable to political liberalism. Other historically important arguments against slavery are unavailable to political liberalism
for similar reasons. American abolitionists of the 1830s and 1840s, for
example, typically cast their arguments in religious terms, arguments
that political liberalism cannot invoke.

How, then, can political liberalism escape the company of
Douglas and oppose slavery without presupposing some comprehensive moral view? It might be replied that Douglas was wrong to
seek social peace at any price; not just any political agreement will
do. Even conceived as a political conception, justice as fairness is not
merely a modus vivendi. Given the principles and self-understandings implicit in our political culture, only an agreement on terms
that treat persons fairly, as free and equal citizens, can provide a reasonable basis for social cooperation. For us twentieth-century Americans, at least, the rejection of slavery is a settled matter. The historical demise of Douglas's position is by now a fact of our political
tradition that any political agreement must take as given.

This appeal to the conception of citizenship implicit in our political culture might explain how political liberalism can oppose slavery

today; our present political culture was importantly shaped, after all, by the Civil War, Reconstruction, the adoption of the Thirteenth, Fourteenth, and Fifteenth Amendments, *Brown v. Board of Education*,[36] the civil rights movement, the Voting Rights Act,[37] and so on. These experiences, and the shared understanding of racial equality and equal citizenship they formed, provide ample grounds for holding that slavery is at odds with American political and constitutional practice as it has developed over the past century.

But this does not explain how political liberalism could oppose slavery in 1858. The notions of equal citizenship implicit in American political culture of the mid-nineteenth century were arguably hospitable to the institution of slavery. The Declaration of Independence proclaimed that all men are created equal, endowed by their Creator with certain unalienable rights, but Douglas argued, not implausibly, that the signers of the Declaration were asserting the right of the colonists to be free of British rule, not the right of their Negro slaves to equal citizenship.[38] The Constitution itself did not prohibit slavery, but to the contrary accommodated it by allowing states to count three-fifths of their slave population for apportionment purposes,[39] providing that Congress could not prohibit the slave trade until 1808,[40] and requiring the return of fugitive slaves.[41] And in the notorious *Dred Scott* case,[42] the Supreme Court upheld the property rights of slaveholders in their slaves and ruled that African-Americans were not citizens of the United States.[43] To the extent that political liberalism refuses to invoke comprehensive moral ideals and relies instead on notions of citizenship implicit in the political culture, it would have a hard time explaining, in 1858, why Lincoln was right and Douglas was wrong.

The Fact of Reasonable Pluralism

The abortion debate today and the Lincoln-Douglas debate of 1858 illustrate the way a political conception of justice must presuppose some answer to the moral questions it purports to bracket, at least where grave moral questions are concerned. In cases such as these, the priority of the right over the good cannot be sustained. A further difficulty with political liberalism concerns the reason it gives for asserting the priority of the right over the good in the first place. For Kantian liberalism, the asymmetry between the right and the good arises from a certain conception of the person. Because we must think of ourselves as moral subjects given prior to our aims and attachments, we must regard the right as regulative with respect to the particular ends we affirm; the right is prior to the good because the self is prior to its ends.

For political liberalism, the asymmetry between the right and the good is not based on a Kantian conception of the person but instead on a certain feature of modern democratic societies. Rawls describes this feature as "the fact of reasonable pluralism" (p. xvii). "A modern democratic society is characterized not simply by a pluralism of comprehensive religious, philosophical, and moral doctrines but by a pluralism of incompatible yet reasonable comprehensive doctrines. No one of these doctrines is affirmed by citizens generally" (p. xvi). Nor is it likely that sometime in the foreseeable future this pluralism will cease to hold. Disagreement about moral and religious questions is not a temporary condition but "the normal result of the exercise of human reason" under free institutions (p. xvi).

Given the "fact of reasonable pluralism," the problem is to find principles of justice that free and equal citizens can affirm despite their moral, philosophical, and religious differences. "This is a problem of political justice, not a problem about the highest good" (p. xxv). Whatever principles it generates, the solution to this problem must be one that upholds the priority of the right over the good. Otherwise, it will fail to provide a basis for social cooperation among adherents of incompatible but reasonable moral and religious convictions.

But here there arises a difficulty. For even if the fact of reasonable pluralism is true, the asymmetry between the right and the good depends on a further assumption. This is the assumption that, despite our disagreements about morality and religion, we do not have, or on due reflection would not have, similar disagreements about justice. Political liberalism must assume not only that the exercise of human reason under conditions of freedom will produce disagreements about the good life, but also that the exercise of human reason under conditions of freedom will *not* produce disagreements about justice. The "fact of reasonable pluralism" about morality and religion only creates an asymmetry between the right and the good when coupled with the further assumption that there is no comparable "fact of reasonable pluralism" about justice.

It is not clear, however, that this further assumption is justified. We need only look around us to see that modern democratic societies are teeming with disagreements about justice. Consider, for example, contemporary debates about affirmative action, income distribution and tax fairness, health care, immigration, gay rights, free speech versus hate speech, and capital punishment, to name just a few. Or consider the divided votes and conflicting opinions of Supreme Court justices in cases involving religious liberty, freedom of speech, privacy rights, voting rights, the rights of the accused, and so on. Do not these debates display a "fact of reasonable pluralism" about justice? If so, how does the pluralism about justice that prevails in modern democratic societies differ from the pluralism about morality and religion? Is there reason to think that, sometime in the foreseeable future, our disagreements about justice will dissolve even as our disagreements about morality and religion persist?

The political liberal might reply by distinguishing two different kinds of disagreement about justice. There are disagreements about what the principles of justice should be and disagreements about how these principles should be applied. Many of our disagreements about justice, it might be argued, are of the second kind. Although we generally agree, for example, that freedom of speech is among the basic rights and liberties, we disagree about whether the right to free speech should protect racial epithets, or violent pornographic depictions, or commercial advertising, or unlimited contributions to political campaigns. These disagreements, vigorous and even intractable though they may be, are consistent with our agreeing at the level of principle that a just society includes a basic right to free speech.

Our disagreements about morality and religion, by contrast, might be seen as more fundamental. They reflect incompatible conceptions of the good life, it might be argued, not disagreements about how to put into practice a conception of the good life that commands, or on reflection would command, widespread agreement. If our controversies about justice concern the application of principles we share or would share on due reflection, while our controversies about morality and religion run deeper, then the asymmetry between the right and the good advanced by political liberalism would be vindicated.

But with what confidence can this contrast be asserted? Do all of our disagreements about justice concern the application of principles we share or would share on due reflection, rather than the principles themselves? What of our debates about distributive justice? Here it would seem that our disagreements are at the level of principle, not application. Some maintain, consistent with Rawls's difference principle, that only those social and economic inequalities that improve the condition of the least-advantaged members of society are just. They argue, for example, that government must ensure the provision of certain basic needs, such as income, education, health care, housing, and the like, so that all citizens will be able meaningfully to exercise their basic liberties. Others reject the difference principle. Libertarians argue, for example, that it may be a good thing for people to help those less fortunate than themselves, but that this should be a matter of charity, not entitlement. Government should not use its coercive power to redistribute income and wealth, but should respect people's rights to exercise their talents as they choose, and to reap their rewards as defined by the market economy.[44]

The debate between liberal egalitarians like Rawls and libertarians like Robert Nozick and Milton Friedman is a prominent feature of political argument in modern democratic societies. This debate reflects disagreement about what the correct principle of distributive justice is, not disagreement about how to apply the difference principle. But this would suggest that there exists in democratic societies a "fact of reasonable pluralism" about justice as well as about morality and religion. And if this is the case, the asymmetry between the right and the good does not hold.

Political liberalism is not without a reply to this objection, but the reply it must make departs from the spirit of toleration it otherwise evokes. Rawls's reply must be that, although there is a fact of pluralism about distributive justice, there is no fact of *reasonable* pluralism.[45] Unlike disagreements about morality and religion, disagreements about the validity of the difference principle are not reasonable; libertarian theories of distributive justice would not be sustained on due reflection. Our differences about distributive justice, unlike our differences of morality and religion, are not the natural outcome of the exercise of human reason under conditions of freedom.

At first glance, the claim that disagreements about distributive justice are not reasonable may seem arbitrary, even harsh, at odds with political liberalism's promise to apply "the principle of toleration to philosophy itself" (p. 10). It contrasts sharply with Rawls's apparent generosity toward differences of morality and religion. These differences, Rawls repeatedly writes, are a normal, indeed desirable feature of modern life, an expression of human diversity that only the oppressive use of state power can overcome (pp. 303–304). Where comprehensive moralities are concerned, "it is not to be expected that conscientious persons with full powers of reason, even after free discussion, will all arrive at the same conclusion" (p. 58). Since the exercise of human reason produces a plurality of reasonable moral and religious doctrines, "it is unreasonable or worse to want to use the sanctions of state power to correct, or to punish, those who disagree with us" (p. 138). But this spirit of toleration does not extend to our disagreements about justice. Because disagreements between, say, libertarians and advocates of the difference principle do not reflect a reasonable pluralism, there is no objection to using state power to implement the difference principle.

Intolerant though it may seem at first glance, the notion that theories of distributive justice at odds with the difference principle are not reasonable, or that libertarian theories of justice would not survive due reflection, is no arbitrary claim. To the contrary, in *A Theory of Justice* Rawls offers a rich array of compelling arguments on behalf of the difference principle and against libertarian conceptions: the distribution of talents and assets that enables some to earn more and others less in the market economy is arbitrary from a moral point of view; so is the fact that the market happens to prize and reward, at any given moment, the talents you or I may have in abundance; libertarians would agree that distributive shares should not be based on social status or accident of birth (as in aristocratic or caste societies), but the distribution of talents given by nature is no less arbitrary; the notion of freedom that libertarians invoke can be meaningfully exercised only if persons' basic social and economic needs are met; if people deliberated about distributive justice without reference to their own interests, or without prior knowledge of their talents and the value of those talents in the market economy, they would agree that the natural distribution of talents should not be the basis of distributive shares; and so on.[46]

My point is not to rehearse Rawls's argument for the difference principle, but only to recall the kind of reasons he offers. Viewing justification as a process of mutual adjustment between principles and considered judgments that aims at a "reflective equilibrium,"[47] Rawls tries to show that the difference principle is more reasonable than the alternative offered by libertarians. To the extent that his arguments are convincing—as I believe they are—and to the extent they can be convincing to citizens of a democratic society, the principles they support are properly embodied in public policy and law. Disagreement will doubtless remain. Libertarians will not fall silent or disappear. But their disagreement need not be regarded as a "fact of reasonable pluralism" in the face of which government must be neutral.

But this leads to a question that goes to the heart of political liberalism's claim for the priority of the right over the good: if moral argument or reflection of the kind Rawls deploys enables us to conclude, despite the persistence of conflicting views, that some principles of justice are more reasonable than others, what guarantees that reflection of a similar kind is not possible in the case of moral and religious controversy? If we can reason about controversial principles of distributive justice by seeking a reflective equilibrium, why can we not reason in the same way about conceptions of the good? If it can be shown that some conceptions of the good are more reasonable than others, then the persistence of disagreement would not necessarily amount to a "fact of reasonable pluralism" that requires government to be neutral.

Consider, for example, the controversy in our public culture about the moral status of homosexuality, a controversy based in comprehensive moral and religious doctrines. Some maintain that homosexuality is sinful, or at least morally impermissible; others argue that homosexuality is morally permissible, and in some cases gives expression to important human goods. Political liberalism insists that neither of these views about the morality of homosexuality should play a role in public debates about justice or rights. Government must be neutral with respect to them. This means that those who abhor homosexuality may not seek to embody their view in law; it also means that proponents of gay rights may not base their arguments on the notion that homosexuality is morally defensible. From the standpoint of political liberalism, each of these approaches would wrongly base the right on some conception of the good; each would fail to respect the "fact of reasonable pluralism" about comprehensive moralities.

But does the disagreement in our society about the moral status of homosexuality constitute a "fact of reasonable pluralism" any more than does the disagreement about distributive justice? According to political liberalism, the libertarian's objection to the difference principle does not constitute a "fact of reasonable pluralism" that requires government neutrality, because there are good reasons to conclude, on due reflection, that the arguments for the difference principle are more convincing than the ones that support libertarianism. But isn't it possible to conclude, with equal or greater confidence, that on due reflection, the arguments for the moral permissibility of homosexuality are more convincing than the arguments against it? Consistent with the search for a reflective equilibrium among principles and considered judgments, such reflection might proceed by assessing the reasons advanced by those who assert the moral inferiority of homosexual to heterosexual relations.

Those who consider homosexuality immoral often argue, for example, that homosexuality cannot fulfill the highest end of human sexuality, the good of procreation.[48] To this it might be replied that many heterosexual relations also do not fulfill this end, such as contracepted sex, or sex among sterile couples, or sex among partners beyond the age of reproduction. This might suggest that the good of procreation, important though it is, is not necessary to the moral worth of human sexual relations; the moral worth of sexuality might also consist in the love and responsibility it expresses, and these goods are possible in homosexual as well as heterosexual relations. Opponents might reply that homosexuals are often promiscuous, and hence less likely to realize the goods of love and responsibility. The reply to this claim might consist in an empirical showing to the contrary, or in the observation that the existence of promiscuity does not argue against the moral worth of homosexuality as such, only against certain instances of it.[49] Heterosexuals also engage in promiscuity and other practices at odds with the goods that confer on sexuality its moral worth, but this fact does not lead us to abhor heterosexuality as such. And so on.

My point is not to offer a full argument for the moral permissibility of homosexuality, only to suggest the way such an argument might proceed. Like Rawls's argument for the difference principle, it would proceed by seeking a reflective equilibrium between our principles and considered judgments, adjusting each in the light of the other. That the argument for the morality of homosexuality, unlike the argument for the difference principle, explicitly addresses claims about human ends and conceptions of the good does not mean that the same method of moral reasoning cannot proceed. It is unlikely, of course, that such moral reasoning would produce conclusive or irrefutable answers to moral and religious controversies. But as Rawls acknowledges, such reasoning does not produce irrefutable answers to questions of justice either; a more modest notion of justification is appropriate. "In philosophy questions at the most fundamental level are not usually settled by conclusive argument," writes Rawls, referring to arguments about justice. "What is obvious to some persons and accepted as a basic idea is unintelligible to others. The way to resolve the matter is to consider after due reflection which view, when fully worked out, offers the most coherent and convincing account" (p. 53). The same could be said of arguments about comprehensive moralities.

If it is possible to reason about the good as well as the right, then political liberalism's claim for the asymmetry between the right and good is undermined. For political liberalism, this asymmetry rests on the assumption that our moral and religious disagreements reflect a "fact of reasonable pluralism" that our disagreements about justice do not. What enables Rawls to maintain that our disagreements about distributive justice do not amount to a "fact of reasonable pluralism" is the strength of the arguments he advances on behalf of the difference principle and against libertarianism. But the same could be said of other controversies, including, conceivably, some moral and religious controversies. The public culture of democratic societies includes controversies about justice and comprehensive moralities alike. If government can affirm the justice of redistributive policies even in the face of disagreement by libertarians, why cannot government affirm in law, say, the moral legitimacy of homosexuality, even in the face of disagreement by those who regard homosexuality as sin?[50] Is Milton Friedman's objection to redistributive policies a less "reasonable pluralism" than Pat Robertson's objection to gay rights?

With morality as with justice, the mere fact of disagreement is no evidence of the "reasonable pluralism" that gives rise to the demand that government must be neutral. There is no reason in principle why in any given case, we might not conclude that, on due reflection, some moral or religious doctrines are more plausible than others. In such cases, we would not expect all disagreement to disappear, nor would we rule out the possibility that further deliberation might one day lead us to revise our view. But neither would we have grounds to insist that our deliberations about justice and rights may make no reference to moral or religious ideals.

The Limits of Liberal Public Reason

Whether it is possible to reason our way to agreement on any given moral or political controversy is not something we can know until we try. This is why it cannot be said in advance that controversies about comprehensive moralities reflect a "fact of reasonable pluralism" that controversies about justice do not. Whether a moral or political controversy reflects reasonable but incompatible conceptions of the good, or whether it can be resolved by due reflection and deliberation, can only be determined by reflecting and deliberating. But this raises a further difficulty with political liberalism. For the political life it describes leaves little room for the kind of public deliberation necessary to test the plausibility of contending comprehensive moralities—to persuade others of the merits of our moral ideals, to be persuaded by others of the merits of theirs.

Although political liberalism upholds the right to freedom of speech, it severely limits the kinds of arguments that are legitimate contributions to political debate, especially debate about constitutional essentials and basic justice.[51] This limitation reflects the priority of the right over the good. Not only may government not endorse one or another conception of the good, but citizens may not even introduce into political discourse their comprehensive moral or religious convictions, at least when debating matters of justice and rights (pp. 15–16).[52] Rawls maintains that this limitation is required by the "ideal of public reason" (p. 218). According to this ideal, political discourse should be conducted solely in terms of "political values" that all citizens can reasonably be expected to accept. Because citizens of democratic societies do not share comprehensive moral and religious conceptions, public reason should not refer to such conceptions (pp. 216–220).

The limits of public reason do not apply, Rawls allows, to our personal deliberations about political questions, or to the discussions we may have as members of associations such as churches and universities, where "religious, philosophical, and moral considerations" (p. 215) may properly play a role.

> But the ideal of public reason does hold for citizens when they engage in political advocacy in the public forum, and thus for members of political parties and for candidates in their campaigns and for other groups who support them. It holds equally for how citizens are to vote in elections when constitutional essentials and matters of basic justice are at stake. Thus, the ideal of public reason not only governs the public discourse of elections insofar as the issues involve those fundamental questions, but also how citizens are to cast their vote on these questions. (p. 215)

How can we know whether our political arguments meet the requirements of public reason, suitably shorn of any reliance on moral or religious convictions? Rawls offers a novel test. "To check whether we are following public reason we might ask: how would our argument strike us presented in the form of a supreme court opinion?" (p. 254). For citizens of a democracy to allow their political discourse about fundamental questions to be informed by moral and religious ideals is no more legitimate, Rawls suggests, than for a judge to read his or her moral and religious beliefs into the Constitution.

The restrictive character of this notion of public reason can be seen by considering the sorts of political arguments it would rule out. In the debate about abortion rights, those who believe that the fetus is a person from the moment of conception and that abortion is therefore murder could not seek to persuade their fellow citizens of this view in open political debate. Nor could they vote for a law that would restrict abortion on the basis of this moral or religious conviction. Although adherents of the Catholic teaching on abortion could discuss the issue of abortion rights in religious terms within their church, they could not do so in a political campaign, or on the floor of the state legislature, or in the halls of Congress. Nor for that matter could opponents of the Catholic teaching on abortion argue their case in the political arena. Relevant though it clearly is to the question of abortion rights, Catholic moral doctrine cannot be debated in the political arena that political liberalism defines.

The restrictive character of liberal public reason can also be seen in the debate about gay rights. At first glance, these restrictions might seem a service to toleration. Those who consider homosexuality immoral and therefore unworthy of the privacy rights accorded heterosexual intimacy could not legitimately voice their views in public debate. Nor could they act on their belief by voting against laws that would protect gay men and lesbians from discrimination. These beliefs reflect comprehensive moral and religious convictions and so may not play a part in political discourse about matters of justice.

But the demands of public reason also limit the arguments that can be advanced in support of gay rights, and so restrict the range of reasons that can be invoked on behalf of toleration. Those who oppose antisodomy laws of the kind at issue in *Bowers v. Hardwick*[53] cannot argue that the moral judgments embodied in those laws are wrong, only that the law is wrong to embody any moral judgments at all.[54] Advocates of gay rights cannot contest the substantive moral judgment lying behind antisodomy laws or seek, through open political debate, to persuade their fellow citizens that homosexuality is morally permissible, for any such argument would violate the canons of liberal public reason.

The restrictive character of liberal public reason is also illustrated by the arguments offered by American abolitionists of the 1830s and 1840s. Rooted in evangelical Protestantism, the abolitionist movement argued for the immediate emancipation of the slaves on the grounds that slavery is a heinous sin.[55] Like the argument of some present-day Catholics against abortion rights, the abolitionist case against slavery was explicitly based on a comprehensive moral and religious doctrine.

In a puzzling passage, Rawls tries to argue that the abolitionist case against slavery, religious though it was, did not violate the ideal of liberal public reason. If a society is not well-ordered, he explains, it may be necessary to resort to comprehensive moralities in order to bring about a society in which public discussion is conducted solely in terms of "political values" (p. 251 n.41). The religious arguments of the abolitionists can be justified as hastening the day when religious arguments would no longer play a legitimate role in public discourse. The abolitionists "did not go against the ideal of public reason," Rawls concludes, "provided they thought, or on reflection would have thought (as they certainly could have thought), that the comprehensive reasons they appealed to were required to give sufficient strength to the political conception to be subsequently realized" (p. 251).

It is difficult to know what to make of this argument. There is little reason to suppose, and I do not think Rawls means to suggest, that the abolitionists opposed slavery on secular political grounds and simply used religious arguments to win popular support. Nor is there reason to think that the abolitionists sought by their agitation to make a world safe for secular political discourse. Nor can it be assumed that, even in retrospect, the abolitionists would take pride in having contributed, by their religious arguments against slavery, to the emergence of a society inhospitable to religious argument in political debate. If anything the opposite is more likely the case, that by advancing religious arguments against so conspicuous an injustice as slavery, the evangelicals who inspired the abolitionist movement were hoping to encourage Americans to view other political questions in moral and religious terms as well. In any case, it is reasonable to suppose that the abolitionists meant what they said, that slavery is wrong because it is contrary to God's law, a heinous sin, and that this is the reason it should be ended. Absent some extraordinary assumptions, it is difficult to interpret their argument as consistent with the priority of the right over the good, or with the ideal of public reason advanced by political liberalism.

The cases of abortion, gay rights, and abolitionism illustrate the severe restrictions liberal public reason would impose on political debate. Rawls argues that these restrictions are justified as essential to the maintenance of a just society, in which citizens are governed by principles they may reasonably be expected to endorse, even in the light of their conflicting comprehensive moralities. Although public reason requires that citizens decide fundamental political questions without reference "to the whole truth as they see it" (p. 216), this restriction is justified by the political values, such as civility and mutual respect, that it makes possible. "The political values realized by a well-ordered constitutional regime are very great values and not easily overridden and the ideals they express are not to be lightly abandoned" (p. 218). Rawls compares his case for restrictive public reason with the case for restrictive rules of evidence in criminal trials. There too we agree to decide without reference to the whole truth as we know it—through illegally obtained evidence, for example—in order to advance other goods (pp. 218–219).

The analogy between liberal public reason and restrictive rules of evidence is instructive. Setting aside the whole truth as we know it carries moral and political costs, for criminal trials and for public reason alike. Whether those costs are worth incurring depends on how significant they are compared to the goods they make possible, and whether those goods can be secured in some other way. To assess restrictive rules of evidence, for example, we need to know how many criminals go free as a result and whether less restrictive rules would unduly burden innocent persons suspected of a crime, lead to undesirable law enforcement practices, violate important ideals such as respect for privacy (exclusionary rule) and spousal intimacy (spousal privilege), and so on. We arrive at rules of evidence by weighing the importance of deciding in the light of the whole truth against the importance of the ideals that would be sacrificed if all evidence were admissible.

Similarly, to assess restrictive rules of public reason, we need to weigh their moral and political costs against the political values they are said to make possible; we must also ask whether these political values—of toleration, civility, and mutual respect—could be achieved under less-restrictive rules of public reason. Although political liberalism refuses to weigh the political values it affirms against competing values that may arise from within comprehensive moralities, the case for restrictive rules of public reason must presuppose some such comparison.

The costs of liberal public reason are of two kinds. The strictly moral costs depend on the validity and importance of the moral and religious doctrines liberal public reason requires us to set aside when deciding questions of justice. These costs will necessarily vary from case to case. They will be at their highest when a political conception of justice sanctions toleration of a grave moral wrong, such as slavery in the case of Douglas's argument for popular sovereignty. In the case of abortion, the moral cost of bracketing is high if the Catholic doctrine is correct, otherwise much lower. This suggests that, even given the moral and political importance of toleration, the argument for tolerating a given practice must take some account of the moral status of the practice, as well as the good of avoiding social conflict, letting people decide for themselves, and so on.

This way of thinking about the moral cost of liberal public reason is admittedly at odds with political liberalism itself. Although Rawls repeatedly states that a political conception of justice expresses values that normally outweigh whatever other values conflict with them (pp. 138, 146, 156, 218), he also insists that this involves no substantive comparison of the political values to the moral and religious values they override.

> We need not consider the claims of political justice against the claims of this or that comprehensive view; nor need we say that political values are intrinsically more important than other values and that is why the latter are overridden. Having to say that is just what we hope to avoid. (p. 157)

But because political liberalism allows that comprehensive moral and religious doctrines can be true, such comparisons cannot reasonably be avoided.

Beyond the moral costs of liberal public reason are certain political costs. These costs are becoming increasingly apparent in the politics of those countries, notably the United States, whose public discourse most closely approximates the ideal of public reason advanced by political liberalism. With a few notable exceptions, such as the civil rights movement, American political discourse in recent decades has come to reflect the liberal resolve that government be neutral on moral and religious questions, that fundamental questions of public policy be debated and decided without reference to any particular conception of the good.[56] But democratic politics cannot long abide a public life as abstract and decorous, as detached from moral purposes, as Supreme Court opinions are supposed to be. A politics that brackets morality and religion too completely soon generates its own disenchantment. Where political discourse lacks moral resonance, the yearning for a public life of larger meanings finds undesirable expressions. Groups like the Moral Majority seek to clothe the naked public square with narrow, intolerant moralisms. Fundamentalists rush in where liberals fear to tread. The disenchantment also assumes more secular forms. Absent a political agenda that addresses the moral dimension of public questions, public attention becomes riveted on the private vices of public officials. Public discourse becomes increasingly preoccupied with the scandalous, the sensational, and the confessional as purveyed by tabloids, talk shows, and eventually the mainstream media as well.

It cannot be said that the public philosophy of political liberalism is wholly responsible for these tendencies. But its vision of public reason is too spare to contain the moral energies of a vital democratic life. It thus creates a moral void that opens the way for the intolerant and the trivial and other misguided moralisms.

If liberal public reason is too restrictive, it remains to ask whether a more spacious public reason would sacrifice the ideals that political liberalism seeks to promote, notably mutual respect among citizens who hold conflicting moral and religious views. Here it is necessary to distinguish two conceptions of mutual respect. On the liberal conception, we respect our fellow citizens' moral and religious convictions by ignoring them (for political purposes), by leaving them undisturbed, or by carrying on political debate without reference to them. To admit moral and religious ideals into political debate about justice would undermine mutual respect in this sense.

But this is not the only, or perhaps even the most plausible way of understanding the mutual respect on which democratic citizenship depends. On a different conception of respect—call it the deliberative conception—we respect our fellow citizen's moral and religious convictions by engaging, or attending to them—sometimes by challenging and contesting them, sometimes by listening and learning from them—especially if those convictions bear on important political questions. There is no guarantee that a deliberative mode of respect will lead in any given case to agreement or even to appreciation for the moral and religious convictions of others. It is always possible that learning more about a moral or religious doctrine will lead us to like it less. But the respect of deliberation and engagement affords a more spacious public reason than liberalism allows. It is also a more suitable ideal for a pluralist society. To the extent that our moral and religious disagreements reflect the ultimate plurality of human goods, a deliberative mode of respect will better enable us to appreciate the distinctive goods our different lives express.

twenty-nine

REMEMBERING RAWLS

John Rawls, America's greatest political philosopher, died last week at the age of 81. Rawls taught philosophy at Harvard from 1962 to 1994. He is best known for his book *A Theory of Justice* (1971), which offers the most compelling account of liberal political principles since John Stuart Mill. In the 1950s and 1960s, Anglo-American political theory was virtually moribund, consigned to irrelevance by linguistic analysis and moral relativism. Rawls revived political theory by showing that it was possible to argue rationally about justice, rights, and political obligation. He inspired a new generation to take up classic questions of morality and politics.

A Theory of Justice is not an easy read. But its distinctive contribution can be seen in the way it develops three key ideas: individual rights, the social contract, and equality. Before Rawls wrote, the dominant conception of justice in the English-speaking world was utilitarian: Laws and public policies should seek the greatest good for the greatest number. Rawls rejected this view as failing to respect individual rights. Suppose, for example, that a large majority despises a minority religion and wants it banned. Utilitarian principles might support the ban. But Rawls argued that certain rights are so important that the desires of the majority should not override them.

If rights cannot be based on utilitarian principles, how can they be justified? Rawls answered this question with a version of social-contract theory based on a novel thought experiment: Imagine making a social contract without knowing whether we are rich or poor; strong or weak; healthy or unhealthy; without knowing our race, religion, gender, or class. The principles we would choose behind this "veil of ignorance" would be just, Rawls argued, because they would not be tainted by unfair bargaining conditions. If we imagined ourselves behind the veil of ignorance, Rawls maintained, we would choose two principles to govern society. The first would require equal basic liberties for all citizens (speech, association, religion). The second would permit only those inequalities of income and wealth that work to the advantage of the least well-off members of society. So it might be just for doctors to make more money than janitors, for example, but only if such pay differentials were necessary to attract talented people to medicine, and only if doing so helped the least advantaged members of society. This is Rawls's famous "difference principle."

Some critics of Rawls's egalitarianism reply that people behind the veil of ignorance might gamble on inequality and choose a principle that gives people the right to keep whatever wealth they can accumulate. Rawls's best answer to this challenge steps outside the contract argument and draws on the moral impulse behind his theory: The reason we do not deserve, as a matter of right, the benefits that flow from the exercise of our talents is that we cannot take credit for those talents in the first place. That a market society values the skills some people happen to have is their good fortune, not a measure of their moral merit. So we should not regard the bounty and prestige the market bestows on athletes and anchormen, entrepreneurs and stockbrokers, academics and professionals, as a reward for superior virtue. Instead, we should design our tax and educational system so the accidents of nature and social circumstance work for the benefit of everyone. This challenges a meritocratic assumption that runs deep in American life: that success and virtue go hand in hand, that the United States is wealthy because it is good. If Rawls is right, the meritocratic assumption should give way to a more generous stance toward those less favored by fortune and circumstance.

Shortly after his retirement, Rawls joined me for a discussion with students in an undergraduate course I teach on justice. I asked him about Immanuel Kant, his philosophical hero. Despite the similarities in their philosophies, did Kant go wrong in concluding that the equality of human beings is "perfectly consistent with the utmost inequality" of material possessions? Rawls answered with a wry evasion: "I want to say that Kant is really, truly a very great man. One doesn't even think of criticizing him without being aware of that. No, I wouldn't say that Kant goes wrong . . . He was ahead of his time. That you get anything at all out of East Prussia in the eighteenth century is wonderful. And that you get Immanuel Kant is a miracle."

It is something of a miracle, or at least a surprise, to find an American philosopher mentioned in the company of Thomas Hobbes, John Locke, Jean-Jacques Rousseau, Karl Marx, and John Stuart Mill. Political philosophy is one of the few intellectual fields to which America's contribution has been meager. Some attribute this dearth to the success of American democracy. Wars of religion, decaying empires, failed states, and class struggles offer richer fare for philosophy than do stable institutions. This may be why the most notable expressions of American political thought have come not from philosophers but from participants in American public life: Thomas Jefferson, James Madison, Alexander Hamilton, John C. Calhoun, Abraham Lincoln, Frederick Douglass, Jane Addams, Oliver Wendell Holmes, Louis D. Brandeis. Rawls is one of the few nonpractitioners of politics to loom large in American political thought.

When Alexis de Tocqueville visited the United States in the 1830s, he observed that "no country in the civilized world pays less attention to philosophy than the United States." Tocqueville's observation was borne out 170 years later by the public notice of Rawls's death.

The major newspapers of Europe—*Le Monde* in France, *The Times, The Guardian, The Independent,* and *The Daily Telegraph* in England—all marked the passing of America's political philosopher with more extensive obituaries than appeared in *The New York Times* or *The Washington Post.* This may suggest that Rawls's egalitarianism has more resonance for European welfare states than for America's market-driven society. But it also reflects the fact that philosophy continues to play a more prominent role in the public discourse of the Old World than the New.

Rawls's modesty was legendary, as was his kindness to students and junior colleagues. I first read *A Theory of Justice* as a graduate student at Oxford in 1975 and made it the subject of my dissertation. When I came to Harvard as a young assistant professor in the government department, I had never met the figure whose great work on liberalism I had studied. Shortly after I arrived, my phone rang. A hesitant voice on the other end said, "This is John Rawls, R-A-W-L-S." It was as if God himself had called to invite me to lunch and spelled his name just in case I didn't know who he was.

thirty

THE LIMITS OF
COMMUNITARIANISM

WHERE COMMUNITARIANISM GOES WRONG

Along with the works of other contemporary critics of liberal political theory, notably Alasdair MacIntyre,[1] Charles Taylor,[2] and Michael
Walzer,[3] my book *Liberalism and the Limits of Justice (LLJ)* has come
to be identified with the "communitarian" critique of rights-oriented
liberalism. Since part of my argument is that contemporary liberalism offers an inadequate account of community, the term fits to
some extent. In many respects, however, the label is misleading. The
"liberal-communitarian" debate that has raged among political philosophers in recent years describes a range of issues, and I do not always find myself on the communitarian side.

The debate is sometimes cast as an argument between those who
prize individual liberty and those who think the values of the community or the will of the majority should always prevail, or between
those who believe in universal human rights and those who insist
there is no way to criticize or judge the values that inform different
cultures and traditions. Insofar as "communitarianism" is another
name for majoritarianism, or for the idea that rights should rest on
the values that predominate in any given community at any given
time, it is not a view I would defend.

What is at stake in the debate between Rawlsian liberalism and
the view I advance in *LLJ* is not whether rights are important but

whether rights can be identified and justified in a way that does not presuppose any particular conception of the good life. At issue is not whether individual or communal claims should carry greater weight but whether the principles of justice that govern the basic structure of society can be neutral with respect to the competing moral and religious convictions its citizens espouse. The fundamental question, in other words, is whether the right is prior to the good.

For Rawls, as for Kant, the priority of the right over the good stands for two claims, and it is important to distinguish them. The first is the claim that certain individual rights are so important that even the general welfare cannot override them. The second is the claim that the principles of justice that specify our rights do not depend for their justification on any particular conception of the good life, or, as Rawls has put it more recently, on any "comprehensive" moral or religious conception. It is the second claim for the priority of right, not the first, that *LLJ* seeks to challenge.

The notion that justice is relative to the good, not independent of it, connects *LLJ* to writings by others commonly identified as the "communitarian critics" of liberalism. But there are two versions of the claim that justice is relative to the good, and only one of them is "communitarian" in the usual sense. Much of the confusion that has beset the liberal-communitarian debate arises from failing to distinguish the two versions.

One way of linking justice with conceptions of the good holds that principles of justice derive their moral force from values commonly espoused or widely shared in a particular community or tradition. This way of linking justice and the good is communitarian in the sense that the values of the community define what counts as just or unjust. On this view, the case for recognizing a right depends on showing that such a right is implicit in the shared understandings that inform the tradition or community in question. There can be disagreement, of course, about what rights the shared understandings of a particular tradition actually support; social critics and political reformers can interpret traditions in ways that challenge prevailing practices. But these arguments always take the form of recalling a community to itself, of appealing to ideals implicit but unrealized in a common project or tradition.

A second way of linking justice with conceptions of the good holds that principles of justice depend for their justification on the moral worth or intrinsic good of the ends they serve. On this view, the case for recognizing a right depends on showing that it honors or advances some important human good. Whether this good happens to be widely prized or implicit in the traditions of the community would not be decisive. The second way of tying justice to conceptions of the good is therefore not, strictly speaking, communitarian. Since it rests the case for rights on the moral importance of the purposes or ends rights promote, it is better described as teleological, or (in the jargon of contemporary philosophy) perfectionist. Aristotle's political theory is an example: Before we can define people's rights or investigate "the nature of the ideal constitution," he writes, "it is necessary for us first to determine the nature of the most desirable way of life. As long as that remains obscure, the nature of the ideal constitution must also remain obscure."[4]

Of the two ways of linking justice to conceptions of the good, the first is insufficient. The mere fact that certain practices are sanctioned by the traditions of a particular community is not enough to make them just. To make justice the creature of convention is to deprive it of its critical character, even if allowance is made for competing interpretations of what the relevant tradition requires. Arguments about justice and rights have an unavoidably judgmental aspect. Liberals who think the case for rights should be neutral toward substantive moral and religious doctrines and communitarians who think rights should rest on prevailing social values make a similar mistake; both try to avoid passing judgment on the content of the ends that rights promote. But these are not the only alternatives. A third possibility, more plausible in my view, is that rights depend for their justification on the moral importance of the ends they serve.

THE RIGHT TO RELIGIOUS LIBERTY

Consider the case of religious liberty. Why should the free exercise of religion enjoy special constitutional protection? The liberal might reply that religious liberty is important for the same reason individual liberty in general is important—so that people may be free to live autonomously, to choose and pursue their values for themselves. According to this view, government should uphold religious liberty in order to respect persons as free and independent selves, capable of choosing their own religious convictions. The respect the liberal invokes is not, strictly speaking, respect for religion, but respect for the self whose religion it is, or respect for the dignity that consists in the capacity to choose one's religion freely. On the liberal view, religious beliefs are worthy of respect, not in virtue of their content but instead in virtue of being "the product of free and voluntary choice."[5]

This way of defending religious liberty puts the right before the good; it tries to secure the right to religious freedom without passing judgment on the content of people's beliefs or on the moral importance of religion as such. But the right to religious liberty is not best understood as a particular case of a more general right to individual autonomy. Assimilating religious liberty to a general right to choose one's own values misdescribes the nature of religious conviction and obscures the reasons for according the free exercise of religion special constitutional protection. Construing all religious convictions as products of choice may miss the role that religion plays in the lives of those for whom the observance of religious duties is a constitutive end, essential to their good and indispensable to their identity. Some may view their religious beliefs as matters of choice, others not. What makes a religious belief worthy of respect is not its mode of acquisition—be it choice, revelation, persuasion, or habituation—but its place in a good life, or the qualities of character it promotes, or (from a political point of view) its tendency to cultivate the habits and dispositions that make good citizens.

To place religious convictions on a par with the various interests and ends an independent self may choose makes it difficult to distinguish between claims of conscience, on the one hand, and mere preferences, on the other. Once this distinction is lost, the right to demand of the state a special justification for laws that burden the free exercise of religion is bound to appear as nothing more weighty than "a private right to ignore generally applicable laws."[6] If an orthodox Jew is granted the right to wear a yarmulke while on duty in an air force health clinic, then what about servicemen who want to wear other head coverings prohibited by military dress codes?[7] If Native Americans have a right to the sacramental use of peyote, then what can be said to those who would violate state drug laws for recreational purposes?[8] If Sabbath observers are granted the right to schedule their day off from work on the day corresponding to their Sabbath, does not the same right have to be accorded those who want a certain day off to watch football?[9]

Assimilating religious liberty to liberty in general reflects the liberal aspiration to neutrality. But this generalizing tendency does not always serve religious liberty well. It confuses the pursuit of preferences with the performance of duties. It therefore ignores the special concern of religious liberty with the predicament of conscientiously encumbered selves—claimed by duties they cannot choose to renounce, even in the face of civil obligations that may conflict.

But why, it might be asked, should the state accord special respect to conscientiously encumbered selves? Part of the reason is that for government to burden practices central to the self-definition of its citizens is to frustrate them more profoundly than to deprive them of interests less central to the projects that give meaning to their lives. But encumbrance as such is not a sufficient basis for special respect.

Defining projects and commitments can range from the admirable and heroic to the obsessive and demonic. Situated selves can display solidarity and depth of character or prejudice and narrow-mindedness.

The case for according special protection to the free exercise of religion presupposes that religious belief, as characteristically practiced in a particular society, produces ways of being and acting that are worthy of honor and appreciation—either because they are admirable in themselves or because they foster qualities of character that make good citizens. Unless there were reason to think religious beliefs and practices contribute to morally admirable ways of life, the case for a right to religious liberty would be weakened. Pragmatic considerations would, of course, remain; upholding religious liberty could still be justified as a way of avoiding the civil strife that can result when church and state are too closely intertwined. But the moral justification for a right to religious liberty is unavoidably judgmental; the case for the right cannot wholly be detached from a substantive judgment about the moral worth of the practice it protects.

THE RIGHT TO FREE SPEECH

The link between rights and the goods rights protect is also illustrated by recent debates about free speech and hate speech. Should neo-Nazis have the right to march in Skokie, Illinois, a community with large numbers of Holocaust survivors?[10] Should white-supremacist groups be allowed to promulgate their racist views?[11] Liberals argue that government must be neutral toward the opinions its citizens espouse. Government can regulate the time, place, and manner of speech—it can ban a noisy rally in the middle of the night—but it cannot regulate the content of speech. To ban offensive or unpopular speech imposes on some the values of others and so fails to respect each citizen's capacity to choose and express his or her own opinions.

Liberals can, consistent with their view, restrict speech likely to cause significant harm—violence, for example. But in the case of hate speech, what counts as harm is constrained by the liberal conception of the person. According to this conception, my dignity consists not in any social roles I inhabit but instead in my capacity to choose my roles and identities for myself. But this means that my dignity could never be damaged by an insult directed against a group with which I identify. No hate speech could constitute harm in itself, for on the liberal view, the highest respect is the self-respect of a self independent of its aims and attachments. For the unencumbered self, the grounds of self-respect are antecedent to any particular ties and attachments, and so beyond the reach of an insult to "my people." The liberal would therefore oppose restrictions on hate speech, except where it is likely to provoke some actual physical harm—some harm independent of the speech itself.

The communitarian might reply that the liberal conception of harm is too narrow. For people who understand themselves as defined by the ethnic or religious group to which they belong, an insult to the group can inflict a harm as real and as damaging as some physical harms. For Holocaust survivors, the neo-Nazi march was aimed at provoking fears and memories of unspeakable horrors that reached to the core of their identities and life stories.

But to acknowledge the harm that hate speech can inflict does not establish that the speech should be restricted. The harm such speech inflicts has to be weighed against the good of upholding free speech. With speech as with religion, it is not enough simply to invoke the claims of thickly constituted selves. What matters is the moral importance of the speech in relation to the moral status of the settled identities the speech would disrupt or offend. If Skokie could keep out the Nazis, why could not the segregationist communities of the South keep out civil-rights marchers of the 1950s and 1960s? The Southern segregationists did not want Martin Luther King, Jr., to march in their communities any more than the residents of Skokie wanted the neo-Nazis to march in theirs. Like the Holocaust survivors, the segregationists could claim to be thickly constituted selves, bound by common memories that would be deeply offended by the marchers and their message.

Is there a principled way of distinguishing the two cases? For liberals who insist on being neutral with respect to the content of speech, and for communitarians who define rights according to the prevailing values of the communities in question, the answer must be no. The liberal would uphold free speech in both cases, and the communitarian would override it. But the need to decide both cases in the same way displays the folly of the nonjudgmental impulse liberals and communitarians share.

The obvious ground for distinguishing the cases is that the neo-Nazis promote genocide and hate, whereas Martin Luther King, Jr., sought civil rights for blacks. The difference consists in the content of the speech, in the nature of the cause. There is also a difference in the moral worth of the communities whose integrity was at stake. The shared memories of the Holocaust survivors deserve a moral deference that the solidarity of the segregationists does not. Moral discriminations such as these are consistent with common sense but at odds with the version of liberalism that asserts the priority of the right over the good and the version of communitarianism that rests the case for rights on communal values alone.

If the right to free speech depends for its justification on a substantive moral judgment about the importance of speech in relation to the risks it entails, it does not follow that judges should try, in each particular case, to assess the merits of the speech for themselves. Nor, in every case involving religious liberty, should judges undertake to assess the moral importance of the religious practice at issue. On any theory of rights, certain general rules and doctrines are desirable to spare judges the need to recur to first principles in every case that comes before them. But sometimes, in hard cases, judges cannot apply such rules without appealing directly to the moral purposes that justify rights in the first place.

One striking example is the opinion of Judge Frank Johnson in the 1965 case that permitted Martin Luther King's historic march from Selma to Montgomery. Alabama Governor George Wallace tried to prevent the march. Judge Johnson acknowledged that the states had the right to regulate the use of their highways, and that a mass march along a public highway reached "to the outer limits of what is constitutionally allowed." Nevertheless, he ordered the state to permit the march, on grounds of the justice of its cause: "The extent of the right to assemble, demonstrate and march peaceably along the highways," he wrote, "should be commensurate with the enormity of the wrongs that are being protested and petitioned against. In this case, the wrongs are enormous. The extent of the right to demonstrate against these wrongs should be determined accordingly."[12]

Judge Johnson's decision was not content-neutral; it would not have helped the Nazis in Skokie. But it aptly illustrates the difference between the liberal approach to rights and the approach that would rest rights on a substantive moral judgment of the ends rights advance.

NOTES
CREDITS
INDEX

19. Is There a Right to Assisted Suicide?

1. See "Assisted Suicide: The Philosophers' Brief," *New York Review of Books*, vol. 44, March 27, 1997.

21. Moral Argument and Liberal Toleration

1. I do not defend the stronger claim that the morality (or immorality) of a practice is the only relevant reason in deciding whether there should be a law against it.
2. 410 U.S. 113 (1973).
3. 478 U.S. 186 (1986).
4. Roe v. Wade, 410 U.S. 113, 162 (1973).
5. Ibid., 153.
6. Thornburgh v. American College of Obstetricians & Gynecologists, 476 U.S. 747, 777 (1986) (Stevens, J., concurring).
7. Eichbaum, "Towards an Autonomy-Based Theory of Constitutional Privacy: Beyond the Ideology of Familial Privacy," 14 *Harv. C.R.-C.L. L. Rev.* 361, 362, 365 (1979).
8. Richards, "The Individual, the Family, and the Constitution: A Jurisprudential Perspective," 55 *N.Y.U. L. Rev.* 1, 31 (1980).
9. Karst, "The Freedom of Intimate Association," 89 *Yale L.J.* 624, 641 (1980). For articles discussing the connection between privacy and autonomy rights, see also Henkin, "Privacy and Autonomy," 74 *Colum. L. Rev.* 1410 (1974); Smith, "The Constitution and Autonomy," 60 *Tex. L. Rev.* 175 (1982); Wilkinson III and White, "Constitutional Protection for Personal Lifestyles," 62 *Cornell L. Rev.* 563 (1977).
10. Karst, "The Freedom of Intimate Association," 641.
11. Carey v. Population Services Int'l, 431 U.S. 678, 687 (1977).

12. Thornburgh v. American College of Obstetricians & Gynecologists, 476 U.S. 747, 772 (1986).

13. Doe v. Bolton, 410 U.S. 179, 211 (1973) (Douglas, J., concurring) (emphasis omitted).

14. Bowers v. Hardwick, 478 U.S. 186, 205 (1986) (Blackmun, J., dissenting).

15. Whalen v. Roe, 429 U.S. 589, 599–600 (1977).

16. Warren and Brandeis, "The Right to Privacy," 4 *Harv. L. Rev.* 193 (1890).

17. Ibid., 195–196.

18. Prosser, "Privacy," 48 *Calif. L. Rev.* 383 (1960) (discussing the ensuing recognition and development of a right to privacy).

19. 367 U.S. 497 (1961).

20. Ibid., 509.

21. Ibid., 519–521 (Douglas, J., dissenting).

22. Ibid., 519.

23. Ibid., 545 (Harlan, J., dissenting).

24. Ibid., 545–546.

25. Ibid., 553.

26. Ibid., 554.

27. 381 U.S. 479 (1965).

28. Ibid., 485–486.

29. Ibid., 486.

30. 405 U.S. 438 (1972).

31. In fact, the case arose when a man was convicted for giving away a contraceptive device at a public lecture. Ibid., 440.

32. Ibid., 453.

33. *Griswold,* 381 U.S. at 485.

34. *Eisenstadt,* 405 U.S. at 453. The Court's opinion in *Eisenstadt* camouflages the shift from the old privacy to the new with a false hypothetical premise: "If under *Griswold* the distribution of contraceptives to married persons cannot be prohibited, a ban on distribution to unmarried persons would be equally impermissible." Ibid. But *Griswold* did not hold that distribution to married persons cannot be prohibited.

35. 410 U.S. 113 (1973).

36. Ibid., 153.

37. Carey v. Population Services Int'l, 431 U.S. 678 (1977).

38. Ibid., 687.

39. Ibid.

40. Ibid. (quoting *Eisenstadt,* 405 U.S. at 453) (emphasis added in *Carey*).

41. Ibid. (quoting *Roe,* 410 U.S. at 153) (emphasis added in *Carey*).

42. Ibid.

43. Ibid., 688.

44. Thornburgh v. American College of Obstetricians, 476 U.S. 747, 772 (1986).

45. Planned Parenthood v. Casey, 505 U.S. 833, 851 (1992).

46. Bowers v. Hardwick, 478 U.S. 186, 190–191 (1986).

47. Ibid., 196.

48. Ibid.

49. Ibid., 204 (Blackmun, J., dissenting) (quoting Thornburgh v. American College of Obstetricians & Gynecologists, 476 U.S. at 777 n.5 (Stevens, J., concurring) (quoting Fried, "Correspondence," 6 *Phil. and Pub. Aff.* 288–289 [1977])).

50. Ibid., 205.

51. Ibid.

52. Ibid., 211.

53. Ibid. In striking down a similar sodomy law, the New York Court of Appeals clearly expressed the idea that government must be neutral among competing conceptions of the good. "It is not the function of the Penal Law in our governmental policy to provide either a medium for the articulation or the apparatus for the intended enforcement of moral or theological values." People v. Onofre, 51 N.Y.2d 476, 488 n.3, 415 N.E.2d 936, 940 n.3, 434 N.Y.S.2d 947, 951 n.3 (1980), *cert. denied,* 451 U.S. 987 (1981).

54. Rawls, "Justice as Fairness: Political Not Metaphysical," 14 *Phil. and Pub. Aff.* 223, 245 (1985); Rorty, "The Priority of Democracy to Philosophy," in *The Virginia Statute for Religious Freedom,* 257 (M. Peterson and R. Vaughan, eds., 1988).

55. 410 U.S. 113 (1973).

56. Ibid., 159.

57. Ibid.

58. Ibid., 160–162.

59. Ibid., 162.

60. Ibid.

61. Ibid., 163.

62. 476 U.S. 747 (1986).

63. Ibid., 797 (White, J., dissenting).

64. Ibid., 796.

65. Ibid., 790. Justice Harlan suggested a similar way of bracketing the moral controversy over contraception in Poe v. Ullman, 367 U.S. 497, 547 (1961) (Harlan, J., dissenting): "The very controversial nature of these questions would, I think, require us to hesitate long before concluding that the Constitution precluded Connecticut from choosing as it has among these various views."

66. Ibid., 777 (Stevens, J., concurring).

67. Ibid., 777–778 (quoting ibid. at 794 (White, J. dissenting)).

68. 478 U.S. 186 (1986).

69. Ibid., 191.

70. The phrases are from Griswold v. Connecticut, 381 U.S. 479, 486 (1965).

71. 478 U.S. at 205 (Blackmun, J., dissenting) (emphasis added).

72. Ibid., 206.

73. Ibid., 217 (Stevens, J., dissenting) (quoting Fitzgerald v. Porter Memorial Hospital, 523 F.2d 716, 719–720 (7th Cir. 1975), *cert. denied,* 425 U.S. 916 (1976)).

74. Ibid., 218–219.

75. Hardwick v. Bowers, 760 F.2d 1202 (11th Cir. 1985), *rev'd,* 476 U.S. 747 (1986).

76. Ibid., 1211–1212.

77. Ibid., 1212 (quoting Griswold v. Connecticut, 381 U.S. 479, 486 (1965)).

78. Ibid., 1212.

79. For individualist readings of *Griswold,* see Eisenstadt v. Baird, 405 U.S. 438, 453 (1972) and Carey v. Population Services Int'l, 431 U.S. 678, 687 (1977).

80. 394 U.S. 557 (1969).

81. Ibid., 564–566, 568 ("This right to receive information and ideas, *regardless of their social worth,* is fundamental to our free society . . . The States retain broad power to regulate obscenity; that power simply does not extend to mere possession by the individual in the privacy of his own home.") (emphasis added) (citation omitted).

82. 51 N.Y.2d 476, 415 N.E.2d 936, 434 N.Y.S.2d 947 (1980), *cert. denied,* 451 U.S. 987 (1981).

83. Ibid., 487–488, 415 N.E.2d at 939–41, 434 N.Y.S.2d at 950–951.

84. Ibid., 488 n.3, 415 N.E.2d at 940 n.3, 434 N.Y.S.2d at 951 n.3.

85. Ibid.

86. Bowers v. Hardwick, 478 U.S. 186, 191 (1986).

87. Lawrence v. Texas, 539 U.S. 558 (2003).

88. Ibid., 562.

89. Ibid., 574, quoting *Casey,* 505 U.S. 833, 851 (1992).

90. Lawrence v. Texas, 567.

91. Ibid., 575.

92. Ibid., 602.

93. Ibid., 604.

94. Ibid., 602.

23. The Procedural Republic and the Unencumbered Self

1. An excellent example of this view can be found in Samuel Huntington, *American Politics: The Promise of Disharmony* (Cambridge, Mass.: Harvard University Press, 1981). See especially his discussion of the "ideals versus institutions" gap, pp. 10–12, 39–41, 61–84, 221–262.

2. See, for example, the conceptions of a "practice" advanced by Alasdair MacIntyre and Charles Taylor. MacIntyre, *After Virtue* (Notre Dame: University of Notre Dame Press, 1981), pp. 175–209; Taylor, "Interpretation and the Sciences of Man," *Review of Metaphysics* 25 (1971), pp. 3–51.

3. John Rawls, *A Theory of Justice* (Oxford: Oxford University Press, 1971); Immanuel Kant, *Groundwork of the Metaphysics of Morals,* trans. H. J. Paton (1785; New York: Harper and Row, 1956); Kant, *Critique of Pure Reason,* trans. Norman Kemp Smith (1781, 1787; London: Macmillan, 1929); Kant, *Critique of Practical Reason,* trans. L. W. Beck (1788; Indianapolis: Bobbs-Merrill, 1956); Kant, "On the Common Saying: 'This May Be True in Theory, But It Does Not Apply in Practice,'" in Hans Reiss, ed., *Kant's Political Writings* (1793; Cambridge: Cambridge University Press, 1970). Other recent versions of the claim for the priority of the right over good can be found in Robert Nozick, *Anarchy, State, and Utopia* (New York: Basic Books, 1974); Ronald Dworkin, *Taking Rights Seriously* (London: Duckworth, 1977); Bruce Ackerman, *Social Justice in the Liberal State* (New Haven: Yale University Press, 1980).

4. This section, and the two that follow, summarize arguments developed more fully in Michael Sandel, *Liberalism and the Limits of Justice* (Cambridge: Cambridge University Press, 1982).

5. Rawls, *A Theory of Justice,* p. 3.

6. John Stuart Mill, *Utilitarianism,* in *The Utilitarians* (1893; Garden City: Doubleday, 1973), p. 465; Mill, *On Liberty,* in *The Utilitarians,* p. 485 (originally published 1849).

7. Kant, "On the Common Saying," p. 73.

8. Kant, *Groundwork,* p. 92.

9. Kant, *Critique of Practical Reason,* p. 89.

10. Kant *Groundwork,* p. 105.

11. Kant, *Critique of Practical Reason,* p. 89.

12. Kant, *Groundwork,* p. 121.

13. Rawls, "The Basic Structure as Subject," *American Philosophical Quarterly* (1977), p. 165.

14. Rawls, *A Theory of Justice,* p. 560.

15. Rawls, "Kantian Constructivism in Moral Theory," *Journal of Philosophy* 77 (1980), p. 543.

16. Mill, *On Liberty,* p. 485.

17. Rawls, *A Theory of Justice,* pp. 101–102.

18. Croly, *The Promise of American Life* (Indianapolis: Bobbs-Merrill, 1965), pp. 270–273.

19. Beer, "Liberalism and the National Idea," *The Public Interest* (Fall 1966), pp. 70–82.

20. See, for example, Laurence Tribe, *American Constitutional Law* (Mineola: The Foundation Press, 1978), pp. 2–3.

21. See Ronald Dworkin, "Liberalism," in Stuart Hampshire, ed., *Public and Private Morality* (Cambridge: Cambridge University Press, 1978), p. 136.

25. The Peril of Extinction

1. George Kateb, "Nuclear Weapons and Individual Rights," *Dissent,* Spring 1986.

26. Dewey's Liberalism and Ours

1. Robert B. Westbrook, *John Dewey and American Democracy* (Cornell University Press, 1991); Stephen Rockefeller, *John Dewey: Religious Faith*

and *Democratic Humanism* (Columbia University Press, 1991); Jennifer Welchman, *Dewey's Ethical Thought* (Cornell University Press, 1995); Debra Morris and Ian Shapiro, eds., *John Dewey: The Political Writings* (Hackett, 1993); Richard Rorty, *Consequences of Pragmatism* (University of Minnesota Press, 1982); Richard J. Bernstein, "John Dewey on Democracy," in *Philosophical Profiles: Essays in a Pragmatic Mode* (University of Pennsylvania Press, 1986), pp. 260–272.

2. *John Dewey: The Early Works,* 1882–1898, Volumes 1–5; *John Dewey: The Middle Works,* 1899–1924, Volumes 1–15; *John Dewey: The Later Works,* 1925–1953, Volumes 1–17, edited by Jo Ann Boydston (Southern Illinois University Press, 1969–1991).

3. Dewey, "The Need for a Recovery of Philosophy" (1917), in *The Middle Works,* Volume 10.

4. Ibid.

5. Dewey, *Liberalism and Social Action* (1935), in *The Later Works,* Volume 11, p. 24.

6. Ibid., p. 25.

7. Ibid., p. 44.

8. See Rorty, *Philosophy and the Mirror of Nature* (Princeton University Press, 1979), and Rorty, *Consequences of Pragmatism* (University of Minnesota Press, 1982).

9. Richard Rorty, "The Priority of Democracy to Philosophy," in Merrill D. Peterson and Robert C. Vaughan, eds., *The Virginia Statute for Religious Freedom* (Cambridge University Press, 1988), pp. 257–282.

10. Dewey, *The Public and Its Problems* (1927), in *The Later Works,* Volume 2, p. 295.

11. Ibid., p. 314.

12. Ibid., pp. 301, 330, 308.

13. Ibid., p. 303.

14. Ibid., p. 324.

15. Ibid., p. 321.

27. Mastery and Hubris in Judaism

1. Halakhic Judaism is the Judaism of those who live in accordance with the precepts of Jewish law.

2. David Hartman, *A Living Covenant: The Innovative Spirit in Traditional Judaism* (New York: The Free Press, 1985), 32.

3. Ibid., 36.

4. Ibid., 3.

5. Ibid., 98.

6. Ibid., 183.

7. Ibid., 99.

8. Ibid., 96.

9. *Midrash Terumah,* chapter 2, quoted in Noam J. Zohar, *Alternatives in Jewish Bioethics* (Albany: State University of New York Press, 1997), 20–21. On religious naturalism, see Zohar, ibid., 19–36.

10. Rabbi Joseph B. Soloveitchik, *Halakhic Man,* trans. Lawrence Kaplan (Philadelphia: Jewish Publication Society of America, 1983; originally published in Hebrew, 1944), 99.

11. Ibid., 107, 109.

12. Hartman, *Living Covenant,* 79.

13. Soloveitchik, "The Lonely Man of Faith," *Tradition* 7:2 (Summer 1965), 35–36, quoted in Hartman, *Living Covenant,* 82.

14. Hartman, *Living Covenant,* 84.

15. Ibid., 88.

16. Ibid., 257.

17. Ibid., 256.

18. Ibid., 260.

19. Ibid., 18.

20. Ibid., 260.

21. David Hartman, *A Heart of Many Rooms: Celebrating the Many Voices within Judaism* (Woodstock, Vt.: Jewish Lights Publishing, 1999), 77–78.

22. Ibid., 78.

23. Ibid., 201–202.

24. Carey Goldberg, "Who Needs Sleep? New Pill Hits Scene," *Boston Globe,* Sept. 22, 2002, A1, A20.

25. Midrash Rabbah, Genesis VIII, 4,5; quoted in Hartman, *Heart of Many Rooms,* 77.

26. Ibid., 77–78.

27. *Mishneh Torah, Avodah Zarah* II, 4; quoted in Hartman, *Heart of Many Rooms,* 106.

28. Ibid., 107.

28. Political Liberalism

1. John Rawls, *A Theory of Justice* (1971).
2. See, e.g., H. L. A. Hart, "Between Utility and Rights," in *The Idea of Freedom*, 77 (Alan Ryan, ed., 1979).
3. See Friedrich A. Hayek, *The Constitution of Liberty* (1960); Robert Nozick, *Anarchy, State, and Utopia* (1974).
4. See Bruce A. Ackerman, *Social Justice in the Liberal State*, pp. 349–378 (1980); Ronald Dworkin, *Taking Rights Seriously,* pp. 90–100, 168–177 (1977); Charles Fried, *Right and Wrong,* pp. 114–119 (1978); Charles E. Larmore, *Patterns of Moral Complexity,* pp. 42–68 (1987); Nozick, *Anarchy, State, and Utopia,* p. 33; Rawls, *A Theory of Justice,* pp. 30–32, 446–451, 560; Ronald Dworkin, "Liberalism," in *Public and Private Morality,* pp. 113, 127–136 (Stuart Hampshire, ed., 1978); Thomas Nagel, "Moral Conflict and Political Legitimacy," *Phil. and Pub. Aff.,* 16, pp. 215, 227–237 (1987).
5. See Immanuel Kant, *Critique of Pure Reason* (Norman K. Smith, trans., St. Martin's Press, 1965) (1788); Immanuel Kant, *Groundwork of the Metaphysic of Morals* (H. J. Paton, trans., Harper & Row, 3d ed., 1964) (1785); Immanuel Kant, "On the Common Saying: 'This May Be True in Theory, but It Does Not Apply in Practice,'" in *Kant's Political Writings,* pp. 61, 73–74 (Hans Reiss, ed., and H. B. Nisbet, trans., 1970); Rawls, *A Theory of Justice,* pp. 30–32, 446–451, 560.
6. See Alasdair MacIntyre, *After Virtue* (2d ed., 1984) [hereafter cited as MacIntyre, *After Virtue*]; Alasdair MacIntyre, *Is Patriotism a Virtue?: The Lindley Lecture* (1984) [hereafter cited as MacIntyre, *Is Patriotism a Virtue?*]; Alasdair MacIntyre, *Whose Justice? Which Rationality?* (1988).
7. See Charles Taylor, "The Nature and Scope of Distributive Justice," in *Philosophy and the Human Sciences, Philosophical Papers,* 2, p. 289 (1985); Charles Taylor, *Sources of the Self: The Making of the Modern Identity* (1989) [hereafter cited as Taylor, *Sources of the Self*].
8. See Michael Walzer, *Spheres of Justice: A Defense of Pluralism and Equality* (1983).
9. See Michael J. Sandel, *Liberalism and the Limits of Justice* (1982); Michael J. Sandel, "The Procedural Republic and the Unencumbered Self," *Pol. Theory,* p. 81 (1984).
10. Michael Walzer comes close to this view when he writes: "Justice is rela-

tive to social meanings . . . A given society is just if its substantive life is lived . . . in a way faithful to the shared understandings of the members." Walzer, *Spheres of Justice,* pp. 312–313. Walzer allows, however, that prevailing practices of rights can be criticized from the standpoint of alternative interpretations of a society's shared understandings. Ibid., pp. 84–91.

11. Much of the debate about liberal political philosophy in the last decade has focused on the "communitarian" critique of liberalism, or, more broadly, on the challenge to the priority of the right over the good. The best overall account of this debate is Stephen Mulhall and Adam Swift, *Liberals and Communitarians* (1992). Edited volumes on the subject include *Communitarians and Individualism* (Shlomo Avineri and Avner de-Shalit, eds., 1992); *Liberalism and Its Critics* (Michael J. Sandel, ed., 1984); *Liberalism and the Good* (R. Bruce Douglass, Gerald M. Mara, and Henry S. Richardson, eds., 1990); *Liberalism and the Moral Life* (Nancy L. Rosenblum, ed., 1989); and *Universalism vs. Communitarianism* (David Rasmussen, ed., 1990). Notable book-length works include Daniel Bell, *Communitarianism and Its Critics* (1993); Will Kymlicka, *Liberalism, Community, and Culture* (1989); Charles E. Larmore, *Patterns of Moral Complexity* (1987); and Stephen Macedo, *Liberal Virtues: Citizenship, Virtue, and Community in Liberal Constitutionalism* (1990). The vast literature on the subject includes among others: Jeremy Waldron, "Particular Values and Critical Morality," in *Liberal Rights,* 168 (1993); C. Edwin Baker, "Sandel on Rawls," *U. Pa. L. Rev.,* 133, p. 895 (1985); Sheyla Benhabib, "Autonomy, Modernity and Community: Communitarianism and Critical Social Theory in Dialogue," in *Zwischenbetrachtungen im Prozess der Aufklaerung,* p. 373 (Axel Honneth, Thomas McCarthy, Claus Offe, and Albrecht Welmer, eds., 1989); Allen E. Buchanan, "Assessing the Communitarian Critique of Liberalism," *Ethics,* 99, p. 852 (1989); Gerald Doppelt, "Is Rawls's Kantian Liberalism Coherent and Defensible?" *Ethics,* 99, p. 815 (1989); Stephen A. Gardbaum, "Law, Politics, and the Claims of Community," *Mich. L. Rev.* 90, p. 685 (1992); Emily R. Gill, "Goods, Virtues, and the Constitution of the Self," in *Liberals on Liberalism,* p. 111 (Alfonso J. Damico, ed., 1986); Amy Gutmann, "Communitarian Critics of Liberalism," *Phil. and Pub. Aff.,* 14, p. 308 (1985); H. N. Hirsch, "The Threnody of Liberalism," *Pol. Theory,* 14, p. 423 (1986); Will Kymlicka, "Liberalism and Communitarianism," *Can.*

J. *Phil.*, 18, p. 181 (1988); Will Kymlicka, "Rawls on Teleology and Deontology," *Phil. and Pub. Aff.*, 17, p. 173 (1988); Christopher Lasch, "The Communitarian Critique of Liberalism," *Soundings*, 69, p. 60 (1986); David Miller, "In What Sense Must Socialism Be Communitarian?" *Soc. Phil. and Pol.*, 6, p. 57 (1989); Chantal Mouffe, "American Liberalism and Its Critics: Rawls, Taylor, Sandel, and Walzer," *Praxis Int'l*, 8, p. 193 (1988); Patrick Neal, "A Liberal Theory of the Good?" *Can. J. Phil.*, 17, p. 567 (1987); Jeffrey Paul and Fred D. Miller, Jr., "Communitarian and Liberal Theories of the Good," *Rev. Metaphysics*, 43, p. 803 (1990); Milton C. Regan, Jr., "Community and Justice in Constitutional Theory," *Wis. L. Rev.*, 1985, p. 1073; Richard Rorty, "The Priority of Democracy to Philosophy," in *The Virginia Statute of Religious Freedom*, pp. 257–282 (Merrill D. Peterson and Robert C. Vaughan, eds., 1988); George Sher, "Three Grades of Social Involvement," *Phil. and Pub. Aff.*, 18, p. 133 (1989); Tom Sorell, "Self, Society, and Kantian Impersonality," *Monist*, 74, p. 30 (1991); Symposium, "Law, Community, and Moral Reasoning," *Cal. L. Rev.*, 77, p. 475 (1989); Charles Taylor, "Cross-Purposes: The Liberal-Communitarian Debate," in *Liberalism and the Moral Life* (Rosenblum, ed.); Robert B. Thigpen and Lyle A. Downing, "Liberalism and the Communitarian Critique," *Am. J. Pol. Sci.*, 31, p. 637 (1987); John Tomasi, "Individual Rights and Community Virtues," *Ethics*, 101, p. 521 (1991); John R. Wallach, "Liberals, Communitarians, and the Tasks of Political Theory," *Pol. Theory*, 15, p. 581 (1987); Michael Walzer, "The Communitarian Critique of Liberalism," *Pol. Theory*, 18, p. 6 (1990); Iris M. Young, "The Ideal of Community and the Politics of Difference," *Soc. Theory and Prac.*, 12, p. 1 (1986); and Joel Feinberg, "Liberalism, Community and Tradition," *Tikkun*, May–June 1988, p. 38. Prior to *Political Liberalism*, Rawls addressed these issues in a number of essays, including "The Idea of an Overlapping Consensus," *Oxford J. Legal Stud.*, 7, p. 1 (1987); "Justice as Fairness: Political Not Metaphysical," *Phil. and Pub. Aff.*, 14, p. 223 (1985); and "The Priority of Right and Ideas of the Good," *Phil. and Pub. Aff.*, 17, p. 251 (1987). In "Political Liberalism," however, he states: "The changes in the later essays are sometimes said to be replies to criticisms raised by communitarians and others. I don't believe there is a basis for saying this" (p. xvii).

12. Rawls, *A Theory of Justice*, p. 560.
13. Ibid., p. 561.

14. Ibid., pp. 574–75.

15. The objection to the conception of the person presented in *A Theory of Justice* does not depend on failing to see the original position as a device of representation. It can be stated wholly in terms of the conception of the person presented in Part III of *A Theory of Justice,* which Rawls now recasts as a political conception. Not only critics, but also defenders of Rawls's liberalism interpreted *A Theory of Justice* as affirming a Kantian conception of the person. See, e.g., Larmore, *Patterns of Moral Complexity,* pp. 118–130.

16. See MacIntyre, *After Virtue,* pp. 190–209; MacIntyre, *Is Patriotism a Virtue?,* p. 8, passim; Sandel, *Liberalism and the Limits of Justice,* pp. 175–183; Taylor, *Sources of the Self,* p. 508.

17. For contemporary examples of comprehensive liberalism, see George Kateb, *The Inner Ocean: Individualism and Democratic Culture* (1992); and Joseph Raz, *The Morality of Freedom* (1986). Ronald Dworkin describes his view as a version of comprehensive liberalism in "Foundations of Liberal Equality," in *The Tanner Lectures on Human Values,* vol. 11, p. 1 (Grethe B. Peterson, ed., 1990).

18. See Rawls, *A Theory of Justice,* pp. 11–12.

19. Ibid., p. 560.

20. Ibid.

21. Ibid., p. 561.

22. The notion that we should regard our moral and religious duties as "self-authenticating from a political point of view" (p. 33) accords with Rawls's statement that "from the standpoint of justice as fairness, these [moral and religious] obligations are self-imposed" (*A Theory of Justice,* p. 206). But it is not clear what the justification can be on such a view for according religious beliefs or claims of conscience a special respect not accorded other preferences that people may hold with equal or greater intensity. See ibid., pp. 205–211.

23. John Rawls, "Kantian Constructivism in Moral Theory: Rational and Full Autonomy," *J. Phil.,* 77, pp. 515, 519 (1980).

24. Rorty, "The Priority of Democracy to Philosophy," pp. 257, 262.

25. Ibid., p. 265.

26. Ibid., p. 268.

27. Ibid., p. 264.

28. Thomas Hobbes, who can be interpreted as advancing a political con-

ception of justice, ensured the priority of his political conception with respect to claims arising from contending moral and religious conceptions by denying the truth of those conceptions. See Thomas Hobbes, *Leviathan*, pp. 168–183 (C. B. Macpherson, ed., Penguin Books, 1985) (1651).

29. Rawls seems to take this view in a footnote on abortion. But he does not explain why political values should prevail even if the Catholic doctrine were true (p. 243 n.32).

30. *Created Equal? The Complete Lincoln-Douglas Debates of 1858*, pp. 369, 374 (Paul M. Angle, ed., 1958) [hereafter cited as *Created Equal?*].

31. Ibid., p. 390.

32. Ibid.

33. Ibid., p. 392.

34. Ibid.

35. Ibid., pp. 388–389.

36. 347 U.S. 483 (1954).

37. Voting Rights Act of 1965, 42 U.S.C. §§1971, 1973 (1988).

38. See *Created Equal?*, p. 374.

39. See U.S. Constitution, art. I, §2, cl. 3.

40. See ibid., art I, §9, cl. 1.

41. See ibid., art IV, §2, cl. 3.

42. Scott v. Sandford, 60 U.S. (19 How.) 393 (1857).

43. See ibid., pp. 404–405.

44. See Milton Friedman, *Capitalism and Freedom*, p. 200 (1962); Milton Friedman and Rose Friedman, *Free to Choose*, pp. 134–136 (1980); Hayek, *The Constitution of Liberty*, pp. 85–86, 99–100; Nozick, *Anarchy, State, and Utopia*, pp. 149, 167–174.

45. Although Rawls does not state this view explicitly, it is necessary in order to make sense of the "fact of reasonable pluralism" and the role it plays in supporting the priority of the right. He notes that reasonable disagreements may arise over what policies fulfill the difference principle, but adds, "this is not a difference about what are the correct principles but simply a difference in the difficulty of seeing whether the principles are achieved" (p. 230).

46. See Rawls, *A Theory of Justice*, pp. 72–75, 100–107, 136–142, 310–315.

47. See ibid., pp. 20–21, 48–51, 120, 577–587.

48. In this paragraph I draw on some of the arguments for and against the

morality of homosexuality that appear in John Finnis and Martha Nussbaum, "Is Homosexual Conduct Wrong?: A Philosophical Exchange," *New Republic*, Nov. 15, 1993, pp. 12–13; Stephen Macedo, "The New Natural Lawyers," *Harvard Crimson*, Oct. 29, 1993, p. 2; and Harvey C. Mansfield, "Saving Liberalism From Liberals," *Harvard Crimson*, Nov. 8, 1993, p. 2.

49. An alternative line of reply might undertake to defend promiscuity and to deny that the goods of love and responsibility are necessary to the moral worth of sexuality. From this point of view, the line of argument I suggest mistakenly seeks to defend the moral legitimacy of homosexuality by way of an analogy with heterosexuality. See Bonnie Honig, *Political Theory and the Displacement of Politics*, pp. 186–195 (1993).

50. It is possible to argue for certain gay rights on grounds that neither affirm nor deny the morality of homosexuality. The question here is whether government is justified in supporting laws or policies (such as gay marriage, for example) on grounds that affirm the moral legitimacy of homosexuality.

51. Rawls states that the limits of public reason apply to all discussions involving constitutional essentials and basic justice. As for other political questions, he writes that "it is usually highly desirable to settle political questions by invoking the values of public reason. Yet this may not always be so" (pp. 214–215).

52. This idea is repeated at several other points (pp. 215, 224, 254).

53. 478 U.S. 186 (1986).

54. See Michael J. Sandel, "Moral Argument and Liberal Toleration: Abortion and Homosexuality," *Cal. L. Rev.*, 77, pp. 521, 534–538 (1989).

55. See Eric Foner, *Politics and Ideology in the Age of the Civil War*, p. 72 (1980); Aileen S. Kraditor, *Means and Ends in American Abolitionism*, pp. 78, 91–92 (1967); James M. McPherson, *Battle Cry of Freedom: The Civil War Era*, pp. 7–8 (1988).

56. I elaborate this claim in Sandel, *Democracy's Discontent* (Harvard University Press, 1996).

30. The Limits of Communitarianism

1. See Alasdair MacIntyre, *After Virtue* (Notre Dame: University of Notre Dame Press, 1981).

2. See Charles Taylor, *Philosophical Papers,* vol. I: *Human Agency and Language;* vol. II: *Philosophy and the Human Sciences* (Cambridge: Cambridge University Press, 1985); and Taylor, *Sources of the Self: The Making of Modern Identity* (Cambridge, Mass.: Harvard University Press, 1989).
3. See Michael Walzer, *Spheres of Justice: A Defense of Pluralism and Equality* (New York: Basic Books, 1983).
4. *The Politics of Aristotle,* 1323a14, ed. and trans. Ernest Barker (London: Oxford University Press, 1958), p. 279.
5. The phrase is from Wallace v. Jaffree, 472 U.S. 38, 52–53 (1985): "Religious beliefs worthy of respect are the product of free and voluntary choice by the faithful."
6. The phrase is from Employment Division v. Smith, 494 U.S. 872, 886 (1990).
7. See Goldman v. Weinberger, 475 U.S. 503 (1986).
8. See Employment Division v. Smith, 494 U.S. 872 (1990).
9. See Thornton v. Caldor, Inc., 474 U.S. 703 (1985).
10. See Collin v. Smith, 447 F. Supp. 676 (1978); Collin v. Smith, 578 F.2d 1198 (1978).
11. See Beauharnais v. Illinois, 343 U.S. 250 (1952).
12. Williams v. Wallace, 240 F. Supp. 100, 108, 106 (1965).

CREDITS

Chapter 1: Originally published in *The Atlantic Monthly,* vol. 227, March 1996; based on Michael J. Sandel, *Democracy's Discontent* (Harvard University Press, 1996).

Chapter 2: Originally published in *The New Republic,* February 22, 1988.

Chapter 3: Originally published in *The New Republic,* September 2, 1996.

Chapter 4: Originally published in *The New Republic,* October 14, 1996.

Chapter 5: Originally published in *The New York Times,* December 29, 1996.

Chapter 6: Originally published in *The New Republic,* October 26, 1998.

Chapter 7: From a talk presented at the John F. Kennedy Library, 2000, drawn from Michael J. Sandel, *Democracy's Discontent* (Harvard University Press, 1996).

Chapter 8: Originally published in *The New Republic,* March 10, 1997.

Chapter 9: Originally published in *The New Republic,* September 1, 1997.

Chapter 10: Originally published in *The New Republic,* January 19, 1998.

Chapter 11: Originally published in *The New Republic,* May 25, 1998.

Chapter 12: Originally published in *The New Republic,* April 13, 1998.

Chapter 13: Originally published in *The New Republic,* May 26, 1997.

Chapter 14: Originally published in *The New York Times,* December 15, 1997.

Chapter 15: Originally published in *The New Republic,* December 23, 1996.

Chapter 16: Originally published in *The New Republic,* December 1, 1997.

Chapter 17: Originally published in *The New Republic,* July 7, 1997.

Chapter 18: Originally published in *The New Republic,* March 2, 1998.

Chapter 19: Originally published in *The New Republic,* April 14, 1997.

Chapter 20: Originally published in the *New England Journal of Medicine,* July 15, 2004.

Chapter 21: Earlier versions of this chapter appeared in the *California Law Review,* vol. 77, 1989, pp. 521–538, and in Michael J. Sandel, *Democracy's Discontent* (Harvard University Press, 1996).

Chapter 22: Originally published in *The New Republic,* May 7, 1984.

Chapter 23: Originally published in *Political Theory,* vol. 12, no. 1, February 1984, pp. 81–96.

Chapter 24: Originally published in *The New York Times,* April 24, 1983.

Chapter 25: Originally published in *Dissent,* Summer 1986, reprinted with permission.

Chapter 26: Originally published in *The New York Review of Books,* vol. 43, no. 8, May 9, 1996.

Chapter 27: Originally published in *Judaism and Modernity: The Religious Philosophy of David Hartman,* ed. Jonathan W. Malino, pp. 121–132, © Ashgate, 2004.

Chapter 28: Originally published in the *Harvard Law Review,* vol. 107, no. 7, May 1994, pp. 1765–1794.

Chapter 29: Originally published in *The New Republic,* December 16, 2002.

Chapter 30: Originally published in Michael J. Sandel, *Liberalism and the Limits of Justice,* 2nd edition, pp. ix–xvi, © Cambridge University Press, 1998. Reprinted with permission.

INDEX

Bush, George H. W., 35, 46
Bush, George W., 1–3, 68, 120
Business, big, 12–17, 22–23, 42–44, 51–52, 57, 154, 193

Calhoun, John C., 250
Campaigns. *See* Political campaigns
Campbell Soup Company, 74
Canada, 78–79
Capitalism, 17–18, 23, 32, 34, 44, 46, 81, 185
Capital punishment, 105, 107, 232
Carey v. Population Services International, 130
Carter, Jimmy, 1, 36–37, 169
Catholicism, 225–226, 241–242, 245, 275n29
Central Intelligence Agency, 61
Centralization, 13–17, 42–44, 52, 170
Channel One, 74–75
Character, of citizens, formation of, 9–10, 20, 25–27
Charities, church-based, 57
Cheerleaders, 97–100
Children, moral character of, 46, 49
Choice, freedom of, 4, 39, 47, 70–71, 114, 144–145, 255; liberal versus republican views, 9–11, 19–22, 27–29; and toleration, 147–148; and unencumbered self, 163, 172; and corruption of the person, 213–215
Christian Coalition, 28
Christianity, 111, 146, 149, 176
Citizenship, 3, 5, 16, 64, 66, 152, 195; formative nature of, 9–10, 20, 25–27; political economy of, 11–12, 17–19, 25–26; republican, 11–12; national, 16, 40, 44; in global economy, 30–32; renewal of, 54, 56; and unencumbered self, 163; and public identity, 219–221; equal, 229–230

Civic conception of freedom, 7, 21, 24, 26
Civic conservatism, 22–23
Civic corruption, 69, 72
Civic education, 16, 25–26, 41, 72
Civic engagement, 11, 41, 194
Civic identity, 16, 27, 30–31, 33–34, 81–84
Civic renewal, 4, 5, 7, 10, 24, 27, 29, 34, 38–39, 49, 53, 56–58, 66, 72, 154
Civility, 5, 54–58, 244
Civil rights, 151
Civil rights movement, 4, 22–23, 36, 40–42, 45, 47, 55, 153, 230, 245, 258–260
Civil society, 55–57
Civil War, 230
Cleveland Browns, 82–83
Clinton, Bill, 2, 7–8, 29, 46–51, 54, 59–62, 68, 93, 108–112
Cloning, 200
CNN, 1, 31, 53
Coercion, 5, 25–26, 47, 49, 70, 132, 233
Cohen, William, 61
Colorado Rockies, 73
Colorado Springs, Col., 74
Commager, Henry, 183
Commercialism, 67, 73–76
Commission on Global Governance, 31
Common assets, 165–167
Common good. *See* Good, common
Communal conservatism, 38–39, 42
Communal liberalism, 39, 41–42
Communal values, 39
Communitarianism, 145–146; and morality, 152–155; Dewey's view of, 190, 193–194; and egalitarianism, 212–213; inadequacy of, 252–255; and freedom of religion, 255–257; and freedom of speech, 257–260
Community, 4–5, 7–8, 51, 145; political, 10–13, 23, 26, 30, 37–45; global, 32–33,

Genetic engineering, 200–205, 207–208, 210

Genocide, 181, 259

Germany, 111, 210, 250

Gingrich, Newt, 52

Global community, 32–33, 53

Global economy, 7, 24, 28, 30–32, 34, 42, 51, 53, 210

Global obligations, 96

Global politics, 29–33

Global warming, 93–96

God, 2, 196–199, 201–204, 206–208, 210

Goldwater, Barry, 21

Good, 157–158, 161; common, 3, 10, 25, 45, 56–57, 103–104, 152–155, 168, 171, 190, 220; priority of right over, 146, 150–155, 157–159, 161, 163, 166, 212–224, 226, 231, 236, 240, 243, 253, 255, 259, 272n11, 275n45; greater, 148, 165

Good life, 4–5, 9, 13, 19, 26–28, 39, 123, 145, 151, 156–157, 191, 212–213, 232–233

Good society, 2–3, 18–19

Gore, Al, 2

Government, big, 12–17, 22–23, 32–33, 52, 57, 63, 194

Government agencies, branding for, 77–80

Government neutrality. *See* Neutrality

Government regulation. *See* Regulation

Great Depression, 17

Great Society, 21–23, 33, 36, 40–42, 52, 166, 193–194

Greece, ancient, 154, 186

Green, T. H., 192

Green Bay Packers, 83–84

Griswold v. Connecticut, 128–130, 137–138, 140, 264n34

Halakhic Judaism, 196–200, 203, 205–207, 269n1

Hamilton, Alexander, 250

Happiness, 148–150, 159

Harlan, John, 126–128, 266n65

Hart, Gary, 7

Hart, H. L. A., 152

Hartman, David, 146, 196–201, 203–209; *A Living Covenant*, 205

Harvard University, 248, 251

Hate speech, 232–233, 257–260

Hayek, Friedrich, 211

Health care, 2, 10, 39, 151, 176, 212, 232–233

Hegel, G. W. F., 190, 192

Hispanics, 99, 102

Historical artifacts, marketing of, 85–88

Hitler, Adolf, 210

Hobbes, Thomas, 250, 274n28

Holidays, compared to vacations, 177–178

Hollywood, 48, 54, 57

Holmes, Oliver Wendell, Jr., 250

Holocaust, 257–259

Holtzman, Elizabeth, 60

Homosexuality, 4, 42, 47, 68, 265n53, 276nn48–50; and liberal toleration, 122–123, 125, 131–132, 136–143; and political liberalism, 236–239, 241–242. *See also* Gay rights

Honor, 97–100, 103–104, 257

Hook, Sidney, 185

Horton, Willie, 46, 49

House Judiciary Committee, 59–62

Housing, 10, 39, 212, 233

Hubris, 201, 203–208, 210

Human finitude, 205–206, 208

Humanism, 198

Human nature, 24–25, 159, 200

Hyde, Henry, 60–62

Identity: civic, 16, 27, 30–31, 33–34, 81–84; national, 33; public, 219–221, 224

Race, 44, 99, 101–103, 233

Racism, 40, 101, 257–260

Railsback, Tom, 61

Rangel, Charles, 60

Rap music, 54, 57

Rawls, John, 113, 145–146, 157–158, 161–165, 191, 248–253; *Political Liberalism*, 146, 221–225, 231, 233–236, 238, 240–243, 245; *A Theory of Justice*, 150, 152, 211–221, 235, 248, 251, 274nn15,22

Reagan, Ronald, 2, 7–8, 22–23, 36–39, 42–43, 46, 52, 66, 169

Reason, public, 239–247, 276n51

Reasonable pluralism, 223–224, 230–239, 275n45

Reconstruction, 230

Reflective equilibrium, 235–238

Reform, 35–36

Regulation, 11, 15, 17–18, 21, 35, 42, 52

Relativism, moral, 147–148, 248

Religion, 4, 22, 28, 68, 220; and the Bible, 2, 110, 112, 196–197; and government neutrality, 39–40, 47, 113–115, 123, 125, 131–134, 138, 141, 145, 147, 191–192, 195, 225–227, 236–239, 253–254, 256–257; Christianity, 111, 146, 149, 176; and intolerance, 146; mastery/hubris in Judaism, 196–210; Catholic view of abortion, 225–226, 241–242, 245, 275n29; and reasonable pluralism, 230–239; and public reason, 240–247; freedom of, 249, 255–257

Religious anthropology, 199–201, 203–206

Religious values, 225

Republicanism, 155; and liberalism, 9–12, 19–22, 26; conception of freedom, 10–12, 19–20; historical context, 11–12, 24–26; risks of, 23–26

Republican Party, 8–10, 35–36, 44, 46–48, 51, 53–54, 60–62, 65–66, 170, 227

Resentment, 97–100

Respect, mutual, 244, 246–247

Retributive justice, 108

Retributive theory of punishment, 105–108

Revelation, divine, 197–198

Rights, 28–29, 97, 99–100, 115, 141, 175–176; individual, 4, 23, 33, 37, 39–42, 122, 145, 149–155, 157, 164–165, 169, 172, 182, 189, 195, 211–212, 248–249, 252–255; private property, 39, 151, 230; priority over good, 146, 150–155, 157–159, 161, 163, 166, 212–224, 226, 231, 236, 240, 243, 253, 255, 259, 272n11, 275n45; civil, 151; economic, 151; social, 151; natural, 188–191; of accused, 232

Riots, ghetto, 22

Robertson, Pat, 239

Rodino, Peter, 60–62

Roe v. Wade, 123, 130, 133–135, 144

Rome, ancient, 149, 177, 210

Roosevelt, Franklin, 17–18, 36, 40, 49, 109, 185

Roosevelt, Theodore, 15–17, 44, 51–53

Rorty, Richard, 146, 191–192, 221–222

Rousseau, Jean-Jacques, 24–26, 250

Royal Canadian Mounted Police, 78–79

Runyon, Marvin, 79

Rush, Benjamin, 25

Ryan, Alan: *John Dewey and the High Tide of American Liberalism,* 183–188, 190–191, 195

Sabbath, 205–209, 256

Sacrifice, shared, 3, 48, 72, 79, 95

St. Clair, James, 59

Same-sex marriage, 1–2, 143, 276n50

Sandel, Michael: *Liberalism and the Limits of Justice,* 252–253

Sandman, Charles, 61